STRATEGIES AND SKILLS FOR MANAGERIAL WOMEN

JOHANNA HUNSAKER
Associate Professor of
Organizational Behavior
University of San Diego

PHILLIP HUNSAKER
Professor of Management
Director of Management Programs
University of San Diego

COLLEGE DIVISION South-Western Publishing Co.

CINCINNATI   DALLAS   LIVERMORE

Publisher:	Roger Ross
Production Editor:	Sue Ellen Brown
Production House:	Ambos Company
Cover and Interior Designer:	Gwene Grunwald
Photo Researcher:	Diana Fears
Marketing Manager:	David L Shaut
Cover Photo:	Gabe Palmer/ The Stock Market

GM85BA

Copyright ©1991

by South-Western Publishing Co.

Cincinnati, Ohio

1 2 3 4 5 6 7 D 6 5 4 3 2 1 0

Printed in the United States of America

Hunsaker, Johanna.
    Strategies and skills for managerial women / Johanna Hunsaker,
Phillip Hunsaker. — 2nd ed.
        p.   cm.
    Includes bibliographic references and index.
    ISBN 0-538-80573-0
    1.   Women executives. I Hunsaker, Phillip .   II Title.
HD6054.3.H86   1991   90-38722
658.4'09'024042—dc20   CIP

CONTENTS

PREFACE

CHAPTER 1

MAKING THE MOVE TO MANAGEMENT

Differences Between Doing and Managing   6
    Traditional Socialization Process for Women, 6; Pressures
    of Female Sex Roles, 7; The Queen Bee Syndrome, 9

Our Historically Sexist Society   9
    Role Models Provided Since Birth, 10; Role Constraints, 13;
    Myths and Stereotypes—and Realities, 14

Overcoming Outdated Conceptions   21

CHAPTER 2

ASSUMING MANAGERIAL ROLES AND FUNCTIONS

A Manager's Wide Range of Roles   32
    Goal Balancing, 32; Conceptualizing, 34; Problem Solving, 34;
    Motivating, 34; Conflict Resolving, 35; Politicing, 35;
    Representing, 35; Decision Making, 36; Flexibility, 36

Functions of Management   36
    Planning, 37; Organizing, 39; Staffing, 41; Staffing Women
    Managers, 43; Leading, 44; Controlling, 48

Variations of the Managerial Process   50
    Interpersonal Roles, 51; Informational Roles, 52; Decision
    Roles, 54

CHAPTER 3

PROJECTING YOUR IMAGE

First Impressions Based on Appearance   66
  Decisions Made by Others, 68; Case Examples, 69; Specific
  Guidelines on Clothing, 70; Guidelines on the Use of Accesso-
  ries, 72; Summary, 73

Assertiveness   73

Proper Business Etiquette   75

Depth of Knowledge   75

Breadth of Knowledge   77

Versatility   78

Enthusiasm   78

Sincerity   79

CHAPTER 4

CAREER DEVELOPMENT

Career Management   88
  Meanings of Career, 88; Career Concepts, 89; Planning Your
  Career, 90

Barriers to Career Development   92
  Low Initial Challenge, 92; Low Self-Actualization Satisfac-
  tion, 93; Lack of Regular Performance Appraisal, 93; Unrealis-
  tically High Aspirations, 93; Low-Visibility; or "Safe"
  Positions, 94; Threat to Superiors, 94; The Glass Ceiling, 94;
  Problems of and Strategies for Reentry Women, 95

Strategies for Career Advancement   96
  Realistic Job Previews, 98; Basic Everyday Tactics, 99

Mentors   101
  What is a Mentor? 102; Is a Mentor Really Necessary? 104;
  What Can a Mentor Do for the Woman Manager? 105; How to

Find a Mentor, 105; Problems Encountered in the Mentor Relationship, 108; Can Women Be Mentors? 110

Career Dilemmas   111
Dual Career Couples, 111; The Mommy Track, 112; Linear Career Crises, 113

Alternative Career Paths   114
Women as Entrepreneurs.114; Working Out of the Home,114; Job Sharing, 115

CHAPTER 5

SELF-MANAGEMENT

Stress Management   128
Souces of Stress, 131; Methods of Dealing with Stress, 133

Time Management   137
Time-Management Techniques, 138; Other Timesaving Ideas, 141

CHAPTER 6

COMMUNICATING EFFECTIVELY

Need for Effective Communication   151

Special Communication Problems for Women   151
Characteristics of Women's Speech Patterns, 152; Reverting to Inappropriate Family-Socialized Behaviors, 154; Ways to Overcome Weak Speech Patterns, 155

Roadblocks to Effective Two-Way Communication   156
Hidden Intentions, 157; Preoccupation with Tasks, 157; Emotional Involvement, 157; Distortions to Match One's Expectations, 158; Misperceptions, 158; Distrust, 159

Listening   159
Poor Listening Habits, 160; Active Listening, 162

Ways to Overcome Sender Barriers
to the Communication Process   163

Use Redundancy, 163; Be Complete and Specific, 163; Claim
the Message As Your Own, 163; Ensure That Your Messages
Are Congruent, 164; Develop Credibility, 164

Developing Persuasiveness in Communication   166

The Need for Adequate Feedback   169
Types of Feedback, 169; Effective Use of Feedback, 173

CHAPTER 7

POWER AND POLITICS

Traditional Power Failures of Women Managers   187

Sources of Power for Women Managers   190
Legitimate Power, 191; Reward Power, 192; Coercive Power,
192; Referent Power, 193; Expert Power, 193; Information
Power, 193; Association Power, 194

Power and the Woman Manager's Career   195
Using Feminine Characteristics to Advantage, 195; Adopting
a Masculine Style of Behavior, 197; Seeking Entry into Old
Boys' Network, 197

Strategies for Enhancing Interpersonal Power   198
Be Assertive, 198; Be Courteous, 199; Direct Your Thinking,
199; Neutralize Resistance, 200; Inoculate the Key Decision
Makers, 201; Use the Media, 201; Build Support Groups, 201;
Gatekeep, 202; Hold Out, 202; Go Around, 203; Threaten to
Resign, 203

Sex as a Power Tactic   203
Flirtation, 204; Dating, 205; Flings, 206; Affairs, 206

CHAPTER 8

DELEGATING AND WORKING EFFECTIVELY WITH GROUPS

Delegating   216
Reasons for Ineffective Delegating, 217; Useful Principles of
Delegating, 218

Delegating to Groups   219

Problems of Women in Groups   221
Sex Ratios of Groups, 221; Overcoming of Female Problems in Male-Dominated Groups, 221

Key Group Processes   222
Communication Patterns, 223; Decision-Making Procedures, 224; Group Role Behaviors, 225; Emotional Issues, 228

Emotional Expression   230
Emotional Styles, 230

Team Building   232
Needs Assessment, 234; Planning and Design, 235; The Team Building Meeting, 236; Diagnosis and Evaluation, 236; Problem Solving, 237; Planning Implementation and Follow-Up, 237

Conducting Effective Meetings   237

CHAPTER 9

DEALING WITH DIFFICULT EMPLOYEES

Mismatch of Manager and Employee Behavioral Styles   248
The Expressive Style, 249; The Driving Style, 249; The Analytical Style, 250; The Amiable Style, 250

Personality Problems of Employees   251
Oversensitive Employees, 251; Hostile or Angry Employees, 252; Negative Employees, 253

Signs of Counterproductive Behavior   254
Disrespect, 254; Lack of Cooperation, 255; Passiveness and Agressiveness, 256

Approaches to Interpersonal Conflict Situations   257
Competing, 258; Accomodating, 260; Avoiding, 260; Collaborating, 261; Compromising, 261

Prevention of Unnecessary Conflict   262
Get Initial Agreement, 262; Offer a Limited Choice of Alternatives, 262; Obtain a Commitment in Advance, 263; Communicate Positive Expectations, 263; Use Compliments as Positive Motivators, 264

CHAPTER 10

HIRING AND FIRING EMPLOYEES

Recruiting Employees   272
    Job Analysis, 272; Recruitment Sources, 273; Laws Relevant
    to Equal Employment Opportunities and Affirmative Action,
    274

Screening Applications   276

The Selection Interview   276
    Interviewing Candidates, 278; Good Questions, 278;
    Ambiguous Questions, 280; Poor Questions, 283

The Hiring Decision   284
    Importance of the Background Check, 284; Methods of
    Checking References, 285

Firing Employees   286

Index   293

PREFACE

In writing the second edition of *Strategies and Skills for Managerial Women*, we wanted to reinforce our belief that the world is changing to be a better place for both men and women, but there is still a long way to go before organizations accept and recognize the benefit of fully integrating women into all phases of organizational life. Traditional female and male stereotypes continue to influence the way organizations function, despite affirmative action laws and an unprecedented insurge of females into the labor force.

Women *do* need to learn the rules that men have created in order to "play the corporate game," but we also strongly believe that women can increasingly socialize men so that the rules *can* change and organizations and individuals will benefit. Many of the current management trends, like participative management, coaching, mentoring, and productivity through people, are things that many women have already been socialized to do, and do well. The redefinition of "good management" is starting to include some traditionally "feminine" characteristics. In our management classes at the University of San Diego, in our consulting work, and in our own lives we are impressed with the fact that women, as well as men, are striving for balance in their lives. The definition of success and careers is being expanded to include a holistic image of a total lifestyle and the plan that emerges as a result of a careful, thoughtful, and meaningful analysis. Women, as well as men, are redefining their work objectives and what they value, and many women do choose to work in the managerial arena. Hence the need for this book.

PURPOSE

This book is designed to provide new women managers, working women aspiring to be managers, and students studying for managerial positions, with the fundamental skills and insights necessary for success. This book is addressed to women who hope to be in management, to those women in management who want to move ahead or reevaluate where they are going, and to both men and women who simply want to become more knowledgeable, skilled, and effective. Many of the managerial skills presented here are the same skills required of any successful manager, male or female. It is important to recognize that women must simultaneously deal with other problems, such as role conflict, dual careers, outdated and stereotypical behaviors, policies, and attitudes, lack of acceptance, and tokenism, which can make the application of these skills more difficult. Both men and women can benefit from awareness of the challenges. Our goal for this book is to provide you with awareness, insights, strategies, and skills to help you design and implement a satisfying and productive career path for yourself.

ORGANIZATION OF THE BOOK

In this book many important problems that you will encounter as a female manager will be highlighted. Current research on topics pertaining to women and comments from practicing women managers are interspersed throughout the chapters. The tone of the book, though, is to be *PRACTICAL AND APPLICABLE* to emerging women managers. Fundamental strategies and skills that can enhance your career are included. These strategies are drawn from our experiences as consultants to large and small organizations, from our university teaching experiences, and from counseling many successful women managers. In the first edition, we surveyed 246 women holding mid-to-upper-level management positions to learn what they viewed as the most beneficial guidelines for women in management. Their insights are included in this book. Additionally, case examples and additional comments that reflect the experiences of our current consulting clients are included. We hope that they will provide valuable ideas and inspiration to help the woman manager in her career.

In Chapter 1, you will become more aware of limiting stereotypes, attitudes, and behaviors—those posed by both women themselves and the external environment. The strategies presented for dealing with them and changing them will be of immediate benefit to male and female readers. This book is action-oriented; that is, we expect you to be able to take the skills presented and develop your own individualized strategies for improving yourself and your career.

Part of the strategy for success is mastering the functions of management discussed in Chapter 2. It takes more than academic competence to achieve success in management. Equally important are the strategies for projecting a positive image, which are presented in Chapter 3; the ways to find and maintain relationships with a mentor are explained in Chapter 4; the determination to master your own life by coping with stress and balancing multiple roles are discussed in Chapter 5. Because a managerial job is people-intensive, you will have to work on your communication skills as suggested in Chapter 6. Power and politics are an organizational reality. Traditionally, women have suffered several types of power failures and Chapter 7 details strategies for acquiring power. Chapter 8 deals with delegation and working with groups to obtain objectives. In Chapter 9 we explain how to deal with difficult employees, especially in conflict situations. Finally, in Chapter 10 we present skills you will need when you hire or fire employees.

ACKNOWLEDGEMENTS
Many people contribute to an effort such as this, and we would like to acknowledge and thank those who helped to make this book possible. We appreciate the comments of our reviewers, especially Dr. Mary Ann Von Glinow of the University of Southern California, who wrote detailed, constructive and much appreciated comments during the review process. Jim Burns, Dean of the School of Business Administration at the University of San Diego, provided research resources and a supportive work environment.

Finally, because this book is about women managers, we owe a debt of gratitude to many female students, clients, colleagues, and friends who have helped us refine our ideas and strategies. Your insights, experiences, and willingness to share have influenced us greatly.

Johanna S. Hunsaker   **Phillip L. Hunsaker**
University of San Diego   **University of San Diego**

STRATEGIES AND SKILLS FOR MANAGERIAL WOMEN

CHAPTER 1

MAKING THE MOVE TO MANAGEMENT

Differences Between Doing and Managing

    Traditional Socialization Process for Women

    Pressures of Female Sex Roles

          Mother

          Seductress

          Pet

          Iron Maiden

    The Queen Bee Syndrome

Our Historically Sexist Society

    Role Models Provided Since Birth

    Role Constraints

    Myths and Stereotypes—and Realities

          Stereotype #1—Men Are Intellectually Superior to Women

          Stereotype #2—Men Value Achievements and Meaningful Work More than Women

          Stereotype #3—Men Are Inherently More Assertive than Women

          Stereotype #4—Women Don't Work for Money

Overcoming Outdated Conceptions

Action Guidelines

Key Terms

Discussion Questions

Chapter Case: Running A Business

Endnotes

Additional Resources

Now that a number of career women have become media celebrities, many people think that women in management experience nothing but nonstop glamour. According to Foxworth, moving into management is sometimes celebrated as becoming **queen of the corporation.**[1] Situated in a luxurious office with a reception area filled with admiring male vice-presidents, the sparkling female executive looks forward to returning home to an approving husband or friend and a chilled bottle of champagne and gourmet dinner he prepared himself.

What a disappointment to discover that the spectacular successes of a few have been so overplayed by the media! Realistic, everyday living and working experiences do not usually match up with what the media portray. The sad truth is that management is still pretty much male territory. According to Felice Schwartz, only two facts matter in business: women have babies and men make rules.[2] If women expect to get into management—and stay there—they will have to learn to cope in this atmosphere. Of course, new women managers need to develop the same skills and insights that new male managers must acquire, but many women are new immigrants to a world of customs and language in which men have been raised all along. Since men also realize this, women must, in addition, prove themselves as "naturalized citizens" as well as competent managers. Women *are* in the work force to stay. This one societal change, perhaps the most sweeping of this century, continues to be ignored or undermanaged in most American companies—the mass movement of women in the workplace.[3]

Since the late 1960s, the number of women in the work force has changed dramatically. Within management ranks their representation has more than tripled, according to Loden.[4] Despite this fact, most organizations pay little attention to the impact the change has had on work and family relationships or traditional management styles. Women entering the work force still must go through an acculturation process.

Women entering management positions straight out of graduate or undergraduate business school programs may have a headstart in acculturation. They have a good idea of how to act "properly." They have had two to four years of working with males in academic settings where they learned and got accustomed to business language, which often consists of male-oriented analogies and parallels. **Game playing, team member,** and **playing hardball** are all common workday terms with which they would be familiar. They also have gained experience in working successfully in male-dominated task groups.

For women reentering the job market after a long absence or those born before World War II who are venturing into it for the first time, the greater cultural shock makes the already stressful new management job even more complicated. Such an experience can result in anything from a momentary annoyance for those adequately prepared, to a devastating emotional jolt for those entering cold. If a wounded ego, disappointment, or bewilderment shows through, it may reinforce any existing negative stereotypes and mark the new woman manager as being bad for company morale and a negative influence on other employees. Consequently, it's important for her to roll with the punches, and learn the game rules as quickly as possible.

American business has barely begun to tap the latent and leadership potential of women. Most organizations have failed to recognize women as essential assets in long-term efforts to increase productivity. Most companies have adopted a business as usual approach toward the influx of women into the workplace.

There are two schools of thought on why women are not getting to the top despite their advances in the past 20 years.[5] The first of these claims that women haven't risen more swiftly in the corporate ranks because of external barriers in their paths. The second school of thought points to internal barriers to success, self-defeating barriers that women exhibit, either consciously or unconsciously, in the job.

One recently published book by Morrison, White, and Van Velsor[6] argues convincingly that women must meet a more stringent set of behavioral criteria than men to make it up the corporate ladder: "This narrow band of acceptable characteristics and actions reflects the multiple expectation of corporate women and the challenge they face blending very disparate qualities. Only certain characteristics traditionally accepted as masculine and some traditionally thought of as feminine are permitted through the narrow band."

Other arguments citing external factors are that men in power have lower expectations for women, women are excluded from old boy networks, women are given powerless positions, and women lack mentor and role models.[7] Those who argue in favor of external factors deny the existence of any attitudinal or behavioral differences between male and female managers in general.

Another school of thought focuses on internal barriers female managers face: the biological fact of maternity and traditional female socialization, the need to be supportive, nurturing, intuitive, sensitive, and communicative.[8]

Each of these views has merit. The successful woman manager must understand both viewpoints. Women do face serious external barriers to success and they do have to grapple with internal issues. This chapter will cover some of the difficulties, both internal and external, that many women encounter when making the move to management.

DIFFERENCES BETWEEN DOING AND MANAGING

The critical shift is from doing to managing. Women have traditionally been *doers*, with specific job descriptions like typists or computer programmers. The results of their efforts have usually been readily observable in terms of documents typed or programs operating. A high degree of security has been provided in their clear-cut responsibilities, behaviors, and tangible feedback available.

As *managers*, women are responsible for accomplishing tasks with and through other people. Consequently, there is no longer a clear-cut definition of performance, outcome, or the reward process. Now the essential variables are more ambiguous. It is not always clear what needs to be done to motivate others, how to measure results, or how to spend time effectively at any given moment. Work such as planning and evaluation is not tangible; and the security of performing mixed, routine tasks has changed to a game of chance—with big risks, but also big rewards.

Traditional Socialization Process for Women

Traditional socialization often imposes internal barriers to women in management. Some of the dimensions of the socialization process discussed in this chapter present barriers to women in making the transition to management. As pointed out by Fenn, female roles usually require short, discrete time intervals that provide a time orientation useful for reacting to and solving specific human needs.[9] In management, however, longer time orientations are needed for activities such as goal setting and planning.

A second difference in women's socialization is that most women do not have the experience of playing in group sports that men do. The argument suggests that understanding and practice in collaborative team efforts are important in developing leadership and supportive work environments. Boys learn early that it is necessary to cooperate with others they may not particularly like in order to have a winning team. Girls place higher emphasis on friendships. According to Hennig and Jardim, girls are more apt to refuse playing games with those they don't like.[10] This carries over into organizational life when women fail to understand that personal likes and dislikes are irrelevant in making the team effective. Colwill has argued more recently that, while the team-sport-organization analogy had some intuitive appeal, there is a lack of any real evidence to support this theory.[11]

In reality most women in organizations are still far from the managerial ranks. A prominent feature of most female occupations, according to Nina Colwill, is that of **helpmate**: assisting others in their work.[12] Typical examples are nurse, secretary, and receptionist. This type of position fosters helplessness and dependency, which are the antithesis of the qualities needed in managers.

Hennig and Jardim[13] also point to women's "overinvestment in specialization," the tendency to become obsessed with technical competence. This limits and makes the transition to management tougher by keeping her so clearly focused on the job at hand that she fails to see the bigger picture.

Pressures of Female Sex Roles

Even when a woman does finally break through into the managerial ranks, she may find that she is the only female manager in her company. If this happens, the male majority may actively pressure her into a female sex role. A common set of *female roles*, discussed below, has been described by Kanter.[14]

Mother. The female manager sometimes finds that she has become a "mother" to a group of male subordinates. They bring their troubles to her and she comforts them. This role is based on the stereotyped assumption that women are nurturing and sympathetic listeners. The consequences of being typecast in a mother role are that: (1) the role is relatively safe from sexual harassment; (2) the "mother" becomes an emotional specialist rather than a task-oriented leader, and this perpetrates a traditional stereotype; (3) the "mother" is rewarded by men for services rendered, rather than for independent leadership.

Seductress.   The dangerous element of sexual competition can interfere with the female manager's effectiveness if she is cast as a sex object by male subordinates, peers, or superiors. If the female manager is typecast as a **seductress** who shares her attentions with many admirers, she may be debased. If, on the other hand, she forms a close alliance with one particular man, she may arouse resentment from the others. If a high-status male becomes her "protector," the seductress may be resented for using her body to get an in with superiors. Although a seductress is rewarded with attention, she experiences much tension and her perceived sexuality interferes with all other characteristics which are now more important for the job and career.

Pet.   The **pet** is a token role where the female is symbolically included in the group like a mascot or cheerleader, but not as an equal or influential figure. She is tolerated more as a cute, amusing novelty than as a competent peer or manager. On the positive side, at least the woman is included in the male-dominated group. On the other hand, she is prevented from demonstrating and developing her managerial competence.

Iron Maiden.   If the new woman manager resists falling into any of the three roles just mentioned, and persists in acting in a task-oriented manner, she often is typecast as the tough, "women's libber" type—the **iron maiden**. This may occur by her simply demanding equal treatment because, in the particular male-dominated setting, no woman has ever done that before. By displaying competence and cutting off sexual innuendoes, she may be seen as threatening to her male counterparts and this could cause resentment and suspicion. Consequently, even behaving in healthy, self-actualizing ways can elicit a male response that traps women in more militant roles than they prefer.

Although these roles differ greatly, they all are ways of casting women as inconsequential minorities. All these roles indicate that this is a woman, not an individual or a competent manager. These roles isolate women from the mainstream and diminish their potential effectiveness. By putting women in these roles, men remain in charge and maintain the status quo. Another role that is often seen in organizations is described in the next section.

The Queen Bee Syndrome

The **Queen Bee**, according to Colwill, is a successful woman who has made it to the top by working harder than most men, and "will be damned if she's going to reach down and help some other woman on the climb."[15] The Queen Bee attempts to close the boardroom doors behind her and keep her hard-earned and well-deserved privileges for herself. If another woman is allowed to approach this lofty perch, it will be through the "I had to suffer, so you will too" syndrome.

A cursory examination of these roles reveals the subtle and not so subtle influence of sex-role stereotypes. It is important to note that women must break through these negative images both for themselves and the men with whom they work. By creating new positive roles that demonstrate both their competence and effectiveness as females, a step is taken toward diminishing the impact of our historically sexist society.

OUR HISTORICALLY SEXIST SOCIETY

Long before little girls and boys grow up to become the victims and the perpetrators of gender-related stereotypes, subtle influences are at work. Very early in their lives children learn about sex roles. They learn these roles through relatively simple patterns that most of us take for granted. Parents throw baby boys up in the air and roughhouse with them. They coo over baby girls and handle them delicately. From the earliest days they choose gender-related colors and toys for their children. They encourage the energy and physical activity of their sons, just as they expect their daughters to be more quiet, docile, and ladylike, and though they love their sons and daughters with equal fervor, many people are disappointed when there is no male child to carry on the family name.

When children enter school, the pattern continues. From the moment children pick up their first book, they are given the message that boys are competent, active, and adventuresome while girls are bungling, inept, dependent, and dumb—capable only of doing domestic chores or making themselves attractive. In many old-edition textbooks, boys are consistently portrayed as being able to ride a rocketship to the moon or perform delicate surgery, while girls are shown almost exclusively baking cakes, doing laundry, helping or watching boys.

By the time men and women enter the workplace, they have been immersed in a sexist society. They have come to hold beliefs about themselves, the world, and the people in it. Some of the views have come consciously, others unconsciously. They come from parents, teachers, media, and advertising—almost every facet of society.

These common cultural stereotypes lead to many of the problems the woman manager encounters when she enters the world of work. By examining the socialization process, a better understanding of the role constraints, myths, and stereotypes that may hinder women can be developed.

Role Models Provided Since Birth

People are socialized from birth to fit the traditional role models provided for them, and the roles provided have been very different for little boys and little girls. Most aspects of traditional child rearing have an impact on later behavior—in particular, aggressive versus passive behaviors, views on competition, the effects of labeling, and the individual's perception of his or her ability to succeed.

In childhood, some behaviors are rewarded or punished, not necessarily overtly, but by subtle clues from both parents. When children are at age four or five, they generally become more aggressive toward their environment. For a little boy, aggression means playing with toys such as guns and cars, roughhousing with Dad, and playing competitive ball games. His aggressive, competitive behavior is usually supported, encouraged, and rewarded by both parents. At this early age he is taught that aggressive behavior is acceptable to his parents (as representatives of the larger society) and that he should strive to actively manipulate his environment.

On the other hand, usually the 5-year-old girl receives her rewards from both parents for acting in a more quiet way. Playing with dolls, cooking, and other types of behavior that model her mother may be reinforced. She is not usually found wrestling on the floor with Dad, out playing catch with him, or playing cowboys and Indians. Most fathers typically reward a 4- or 5-year-old daughter by giving her love and attention in return for her relinquishment of aggressive behavior. She understands from subtle cues which behavior is not ladylike and for fear of losing her mother's love, she may choose to identify with her mother to please both parents.

Hennig and Jardim, in their classic book *The Managerial Woman*, hold that the socialization differences described above result in males being able to use aggression constructively, whereas females are socialized to be weak and subordinate.[16] They explain that boys are more valued by society for their active engagement with their environment while girls, receiving different cues from both parents, learn passivity as an expectation and acquire a "second-class citizen" stature. Boys also learn, through their childhood activities, to believe more in their own ability to control fate (and outcomes), whereas girls are given little opportunity to experiment with situations in which initiative and risk are required.

The child's actual play also affects the self-image. Recently much has been written about team sports as an outlet for male aggression and, more importantly, as a way of learning the rules of competition. Males participate in team sports from as early as age five and learn that winning and losing are each acceptable. Soccer, football, and baseball provide a way of learning cooperation and competition, specialization, leadership, how to handle criticism, and the need for alternative plans and goals.

Most women born before the 1970s were not encouraged as children to participate in team sports. When they were 5-year-olds, they engaged in activities that were seen as feminine—such as taking ballet lessons and helping Mom in the kitchen—and as more acceptable to society. What most of these women have missed when growing up has been the opportunity to learn a sophisticated manipulation of their environment: how to win or lose, and the rules of game playing. Not having had exposure to comfortable competition, most of them have had to compete on another level—physical appearance. Winning or losing has become an entirely different experience, tied to less intellectual pursuits.

Fortunately, today some things *have* changed. Since the mid-1970s, soccer teams with elementary school-age girls on them are common.

Illus. 1.1
Because of changing role standards for the girls of today, the women of tomorrow will have a more competitive edge in the workplace.

Softball teams are popular for girls as well as for boys. Although seemingly insignificant, these types of changes will go a long way in breaking down the traditional male/female roles in the socialization process. They cannot, however, help the adult woman who has already started her managerial career and is burdened with traditional strategies.

Society, through its process of socialization, has considered masculinity synonymous with strength, dominance, and power, and has reinforced the male's attitudes regarding his own powers. Simultaneously, it has reinforced the female's feelings of weakness, inadequacy, and lack of control over her environment.

Many women's expectations remain relatively low despite education. A 1985 study of Stanford MBAs found that women graduates had lower ultimate salary hopes and expectations. On the average, women's peak salary expectations were less than 40 percent of men's.[17] Another study of educated women of all ages found that though women did not fear success, many wondered if their achievements were worth the price.[18]

And there *is* a price. Women's careers often demand sacrifices at home, with childbearing, organizational factors, and other barriers hindering their careers. However, lower expectations also tend to function as self-fulfilling prophecies, discouraging women from progressing. Role-constraints play a big part in this phenomena.

Role Constraints

The socialization process leads to role constraints: "What I *must* do because I am a Male/Female. What I *cannot* do because I am a Female/Male." These role constraints often lead to assumptions about what behaviors are appropriate and desirable for members of each sex. Choosing to depart from traditional male/female roles involves shedding old values and adopting new ones. This is easier to talk about than to do.

Not too long ago the authors conducted an informal experiment with graduate students enrolled in an MBA program. The authors thought perhaps this group might not feel as constrained by their gender as the average population. They asked the students to complete a questionnaire including the following unfinished sentences:

"Because I am a female . . . ."

"Because I am a male .. . ."

The responses revealed the overwhelming impact of the socialization process and the widespread existence of gender-related role constraints. Here are some typical answers.

1. Because I am a female, I am still trying to develop my career outside of my home—mainly because I felt my responsibility to my family comes first.

2. Because I am a female, men find it hard to accept my intelligence and aggressive attitude. Oftentimes I'm forced to role-play a passive person in order to get something that I want instead of being able to be my true self. Men can't handle being less smart than a woman.

3. Because I am a male, I feel compelled to be a success in every endeavor I take on.

4. Because I am a male, I feel obligated to be protective toward women and small children; also, to be responsible for the more important decisions made.

These comments show the effects of socialization and subsequent role constraints. A summary of the comments gathered is illustrated in Figure 1-1. These data demonstrate that constraints are felt by both men and women as a result of their socialization process.

FIGURE 1-1

SUMMARY OF RESPONSES ON ROLE CONSTRAINTS

Because I am a male . . .

I must be successful.
I must be the dominant figure.
I have more responsibilities: I
    must go to school and get
    a good education; I must be
    competitive.
I feel strong and determined.
I must wear the pants in the family.
I must take care of my wife
    financially.
I must dominate.
I can be rowdy and crude.
I can't cry in public.
I must be aggressive.
I have unlimited freedom.

Because I am a female . . .

I must work twice as hard to prove
    myself.
I must be responsible to family first
I must play passive.
I can't play competitive sports.
I am emotional.
I have role restrictions.
I have barriers to what I want.
I must accept the roles of today
    and make the most of it
I find it hard to get into the good
    old boys' network.
I must be cautious of my behavior.
I had stricter rules as a child.
I can cry to get my own way.

Can you think of others that have impeded or constrained decisions you have made?

Myths and Stereotypes—and Realities

There is little systematic information upon which to base assumptions of differential managerial ability between sexes. Most "known" differences are based on stereotypes. **Stereotypes** are *assumed* differences, social conventions or norms, learned behaviors, attitudes, and expectations. Stereotyping simplifies the perceptual process by allowing us to evaluate an individual or a thing on the basis of our perception of the group or class to which he, she, or it belongs.

Sex-role stereotyping is a major complication for women aspiring to, or currently in, management. A sampling of the widely accepted notions about women and work includes:

- Women cannot coordinate careers with family demands.
- Women cry in crisis situations.
- Women are not suited emotionally or intellectually for jobs traditionally held by men.
- Women are not committed to their jobs and regard jobs as temporary measures.
- Women cannot travel for business.

These myths and stereotypes and countless others are "based on fears, desires, needs, and emotions—not reality," and this makes the task of dispelling them more difficult.[19] Facts are useful when dealing with logic and thoughtful analysis, not emotions. Dispelling deeply ingrained attitudes and associated social pressures is difficult.

Some of the common stereotypes that impede women's progress in the work force need closer scrutiny. The perpetuation of the following stereotypes has limited many a woman's drive to seek managerial positions.

Stereotype #1. Men Are Intellectually Superior to Women.
Research comparing men and women on aptitude tests does not support this view. The research shows that females, in general, achieve well in their early school years. They do not differ from males in intellectual abilities, methods of learning, creativity, or cognitive style. The most consistent finding is that women surpass men on tests of verbal aptitude. Young girls tend to excel in tests of memory and in scholastic achievement. However, this achievement tends to diminish as they reach adolescence and adulthood. Nevertheless, scholastic achievement and femininity are incongruent.

The stereotype of the ideal woman discourages her expression of intellectual abilities, however. Hollander found that when the grade point average of high school males increased, their self-esteem also increased; whereas, the self-esteem of females *decreased* with increases in grade point average.[20]

Perpetuation of this outmoded stereotype means a woman manager is often torn between the desire for approval and the need to achieve and demonstrate her competence. Most women managers have made concessions that men do not have to make, and these concessions lessen the expression of female competence. A confrontation among men who hold conflicting ideas is usually perceived as healthy and natural. The same behavior by women, on the other hand, might be viewed as aggressive and bitchy.

Stereotype #2. Men Value Achievements and Meaningful Work More than Women. Research indicates that women are motivated by many of the same job elements as men. Both males and females have similar job characteristic-preferences-commitment and find intrinsic satisfaction to be more important than extrinsic motivators. In other words, the work itself satisfied both the women and men. There were no differences between the sexes in the expressed importance of the intrinsic factor. Parents, teachers, and even playmates help instill a sense of the importance of work. A healthy definition of work commitment includes the belief that work is good and makes one feel more worthwhile and important. Chusmir and Durand, in their 1987 study, reported no biological effect on job and work commitment by gender.[21]

Additional research has elaborated on the similarities between male and female managers. Donnell and Hall found that male and female managers have no significant differences in their managerial style.[22] Renwick discovered that men and women have similar attitudes toward conflict resolution.[23] Brief and Oliver revealed that women have the same feelings about work as men.[24] Finally, Birdsall found that male and female managers' communication style with subordinates was basically the same.[25]

Despite these similarities, several studies have highlighted some critical differences that undoubtedly have handicapped women in their quest to convince companies of their knowledge and abilities. First, some research demonstrates that women have traditionally had a self-image problem. For example, Prather found that women are not too often taken seriously as people.[26] As a result, they tend to have low self-esteem. Low self-esteem combined with a low self-image can be crippling.

Fear of success is another problem women face. Dowling labeled the fear of success the **Cinderella complex.**[27] She described the tendency of some women to sabotage their careers because of the fear that, if they are *too* successful, they won't appeal to "Prince Charming."

Women often self-select themselves away from certain types of jobs. Heinen found that many women having high achievement levels traditionally channeled this need in socially acceptable ways.[28] This usually means getting into jobs perceived as female, like nursing and teaching. These fit nicely into the roles for which girls are socialized— and which threaten no one. This viewpoint, however, leads to problems for the woman pursuing a traditionally male career.

In corporate life, having a traditional view presents the aspiring woman with a double-edged sword. Taking on the "male" traits and attributes needed for a management role may leave her feeling less feminine, more dominant, and more aggressive than comfort allows. If she fails to demonstrate these qualities, however, she will not even merit consideration for the position, let alone advancement up the organizational ladder.

These required behaviors often conflict with the desired self-image and contribute to a fear of success. Many women are reluctant to enter the management field since they may view the requisites for successful performance as being inconsistent with their self-image. They view success as unfeminine and therefore undesirable. Hull stated that the biggest barrier to female success is insecurity.[29]

Men, already established in managerial roles, usually do not help resolve this conflict. Often, with the entry of women into leadership positions, men fear losing power, authority, control, and identity. The role of protector and provider reinforced in their childhood is now threatened. In addition, competition will be keener for the dwindling number of top management jobs. Stanek says that, with women in the running, there will be twice as many able, hard-working, and dedicated top managers to choose from.[30]

It is important to note, however, that women's role in our society is rapidly changing and the old rules may not be applicable for long. Koff and Handlon, after a six-year study into the factors causing success or failure of women in management positions, discovered that successful women view achievement as female-appropriate behavior.[31] They found that while many women with low self-esteem are prone to "stay put" because of fear of failure, disloyalty to a peer group, or conflict with tradition, other women are high achievers and can be described as pioneers. Those in the latter group expect to be successful. They are willing to take risks and their strong upwardly-mobile motivations are made possible, in part, by their very positive sense of self-worth.

For older or noncollege-educated women, success in managerial roles may still require some rethinking of an appropriate self-image. But as more and more women enter the work force and have success-ful careers, this image should change to a positive one. Currently, females comprise approximately 50 percent of the undergraduate and graduate business school enrollments. This equal career preparation and socialization may do much to eliminate the traditional conflict between positive self-image and career success, areas especially troublesome for women managers.

Stereotype #3. Men Are Inherently More Assertive than Women. The "ideal" stereotypes of the aggressive, driving male and the sweet, passive female are well-known. In fact, American women do generally tend to score lower than men on personality measures of dominance. However, the argument could be made that this result occurs because of cultural values rather than a basic biological difference.

Heinen et al. found that cultural conditioning tends to cause women to hide negative feelings such as hostility or aggressiveness.[32] When facing conflict, most women tend to run away or attempt to smooth over hostile feelings between people. For this reason, manag-ing conflict can be particularly difficult for females. Alpander and Guttman confirmed the tendency toward a "relationship" orientation by women, which is not wholly surprising.[33] It has been customarily accepted that women in the working world are more aware of, and concerned about, the human interrelationships in a working group than men. This is possibly due to their family orientation and caring instincts.

This tendency of women to be more relationship-oriented should not be viewed as a deficit. Effective leadership requires both task- and relationship-oriented behaviors. Men, traditionally, have been high on task but low on relationship dimensions. This was one reason why sensitivity training caught on so well in the business world. On the other hand, research on female leadership, according to Heinen et al., indicates that women can assimilate and learn the task roles requiring influence and assertiveness.[34] An example of this phenomenon is the current popularity of assertiveness training seminars for women. Carr-Ruffino advocates the rule: *Go directly to the persons involved*.[35] She argues that women can become comfortable with behaving assertively in work situations. With proper reconditioning, both men and women can become proficient in the task and relationship roles required for effective management.

Stereotype #4. Women Don't Work for Money. Women work for the same reasons men work: economic, enjoyment, and societal expectations. The so-called traditional American family, long pictured as a working husband with a wife who remained at home with the children, is becoming less and less common. In fact, married-couple households, with or without children, have become a much smaller proportion of the total: Just over half (54 percent) of all households consisted of a married couple in 1985 versus nearly 70 percent in 1969. Married couples in which the wife did *not* work constituted a minority of both black and white married-couple households in 1985.[36]

One of the most dramatic economic changes of the last few decades has been the movement of American women into the labor market. Not only has the two-earner household become the norm among married couples, but the number of women who are the primary—or only—earners in their own households continues to grow. The numbers show that unmarried women have had relatively high labor force participation rates, at least as far back as 1950. Between 1950 and 1985, the labor force participation rate of never-married women drew increasingly close to that of all men, which fell steadily over this period. The real revolution in female labor force participation occurred among married women, especially those with children. More than half of all mothers with preschool children, only 12 percent of whom were in the labor force in 1950, were working or looking for paid work by 1985. Particularly large increases in the labor force participation rate of mothers of very young children occurred between 1980 and 1985.[37]

The current economy strains even high-income households and is devastating to middle-class and poor families. The divorce rate in the United States has climbed consistently upward since 1960.

Eighty-seven percent of all single-parent households are families headed by women, with over one-third of these designated poor.

In addition to the economic motivation of coping with today's economy, the authors' survey of working women indicated other reasons why women enter the labor force. One woman manager eloquently stated:

I'm amazed when it is assumed that women are not interested in, or motivated by, money. We women learn early that money and power go hand in hand. We observed our mothers and have ourselves been in positions of having to ask for money or being allocated a certain sum for household and personal use. Money probably has more importance to us than to the average male, who is accustomed to producing and controlling it.

Many women also work for enjoyment. They're motivated because working brings personal satisfaction and fulfillment. Women who like to work, who incorporate their work as an integral part of

Source: Comstock, Inc

Illus. 1.2   Women who like to work and who incorporate their work as an integral part of themselves are among the most committed of employees.

themselves, are often among the most committed of employees and are often able to overcome personal and family problems through career involvement.[38]

In today's changing economic environment, two salaries are often necessary for the family to maintain desired life styles. Because the traditional American culture promotes men working outside the home and women working inside the home, society tends to view a woman's decision to take on a paying job as an extension of her regular family duties.

The ultimate consequence of sex-role stereotypes is that they may become self-fulfilling. Women who have been socialized most of their lives to be passive, ladylike, dependent, cooperative, and accepting have come to either 1) believe in these notions, or 2) struggle with the conflict of not believing them, but not being able to disprove them. Men in our society also believe most of these stereotypes. What is set in motion, as a result of these traits ascribed to women, is the following self-fulfilling prophecy: "If everyone (society) sees me as passive, or lacking the ability to control my life, then I must be that way for society tells me what I am. I will then act in ways to confirm those images, for that is what is expected."

In summary, most of today's women, from early childhood, acquired a socialized role, i.e., wife and mother, with accompanying behaviors and images of appropriateness for that role. Faced with entry into a "work" organization, they believe that success is good provided it does not interfere with their feminine role and does not threaten the "more superior" male.

OVERCOMING OUTDATED CONCEPTIONS

Faced with the realities of the psychological, social, and organizational barriers, one wonders, "Is there a future for women in management?"

The answer is yes. A look at demographics provides an appreciation that opportunities exist. More women than ever before are participants in the labor force, and they continue to enter the managerial ranks at ever increasing rates. Women's opportunity to enter at the lower management ranks has increased significantly in this century. In 1900, 3 percent of management positions were held by women; in 1950, 12 percent; in 1980,

26 percent; and in 1983, 33 percent. Unfortunately, the number of women at the very highest level of corporate management is still relatively small.[39]

Several conditions contribute to the increase of women in management positions: longer life expectancy, smaller families, rising educational levels, and economic necessity. Many other factors enhance the eligibility of, and need for, women in managerial roles. These include:

1. A shift from product to service businesses in the American economy.

2. Changes in family roles and in public attitudes.

3. Increased employment opportunities in managerial positions due to organizational growth, branching, and decentralization.

4. Changes in values and life-styles.

5. Legal requirements for nondiscrimination, equal opportunity, and equal pay.

6. Increased internationalization of business.

Despite the fact that women have entered the work force and are here to stay, many uphill struggles still exist. Certainly more women work, but the number of women who attain prestige and high level managerial positions is relatively few. The visibility of those female success models who have broken through the **glass ceiling** of top level management include: Ellen Hancock, 40, head of IBM's $5.5 billion Communications-Business Division (compensation, $250,000); Ellen Marram, 40, President, Grocery Division, Nabisco ($250,000); Roxanne Decyk, 34, Senior Vice-President of Administration, Navistar ($200,000); and Diana Harris, 44, Vice-President of Corporate Development, Bausch and Lomb ($175,000).[40]

These media celebrities and highly visible success stories of women rising to the top are sometimes used to obscure some hard facts. Many observers feel that the rate of advancement for women and minorities has actually slowed.[41] A recent study spanning a 16-year time period found race and gender bias increased through the mid 1970s–1980s as competition for management jobs became more intense and government intervention lessened.[42] Ann Morrison and her co-authors found[43] in their study of women in the top of America's largest corporations that the obstacles related to the **glass ceiling** that kept women from systematically progressing to top management in the 1970s will continue to impede their progress into the next several decades. The authors coined the term **glass ceiling** to describe a barrier so subtle it is transparent, yet so strong that it prevents women from moving up the corporate hierarchy simply because they are female.

So, in conclusion, there *is* room for women in management, but the move may not be an easy one. Women are judged by different standards than their male colleagues. Organizations have not recognized the full impact women in the work force have made. It is not "business as usual."

ACTION GUIDELINES

There is a need for both individuals and organizations to reexamine stereotypes and distorted perceptions if women are to adapt and take advantage of existing opportunities. The primary responsibility, however, is with aspiring women managers themselves. After all, they bear the primary responsibility for their own career success. How they manage their own careers will have an impact on changing their organizations and on overcoming outdated conceptions.

Keeping in mind this process, two very basic assumptions about both men and women can help. These are:

1. Human beings have the ultimate choice of creating and acting on alternatives.

2. Human beings need to be true to themselves, *even* if it means not "fitting" into society.

Women accepting these assumptions will have a better chance at breaking both visible and invisible barriers than those who rely on outdated conceptions and stereotypes to mold their lives. If women have accepted these assumptions, they are ready for the subject of the next chapter—the basics that are essential to performing successfully as a manager.

KEY TERMS

Cinderella complex — the tendency of some women to sabotage their careers because of fear of success

glass ceiling — a subtle, transparent, and hard barrier that serves to prevent women from moving up the corporate ladder

helpmate — a feature of most female occupations which consists of assisting others in their work

iron maiden — a female sex role which typecasts a woman as the tough type who acts in a task-oriented manner

mother role — a female sex role based on the stereotyped assumption that women are nurturing and sympathetic listeners

pet — a token role where the female is symbolically included in a management group like a mascot or cheerleader, but not as an equal or influential figure

Queen Bee — a successful woman who has made it to top management by working harder than most men and who keeps her hard-earned and well-deserved privileges for herself

seductress — a female sex role in which a manager is typecast by male subordinates, peers, or superiors as a sex object who shares her attentions with many admirers

stereotypes — assumed differences, social conventions or norms, learned behaviors, attitudes, or expectation

DISCUSSION QUESTIONS

1. Name the female and male role models that our "historically sexist society" has ascribed to us throughout our lives.

2. Account for some of the socialization factors that separate women form the world of male customs and language that men have been raised in. What are these factors?

3. Describe the effects of the male/female role model socialization as they manifest their barriers upon a new female manager's task-accomplishment strategies.

4. Describe the difficulties a female manager could face in organizations and outline the possible strategies to effectively counter these difficulties.

5. Discuss the concept of the glass ceiling.

CHAPTER CASE

RUNNING A BUSINESS

Joann Zuercher was only out of college five years when her father died suddenly from a heart attack. As an only child with a mother who had never worked in business, Joann responded to her mother's request that she run the family cheese business, Swissche Inc. She gave notice as an assistant buyer for a large Federated department store in order to take over her new responsibility.

Her business was started by her father in 1960 and since then had grown and prospered. By 1989, Swissche Inc. (annual sales exceeded $30 million) had 18 stores, 110 full-time employees, and another 60 part-time employees. Almost all of the full-time employees were male.

Each store had its own manager and assistant manager, but all important decisions had been made by Joann's father. As a result, none of the current store managers were deemed capable of running the business. Joann's mother had inherited the business, but she did not feel capable of running the business and so she counted on Joann. After all, Joann did have a business degree. As an only child Joann felt obliged to respond.

Joann had worked for her father during vacations from the University, and thus, in a very superficial way she knew something about the business. Her previous work in retailing had been fun. She worked with many women as well as men. The evening before she went to work, though, she wondered how she would get along with the mostly long-term male workers at Swissche who had a lot of loyalty to her father. She hoped that her degree in business administration and her previous retailing experience had prepared her for what was to come.

QUESTIONS

1. What problems do you think Joann will face with her employees?
2. Is her prior work experience transferable to Swissche? Explain.
3. If you were Joann, what would you anticipate your problems might be?
4. Which of Kanter's roles do you think the male employees would stereotype Joann as? How would this affect her ability to function as a manager at Swissche?

ENDNOTES

[1] J. Foxworth, "They're Still the New Kids on the Block," *Prime Time* (October, 1981): 50-55.

[2] F. Schwartz, "Management Women and the New Facts of Life," *Harvard Business Review* (January-February, 1989): 65-76.

[3] M. Loden, "Recognizing Women's Potential: No Longer Business as Usual," *Management Review* (December, 1987): 44-46.

[4] M. Loden, Ibid.

[5] Dale Feur, "How Women Manage," *Training* (August, 1988): 23-31.

[6] A. Morrison, R. White, and E. Van Velsor, *Breaking the Glass Ceiling: Can Women Reach the Top of America's Largest Corporations?* (Reading, MA: Addison-Wesley, 1987), 20.

[7] D. Feur, Ibid.

[8] F. Schwartz, Ibid.

[9] Margaret Fenn, *Making It in Management: A Behavioral Approach for Women Executives (Englewood Cliffs, NJ: Prentice-Hall, 1978),* 46.

[10] Margaret Hennig and Anne Jardim, The Managerial Woman (New York: Pocket Books, 1978).

[11] Nina Colwill, *The New Partnership: Women and Men in Organizations* (Palo Alto, CA: Mayfield Publishing Co., 1982), 41.

[12] Ibid., 26.

[13] M. Hennig and A. Jardim, Ibid.

[14] R. Kanter, "Women in Organizations: Sex Roles, Group Dynamics, and Change Strategies," in A. Sargent (ed.), *Beyond Sex Roles* (St. Paul: West Publishing Co., 1977).

[15] Colwill, op. cit., 43-44.

[16] M. Hennig and A. Jardim, op. cit., 76-81.

[17] R. Eckstrom, "Women in Management: Factors Affecting Career Entrance and Advancement," Selection 2, No. 1 (Spring, 1985): 29-32.

[18] M. A. Paludi and J. Fankell-Hauser, "An Ideographic Approach to the Study of Women's Achievement Striving," *Psychology of Women Quarterly*, 10 (1986), 89-100.

[19] L. J. Pickford, "The Superstructure of Myths Supporting the Subordination of Women," in B. A. Stead, *Women in Management* (Englewood Cliffs, NJ: Prentice-Hall, 1985), 165-174.

[20] J. Hollander, "Sex Differences in Sources of Social Esteem," *Journal of Consulting and Clinical Psychology*, 38 (1972): 343-347.

[21] L. Chusmir and D. Durand, "The Female Factor," *Training and Development Journal* (August, 1987): 32-37.

[22] S. Donnell and J. Hall, "Men and Women as Managers: A Significant Case of No Significant Difference," *Organizational Dynamics*, 8 (1980): 60-77.

[23] P. A. Renwick, "The Effects of Sex Differences on the Perception and Management of Superior-Subordinate Conflict: An Exploratory Study," *Organizational Behavior and Human Performance*, 19 (1977): 403-415.

[24] A. P. Brief and R. L. Oliver, "Male-Female Differences in Work Attitudes Among Retail Sales Managers," *Journal of Applied Psychology* (1976): 526-528.

[25] D. Birdsall, "A Comparative Analysis of Male and Female Managerial Communication Style in Two Organizations," *Journal of Vocational Behavior*, 16 (1980): 183-196.

[26] Jane Prather, "Why Can't Women Be More Like Men—A Summary of the Sociopsychological Factors Hindering Women's Advancement in the Professions," *American Behavioral Scientist*, 15 (1971): 172-182.

[27] Colette Dowling, *The Cinderella Complex* (New York: Simon and Schuster, 1981).

[28] J. Stephen Heinen et al., "Developing the Woman Manager," *Personnel Journal* (May, 1975): 282-289.

[29] J. B. Hull, "Female Bosses Say Biggest Barriers Are Insecurity and Being a Woman," *Savvy* (November 2, 1982).

[30] Lou W. Stanek, "Women in Management: Can It Be a Renaissance for Everybody?" *Management Review* (November, 1980): 44-48.

[31] Lois A. Koff and Joseph H. Handlon, "Women in Management: Keys to Success or Failure," *Personnel Administrator* (April, 1975): 24-28.

[32] Heinen et al., op. cit.

[33] G. G. Alpander and J. E. Guttman, "Contents and Techniques of Management Development Programs for Women," *Personnel Journal* (February, 1976): 26-79.

[34] Heinen et al., op. cit.

[35] Norma Carr-Ruffino, *The Promotable Woman* (Belmont, CA: Wadsworth Publishing Co., 1985), 168-169.

[36] S. Rix, *The American Women 1988-1989* (New York, NY: W. W. Norton and Company, 1988).

[37] S. Rix, Ibid.

[38] L. Chusmir and D. Durand, op. cit.

[39] U.S. Department of Labor, Bureau of Labor Statistics, *Employment and Earnings* (January, 1988).

[40] "Corporate Women," 75-76; "Big Change at Big Blue," *Business Week* (February 15, 1988): 92-98.

[41] A. Morrison and M. Von Glinow, "Women and Minorities in Management," unpublished paper (1989).

[42] A. Morrison and M. Von Glinow, Ibid.

[43] A. Morrison et al., op. cit.

ADDITIONAL RESOURCES

Baron, James and Bielby, William. "A Woman's Place is With Other Women," *Sex Segregation in the Workplace: Trends, Explanations, Remedies.* Washington: National Academy Press, 1984, 25-55.

Blotnick, Srully. *Otherwise Engaged: The Private Lives of Successful Career Women.* New York: Facts on File Publications, 1985.

Catalyst, "The Glass Ceiling: A Closer Look." *Perspective* (October, 1987): 53B. Chusmir, Leonard and Durand, Douglas, "The Female Factor." *Training and Development Journal* (August, 1987): 32-37.

Collins, Eliza, *Dearest Amanda . . . An Executive's Advice to Her Daughter.* New York: Harper and Row, Publishers, 1984.

Colwill, Nina. "Men and Women in Organizations: Roles and Status, Stereotypes and Power." in Karen Koziara, Michael Moskow, and Lucretia Tanner (eds.), *Working Women, Past, Present, Future*, Industrial Relations Research Association, BNA Books, 1987, 97-117.

Harragan, Betty L. *Games Mother Never Taught You: Corporate Gamesmanship for Women*. New York: Warner Books, 1977.

Hennig, Margaret and Jardim, Anne. *The Managerial Women*. Garden City, New York: Anchor Books, 1981.

Kanter, Rosabeth. *Men and Women of the Corporation*. New York: Basic Books, 1977.

Morrison, Ann M., White, Randall P., and Van Velsor, Ellen. *Breaking the Glass Ceiling: Can Women Reach the Top of America's Largest Corporations?* Reading, MA: Addison Wesley, 1987.

CHAPTER 2

ASSUMING
MANAGERIAL ROLES
AND FUNCTIONS

A Manager's Wide Range of Roles
    Goal Balancer
    Conceptualizer
    Problem Solver
    Motivator
    Conflict Resolver
    Politician
    Diplomat
    Decision Maker
Functions of Management
    Planning
        Women as Planners
        Planning Aids
        Evaluation of Planning Effectiveness
    Organizing
        Women as Organizers
        Organizing Aids

Functions of Management (Continued)
    Staffing
        The Staffing Process
        Women and Staffing
    Leading
        Women as Leaders
        Leadership Guidelines
        Leadership Dilemmas for Female Managers
        Task and Relationship Behaviors
    Controlling
        Women as Controllers
        Controlling Aids
Variations of the Managerial Processes
    Interpersonal Roles
    Informational Roles
    Decision Roles
Action Guidelines
    Avoid Traditional Female Roles
    Develop Business Acumen
    Clarify Managerial Role Expectations
    Become Proficient in the Functions of Management
Key Terms
Discussion Questions
Chapter Case: The New Director of Quality Inspection
Endnotes
Additional Resources

Having obtained a managerial position, it is important to measure up to expectations in order to keep the position and to move on to positions of greater responsibility. Important questions include: What does the organization expect of a manager in terms of performance? What are the main elements of managing? What are the manager's responsibilities as a leader? This chapter will provide women with strategies for successfully establishing credibility as managers. The first step is a clear understanding of the manager's job, which is diagrammed in Figure 2-1.

A MANAGER'S WIDE RANGE OF ROLES

Essentially, the manager's job is to make efficient and effective use of the organization's resources, such as people, time, money, technology, machinery, and information, to accomplish the organization's goals. Managers are in charge of specific tasks and must see to it that they are done successfully. Successful task accomplishment is the primary basis for evaluating managerial performance. In addition, managers are responsible for the actions of their subordinates. *The success or failure of subordinates is a direct indication of managerial effectiveness.* Consequently, it is important to put aside personal feelings toward subordinates and build a cooperative and supportive task team. Managers at every level are delegated to do this within their own unique area of responsibility. The organization provides the specific goals, policies, operating systems, personnel, and other physical resources. The manager is entrusted with making decisions and producing the desired results leading to organizational goal accomplishment. The manager accomplishes these objectives through the functions of planning, organizing, staffing, leading, and controlling, which are discussed in depth later. To be effective in performing these managerial functions, a manager will assume a wide range of roles.[1]

Goal Balancing

Because organizational resources are limited, a manager must strike a balance between the organization's various goals and needs. One strategy

FIGURE 2-1

THE MANAGER'S JOB

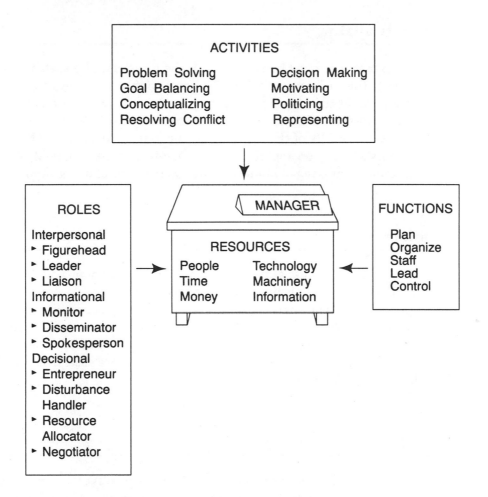

is to arrange each day's tasks in order of priority. It helps to complete the most important tasks right away, and relegate to a lower priority those that can be done later. The effective use of time (a manager's most valuable resource) is discussed in Chapter 5.

A manager also must decide *who* is to perform each particular task based on each subordinate's area of expertise and the various projects that need to be accomplished. This requires analytical skills and assertiveness that a manager may not have developed in previous nonsupervisory positions.

Conceptualizing

A manager must be able to think about tasks in the abstract as they relate to the entire organization. This means that managers must always keep in mind the bigger picture, i.e., the larger organizational goals, as well as the goals of their units. Managers also must be able to balance the short-term results of their units with the long-term outlook. This means not only staying on top of things in day-to-day management, but also continually thinking of innovative and better ways of doing things.

Problem Solving

A manager must anticipate extraordinary situations and be adept at identifying and analyzing real problems when they do occur. After a thorough problem analysis, it is the manager's responsibility to develop alternative solutions and to decide the best course of action. This requires the manager to accept responsibility for decisions that affect others and a move from passive, supportive, reactive roles to more assertive, proactive, decision-making ones.

Motivating

New managers quickly learn that to do an effective job, it is necessary to rely not only on their subordinates and supervisors, but also on their peers and other staff members in the organization. In fact, management can be defined as the process of accomplishing organizational goals through the efforts of other people. This means it is important to reinforce working relationships upward, downward, and laterally within the organization. Managers act as influence channels in all these directions within the organization. Communicating information clearly on what needs to be done and the consequences for those responsible is one of the most important aspects of a manager's job.[2]

Conflict Resolving

Since organizations are made up of people with differing needs and values, disagreements often occur. Conflict can provide opportunities for growth and creativity. Disagreements also can have negative effects on morale and productivity if they are not managed appropriately. Although no manager wants conflict to become disruptive, sometimes it does. The manager's responsibility is to ensure that conflict produces constructive change and new ideas rather than disruptions. New managers who move from women's traditional *doer* roles that have not required them to take charge in resolving conflict and hostilities need to concentrate on being more assertive in conflict situations through understanding, acceptance, and decisive actions.

Politicking

Because of limited resources in an organization and individual differences in goals and values, a manager must be adept at persuading and compromising in order to promote personal, departmental, and organizational goals. Every effective manager plays politics by developing networks of mutual obligations with other managers in the organization. At times this also includes building alliances and coalitions that can be drawn on to win support for critical proposals, decisions, or activities. It also involves managing interpersonal conflicts with subordinates, peers, and superiors in a productive fashion. To develop the necessary rapport and to make contacts, it often helps if managers become involved in informal leisure activities such as picnics, special interest clubs, and sports.

Representing

A manager is the official representative of a working unit in the organization. When attending organizational meetings or dealing with clients, customers, or governmental officials, managers are considered to be representatives of the entire organization and of their units in particular. This has important image implications for both the manager and the organization. Effective communication both within the working group and between the manager and external entities is vital. Not only are these liaisons vital for securing the resources and outcomes desired by the work group, but they also have a crucial impact on the manager's career.

Decision Making

Since no organization runs smoothly at all times, there is no limit to the number and type of problems that may occur. Managers are the ones who are expected to come up with the solutions to difficult problems and to follow through on decisions even when such actions may be unpopular. For example, it may sometimes be necessary to terminate an employee or make unpopular work assignments. In such situations, personal feelings should be put aside in deference to overall organizational effectiveness.

Flexibility

The summary given above does not begin to exhaust the list of roles that a manager must fill. It does, however, emphasize that managers need to change hats frequently and be aware of what particular role is fitting at a given time. The ability to recognize and switch into appropriate roles is a mark of an effective manager.

Unfortunately, as new women managers seek to perform in these roles, they may be subject to conflict with men who are unaccustomed to being answerable to women. As women move into the male domain of organizational responsibility and decision making, men may feel threatened by having to take orders from a woman, and may waste time and energy resisting her authority. Women, too, may feel uncomfortable wielding power over men.[3] As more and more women enter the ranks of management, they are learning to overcome these barriers by developing a careful balance between assertiveness, competence, and charisma.

FUNCTIONS OF MANAGEMENT

Regardless of the type of organization—educational, business, governmental, military, or social—there are basic managerial functions, or processes, that must be carried out. **Management** is the process of *planning, organizing, staffing, leading, and controlling* the efforts of organizational members and using organizational resources to achieve stated organizational objectives.[4] Whether managers supervise three people or dozens of subordinates, they will all perform these functions at one time or another.

Planning

Goals, or objectives, are the results sought. **Planning** is the process of determining goals and how they are to be achieved. No matter how laudable a goal may be, nothing usually happens until a plan of action is developed to achieve it. New Year's resolutions are common examples of unmet goals due to a lack of planning. A plan provides the design for specific courses of action to assure the completion of tasks necessary to accomplish the goal.

Women as Planners. The traditional female *doer* jobs are confined to specific daily tasks and procedures where women carry out plans of others rather than formulate their own. For many new women managers, planning is a new dimension of their jobs, due, in part, to earlier helpmate roles where they acted in supportive ways, as assistants to men. These roles result in a detachment from goal setting and planning.

When given the opportunities and experience, women are just as good at organizational planning as men. Women's potential for planning is identical to men's based on skill levels in abstract reasoning, analytical thinking, achievement motivation, and adaptability.[5] Countless women have always proved this point more pragmatically in mainstream planning ventures in the areas of politics, philanthropy, religious work, and other service-related organizations. Now their planning skills are being recognized financially in business organizations.

Planning Aids. To be successful, a plan must have the *support* of upper management as well as those subordinates who will implement it. Plans must be compatible with other current objectives with regard to timeliness and impact. They also must be clearly understood by subordinates and flexible enough to undergo necessary modifications and revisions. It is helpful to facilitate commitment through involvement

Illus. 2.1   The planning skills of abstract reasoning, analytical thinking, achievement motivation, and adaptability are necessary in business organizations.

of all implementers in the determination of both objectives and plans.[6]

The prerequisite to planning is *clarity of objectives*. The goal may already be officially expressed, or it may have to be established anew. In either case, the manager might codify the goal in a clear, written statement and communicate it to all concerned. It may be necessary, for example, for a manager to issue an explicit memo stating that her goal is to have the highest quality output of any department as measured by the number of returned products.

Next, the manager *gathers all pertinent data* and *analyzes* them to *establish reasonable premises* in order to generate realistic *alternative plans*. After determining the most promising plan, the manager puts it into action by specifying its timing, specific activities and responsibilities, and control points. Finally, the manager *communicates* the plan to all subordinates, peers, and supervisors who may be affected so as to *determine who will be responsible* for what, where, and when.[7]

Evaluation of Planning Effectiveness. There are two main tests that determine the effectiveness of a plan:

1. The first test measures the extent to which the plan facilitates the *attainment of the objectives.*

2. The second test identifies the extent to which the *gains* attributable to the plan *outweigh* the associated *costs* (e.g., time, money, effort) spent on preparing and executing it.

Checkpoints to be considered when evaluating a plan's chances of meeting the above criteria include: compatibility with other current goals, accessibility of resources required, extent of involvement of all concerned, and degree of acceptance by other managers and subordinates who must implement it. If the plan meets these criteria, it is time to organize resources and schedule the activities necessary to make it work.

Organizing

Plans must be translated into action by establishing priorities, assigning responsibilities, and developing time schedules. The necessary human and material resources must be assembled. Tasks must be defined for individuals and groups, and the responsibilities for results established. Thus, the organizing function starts with, and builds upon, the results of previous planning to develop an organizational structure. Through the resulting structure, the manager hopes to accomplish the goals determined in the planning stage. **Organizing** is deciding who is going to do what, and how people and activities will be related.

The importance of the organizing function can be seen clearly in a simple story from "Sesame Street," a children's educational television program.[8] The story begins when the King decides that he and all of his subjects will have a picnic. The King calls his subjects together, announces the picnic, and tells them to bring watermelon, potato salad, etc. The subjects leave to prepare the food. On returning to the picnic, it is discovered that everybody brought potato salad and nothing else. Needless to say, the King expresses his disappointment at having no watermelon. Lo and behold, everyone takes the potato salad home and returns with watermelon! Finally, someone suggests that the subjects divide the task up and assign different things for different people to bring. The story closes with a successful picnic.

While the story is simple (and may even be foolish to some), it illustrates the importance of organizing—of dividing up the total work to be done, defining everyone's duties and responsibilities, and delegating the authority necessary to perform the duties and responsibilities.

Organizing is a tool for making order possible in the performance of activities—it makes possible cooperation and coordination. Without organizing, chaos is likely to occur because no one knows who is responsible for performing each activity. More specifically, without organizing there is no effective way to prevent duplication of activities, nor is there any means of assuring that all necessary activities are performed.

Organizing results in a task system tied together by authority relationships. This takes place through the process of **delegation** where (1) *responsibility* for duties and tasks is assigned, and (2) *authority* to perform the duties and tasks is granted. The amount of authority delegated depends upon situational factors such as the nature of the tasks, the level of subordinate ability, the results expected, and the need for coordination.

Women as Organizers. Because women tend to overspecialize in one particular area or task and become the experts, they often develop a block against delegating to less skilled subordinates.[9] Previously held helpmate-type jobs also may have provided little in the way of responsibilities requiring delegation. In addition, new women managers sometimes are so eager to prove their ability that their quest to show results and earn their wings gets in the way of delegating certain duties. President Dwight D. Eisenhower made an observation that shows the folly of this approach: "There's no telling how much one can accomplish so long as one doesn't need to get all the credit for it."

The above quotation demonstrates the main advantage of delegating responsibilities—it allows the manager to multiply herself, that is, to accomplish many more activities by getting results through other people. It also frees her to do the things only she can do. Finally, it helps develop subordinates. When she delegates, she makes better use of her human resources, develops supervisory depth when she is away, and paves the way for even greater recognition in the long run.

Organizing Aids. After overcoming any unwillingness to let go of things that others can do, several things can be done to make sure that delegation is effective.

1. Make sure that the objectives, timing, and processes are clear.

2. Indicate the standards and control points by which the work will be judged.

3. Assure the subordinate that the manager is available when needed for necessary advice.

4. Make sure that the subordinate is qualified to handle the task.

5. Make sure that the necessary resources to get the job done are made available to the delegates.

6. Build in the necessary authority and announce it to all people involved.

The above guidelines will aid the manager in effective task accomplishment, but they do not eliminate her supervisory responsibilities. She still must motivate the subordinates involved and follow through during the process so that mistakes can be intercepted and corrected. These are the tasks of the management functions of leading and controlling. It is easier to lead and control qualified and committed subordinates, however. This type of subordinate can be obtained through the staffing function.

Staffing

Because people are the most critical resource in any organization, the selection, training, and development of employees are among a manager's most critical tasks. **Staffing** is the managerial function that deals with recruiting, placing, training, and developing organizational members.

The Staffing Process. Because most organizations experience a constant turnover of personnel over time, the staffing process is best conceived of as a series of steps that are performed on a continuing basis to ensure that the organization has the best qualified people in the right positions at all times. The eight major components in the staffing process are briefly described below.[10]

Human resource *planning* ensures that the current and future personnel needs of the organization are met. This function includes the analysis of skills needed, predicted vacancies, and projected expansions or reductions as compared to the labor market demographics. It also involves assuring that equal employment opportunity guidelines are strictly followed and supported in spirit as well, especially by women managers.

Recruitment is the process of attracting candidates for current or projected job openings. Candidates are located through such sources as advertisements (in newspapers, professional journals, radio, or college campus placement offices), employment agencies, and current employees.

Selection is the process of evaluating and choosing from among job applicants. Aids in selection include application forms, resumes, interviews, employment tests, and reference checks. Selection activities, such as interviewing, add increased complexity because of today's changing demographics and more multi-dimensional legal and ethical considerations.

Orientation helps the recruits adjust and fit into the organization. Orientation activities include introducing new employees to current employees, providing them with information on all relevant company policies and procedures, and attending lunches, briefings, and meetings. It also includes the more subtle socialization process that addresses such informal issues as how men and women interact in the system, whether they are treated equally or differentially, and how the organization reacts to affairs.

Training helps employees increase their skills and contributions to the organization. It may be for the purpose of improving their performance in their current job or preparing them for promotions and additional responsibilities.

Performance appraisal compares the employee's actual performance with established criteria and standards. Feedback is then provided to correct deviations or to reward behavior that is acceptable.

Transfers shift personnel among jobs in the organization. **Vertical** transfers are promotions or demotions. **Lateral** transfers are from one position to another at the same level or to a different location.

Separation involves resignations, layoffs, discharges, or retirements. Retirements may be anticipated through earlier human resource planning, but the study of other types of separations can provide insights into the effectiveness of such matters as the pay scale, management style, selection, and training.

Staffing Women Managers

Human resource staffers are coming to realize that, to recruit the most capable managerial talent, they must look to the creative resources in the female work force. In 1986, approximately 36 percent of all managers in American industry were women.[11] Although this is more than double the proportion 20 years ago,[12] of the 43 million women in America's work force in 1988, only 6 percent are classified as middle managers and only 1 percent have achieved positions in top management.[13] Consequently, the supply of potential women managers is growing.

Past practices placed many women in traditional female positions without opportunities for grooming for management positions. To counter these practices, many business and government organizations, such as the State of California, have developed training programs to reeducate employees for positions as managers.[14] These programs are often sponsored entirely by the government to improve quality and keep organizations competitive. They help provide higher quality staff without the recruiting effort, by upgrading the skills and attitudes of current employees.

A second increase in the supply of qualified women for managerial positions has arisen from significant demographic changes, such as the dramatic increase in women's educational levels. Today, women make up to one-half of graduate business classes, which is quite an improvement over the early '60s, when women weren't admitted at all at most schools.[15]

Finally, the rising cost of living has increased the number of women seeking managerial positions which not only pay more than traditional female-occupied positions, but also allow for substantially more satisfaction and personal development.

Illus. 2.2   The number of women now qualified for managerial positions has been influenced by demographic changes such as the dramatic increase in women's educational levels.

Leading

Leading is the function that links the manager's planned objectives and the achievement of those objectives. The planning, organizing, and staffing functions are preparation for achievement. Through the leadership function, the action needed to actually reach objectives is initiated and maintained.[16]

Leadership involves communicating the what and how of job assignments to subordinates and motivating them to accomplish the tasks necessary to achieve organizational objectives. It is the most interpersonal function of management. These components of leadership are so important that a separate chapter on motivation and communication (Chapter 6) is devoted to them.

Looking at well-known examples of effective female leaders, such as Elizabeth Dole, Queen Elizabeth I, Margaret Thatcher, Florence Nightingale, Susan B. Anthony, Indira Gandhi, and Clara Barton, demonstrates that a great variety of personalities and styles can be equally effective. Leadership is not a matter of who the person is, but *how* that person influences others. It is situational, and different jobs require different leadership styles. Leadership is also the creation and cultivation of an appropriate organizational climate in which people can grow as they contribute to the organization's objectives. Through a combination of technical, human, and conceptual skills, the effective leader can persuade others to work enthusiastically and competently toward defined organizational objectives.

Women as Leaders. The above examples of female leaders indicate that women can rise to prominent leadership positions, but the vast majority of organizational leaders today are men. Women usually occupy lower status, less influential positions. In 1986, only 1.7 percent of the corporate officers of Fortune-500 companies were women.[17] What keeps more women from moving into leadership positions?

Some of the answers are evident in commonly accepted myths and stereotypes. Many top executives believe that women aren't tough enough to handle the job. At the same time, women are expected to retain a certain amount of femininity. Corporate women today face the challenge of blending very disparate qualities, while staying within a narrow band of acceptable characteristics and actions.[18]

Inherent in early writings was a prevalent view that women make poor managers. Douglas McGregor, in *The Professional Manager*, has written that the model of a successful manager in American society is based entirely on masculine traits like competitiveness, aggressiveness, and firmness.[19] The model does not include feminine traits like softness, dependency, or emotionality. This type of stereotype indirectly contributes to the belief that men are not usually effective when working for women and that women's more expressive traits interfere with their leadership potential. Still, a gradual shift is taking place as businesses today are beginning to favor the more participative styles of management over competitive and power-oriented ones.[20] This "affiliative" style of management is more compatible with women's expressive social conditioning.

Another problem is the small number of visible women leaders to serve as appropriate female role models. New female managers have few examples to identify with and to emulate. This also results in an ineffective upper echelon network to facilitate female promotions.

Leadership Guidelines. Although there are no universal characteristics of effective leaders, there are valuable assets that a manager can develop more fully to enhance her leadership effectiveness. Some of those pointed out by the American Management Association are summarized below:[21]

Performance is carrying out current duties exceptionally well. Competence in doing one's job generates respect from subordinates and motivates them to be effective also in their jobs.

Initiative is demonstrated by being a self-starter. Subordinates look to their managers to point them in the right direction and to provide the structure in which they can perform their activities.

Acceptance through gaining respect and winning the confidence of others is crucial. A key to being accepted by others is to treat them with respect and to listen carefully when they try to express their needs and concerns.

Good judgment and reaching sound conclusions based on all of the evidence available in a situation where a decision has to be made is also vital. Effective **communication** with people at all levels is a key to obtaining all the necessary information for efficient decision making. It is also crucial in having decisions implemented properly. Because of its pivotal role in effective management, communication skills are dealt with more completely in Chapter 6.

Credibility can also be established through **accomplishment**— the amount and quality of work produced. Accomplishment depends on the effective use of one's own time in getting tangible outcomes completed. Time management is discussed in more detail in Chapter 5.

Flexibility in coping with change and adjusting to the unexpected is a survival prerequisite in the life of a manager. In working with different personalities and different situations, it is extremely important to be able to see things from different points of view and to adapt one's own interpersonal style to meet the needs of changing situations.

Objectivity through the control of personal feelings builds respect as a manager mediates conflicts in an open-minded manner. In dealing with a group of subordinates, it is extremely important not to appear biased. The manager should demonstrate that she has considered all the relevant facts involved in making objective decisions, especially when the results affect those working for her. When a manager is mediating between subordinates, it is crucial to show honesty, integrity, and fairness, to create perceptions of equitable treatment.

Leadership Dilemmas for Female Managers. In addition to the above guidelines, certain traits create specific problems for women managers. Following are several sets of conflicting expectations that women must reconcile to succeed in corporate life.[22]

Women need to take risks and be consistently outstanding earlier in their career than men. This may include taking a job or assignment in a different part of the business to broaden your experience.

Women need to appear tough but not macho. This includes being assertive, taking decisive action, and being cool under pressure. However, women must walk a fine line between being tough and keeping a certain amount of femininity.

Women need to be ambitious but not expect equal treatment. Putting career ahead of family is one thing that many women will not do. Even for those who do, however, a recent survey[23] has shown that women managers are still paid less than their male counterparts, and are not successful getting into the good old boys networks.

Women need to assert themselves and take responsibility, but still follow others' advice. It is important that women managers be accountable for business performance and take responsibility for managing their own careers. Women must also recognize when to solicit advice from their superiors, and what to do with that advice.

Task and Relationship Behaviors. In order for work groups to operate effectively, two major aspects of the leadership function must be exhibited. The first is the **task-related** (or problem-solving)

Behavior that is aimed at accomplishing the objectives of the group itself. The second is the **relationship-related behavior** that involves maintaining rapport and commitment within the group. This includes anything that helps the group to operate more smoothly and to feel good about the other members within the group.

At times a task-related behavior, such as forcefully encouraging the group to make an important decision or to get on with the job, is more important than a relationship-related behavior like mediating group disagreements. An individual who can perform both roles successfully is in a much better position to be an effective leader.

The degree of effectiveness that a leader exhibits is most appropriately measured by the accomplishments of her followers. This in turn depends on how much the followers understand about the goals they are pursuing, how they perform, how unified they are in their work setting. and how committed they are toward the attainment of organizational goals. The effective leader, therefore, determines the most appropriate and productive behavior for herself in dealing with her subordinates, depending on her relevant goals, environment, and leadership abilities. She also integrates the organizational values, group values, and individual values effectively in order to attain the company goals over the long run.

In addition to giving subordinates legitimate directions, the leader, by definition, must be able to influence followers to carry out these directions effectively. A manager, for example, may direct a subordinate to perform a certain task, but it is her *continuous* influence over that subordinate that will determine if the task is carried out properly. The control system she establishes and the way she uses it are key components in making sure that the expected results are achieved.

Controlling

Controlling involves monitoring what is actually happening and correcting deviations from the plan. The best attempts at planning, organizing, staffing, and leading do not always produce the anticipated results. Controlling is the function that makes sure the other management functions pay off. It also serves as the link to future planning, organizing, staffing, and leading.

Three basic elements in the control process are: (1) establishing valid, realistic standards of performance; (2) measuring actual performance against established performance standards, and (3) using the feedback process to take corrective measures to improve situations. Unless there are standards against which performance can be measured, control is impossible. Specific standards can be developed from the performance goals themselves. Examples of standards are units of output produced, the time taken to accomplish certain activities, or any other factor indicating goal achievement.

Once the manager has clearly defined and communicated standards for performance, she can begin to measure the actual results. This includes the collection of data and comparison to the control standards. Conclusions can then be reached regarding performance effectiveness. If deviations from established standards are found, the manager must first identify and analyze the real cause of the deviation. The results of this deviation may be either positive or negative. A positive performance should be complimented with sincere praise or financial rewards. If the result is negative, the manager must plan and initiate corrective action.

Women as Controllers. The primary barrier to effective controlling is the negative image often associated with it. Most people do not enjoy being considered as the person who checks up on others by constantly looking over their shoulders. Also, disciplining and reprimanding subordinates whose behavior deviates from accepted standards is not a pleasant task. For some new women managers, these actions may appear to be out of character. Thus, controlling may present internal as well as interpersonal conflicts for them.

New woman managers should bear in mind that the purpose of control is positive in that it facilitates the accomplishment of organizational objectives. As a result, it benefits all involved in many direct and indirect ways. Also, many of the negatively viewed aspects of controlling can be made more palatable by dealing with them in a positive, problem-solving way. Chapter 9 presents some guidelines for dealing with problem employees.

Controlling Aids. Many techniques can aid in implementing the controlling process. The most useful are **budgets, work standards,** and **time schedules.** Other techniques include **direct observations, progress reports,** and **formal performance evaluations.** If corrective action is warranted, it can be taken through positive activities like **interviewing, counseling,** and **joint problem solving**. The following criteria can be used by the woman manager to evaluate the effectiveness of any control system she installs.

1. Is the system economical? It makes no sense to invest more resources in the control process than the activity itself might save. It is important to include time as a resource in this cost/benefit calculation.

2. Is it efficient? The best time to learn of deviations, particularly negative ones, is before they occur. Since this is seldom possible when dealing with people, the next best thing is to make sure negative deviations are reported in time to make appropriate corrections.

3. Is it understandable? Clear, unambiguous feedback is just as important to subordinates as it is to managers. Managers must clearly understand what went wrong and why. Subordinates must clearly understand what needs to be done when taking corrective actions.

4. Is it acceptable? People who use and are affected by controls must believe that they are fair and useful. An acceptable control system provides the basic motivation to use controls properly. A fundamental prerequisite to acceptance involves an understanding of the system, how it works, and why it is necessary.

VARIATIONS OF THE MANAGERIAL PROCESSES

Every manager must plan, organize, staff, lead, and control, but different managers may go about these activities in different ways. The manager of a small antique shop may plan quite a bit less formally than an engineering department manager charged with designing and supplying small mechanical parts to large aerospace companies. A manager in a newly formed company may find that more time is required in coordinating work since a new organization requires the right sequencing of activities of many different and independent groups. Every manager will have different problems and ways of solving them. If a manager has workers who are engaged in routine, monotonous work, different styles of motivation are required for those workers than the styles appropriate for people working in fast-paced occupations with a lot of excitement and challenge.

The emphasis on the different managerial processes also varies depending on the manager's position in the organizational hierarchy. Upper level executives spend more time planning, while lower level supervisors spend more time controlling. The types of decisions made at the top levels have broader perspectives and longer time horizons than those made at the lower levels that are more specific and sometimes more urgent. All managers must manage, but the appropriate techniques vary according to management level.

The previous descriptions of planning, organizing, staffing, leading, and controlling evoke images of management as rational, systematic, and reflective. However, several researchers who have spent a considerable amount of time observing managers in action agree that, in reality, management is more chaotic than systematic, and more emotional than rational. The manager's day is fractured into an astonishingly large number of contacts with different people and different problems. Henry Mintzberg systematically studied managers on a daily basis and reported what they actually do in his book, *The Nature of Managerial Work*. In general, Mintzberg found that managers can expect no concentration of efforts; rather, managers' activities are characterized by brevity, fragmentation, and variety. There is no break in the pace of activity from the time a manager arrives in the morning until he or she leaves in the evening. On an average day, managers open 36 pieces of mail, make 5 phone calls, and attend 8 meetings. A true break seldom occurs. The best that most managers can hope for is coffee during meetings and lunch during formal business meetings.[24]

Based on his observations of actual managers on the job, Mintzberg concluded that within their functions, managers perform ten different but highly related roles. These roles refer to behaviors attributable to the managerial job. These roles are described in Table 2-1, as they relate to interpersonal relationships, information transfer, and decision making.

Interpersonal Roles

Figurehead roles are ceremonial and symbolic duties that all managers are required to perform from time to time, like giving out achievement certificates. The leadership role includes activities like motivating and controlling subordinates. The liaison role involves interacting with individuals or groups outside the organization or work group.

Informational Roles

All managers should monitor information from outside their organization through magazines and talking with others. They also act as disseminators of this information to internal organizational members. Finally, managers perform as spokespersons when they represent the organization to outsiders.

TABLE 2-1

MINTZBERG'S MANAGERIAL ROLES

Role	Description	Identifiable Activities
Interpersonal		
Figurehead	Symbolic head; obliged to perform a number of routine duties of a legal or social nature	Ceremony, status requests, solicitations
Leader	Responsible for the motivation and activation of subordinates; responsible for staffing, training, and associate duties	Virtually all managerial activities involving subordinates
Liason	Maintains self-developed network of outside contacts and informers who provide favors and information	Acknowledgements of mail; external board work; other activities involving outsiders
Informational		
Monitor	Seeks and receives wide variety of special information (much of it current) to develop thorough understanding of organization and environment; emerges as nerve center of internal and external information of the organization	Handling all mail and contacts categorized as concerned primarily with receiving information (e.g., periodic news, observational tours)

TABLE 2-1 MINTZBERG'S MANAGERIAL ROLES (Cont'd)

Role	Description	Identifiable Activities
Disseminator	Transmits information received from outsiders or from other subordinates to members of the organization; some information factual, some involving interpretation and integration of diverse value positions of organizational influences	Forwarding mail into organization for informational purposed, verbal contacts involving information flow to subordinates (e.g., review sessions, instant communication flows)
Spokesperson	Transmits information to outsides on organization's plans, policies, actions, results, etc.; serves as expert organization's industry	Board meetings; handling mail and contacts involving transmission of information to outsiders
Decisional		
Entrepreneur	Searches organization and its environment for opportunities and initiates "improvement projects" to bring about change; supervises design of certain projects as well	Strategy and review sessions involving initiation or design of improvment projects
Disturbance Handler	Responsible for corrective action when organization faces important, unexpected disturbances	Strategy and review sessions involving disturbances and crises
Resource Allocator	Responsible for allocation of oraganization resources of all kinds—in effect the making or approval of all significant organizational decisions	Scheduling; requests for authorization; any activity involving budgeting and the programming of subordinates' work
Negotiator	Responsible for representing the organization at major negotiations	Negotiation

Source: Henry Mintzberg, "The Nature of Managerial Work" (New York: Harper & Row, 1973): 93-94

Decision Roles

Managers initiate and oversee new projects as an entrepreneur. They take corrective action as a disturbance handler. Managers are resource allocators and also negotiators when bargaining is required.

Just how managers perform their functions in this whirlwind of activity was the subject for another group of researchers. One study questioned 452 managers from 11 management levels in companies that ranged in size from 100 to more than 4,000 employees. They were asked about how much of the workday they spent on 8 different activities. The results are listed in Table 2-2.

TABLE 2-2

PERCENTAGE OF WORKDAY SPENT BY MANAGER ON EIGHT ACTIVITIES

Activities	Top Managers	Middle Managers	First-Level Managers
Planning	28%	18%	15%
Organizing	36%	33%	24%
Leading	22%	36%	51%
Controlling	14%	13%	10%

Source: Adapted from Stephen P. Robbins, *Management*, Second Edition (Englewood Cliffs, N.J.: Prentice-Hall, 1988): 12.

Another study of executives found that fast track managers devoted only 32% of their time to the traditional tasks of planning and controlling, and more in areas of routine communicating (29%), human resource management (20%), and networking (19%), depending upon their political ambitions or organizational climate[25] Furthermore, the differences in activities by rank, indicated in Table 2-2, are especially important for women managers, who for the most part have penetrated lower management, but failed to gain access to upper management.[26]

Given this information, it is evident that although planning, organizing, leading, and controlling are necessary, most managers find themselves attempting these activities under conditions of brevity and fragmentation. The nature of managerial work is extremely fast paced. A manager has to deal with constant interruptions, handle many problems simultaneously, and juggle priorities for action. The new manager is the leader in her field who actualizes for the members of her group the common goal to be achieved. She organizes their experience and ability, molds them into a team, and works *with*, and not *through*, the members of her group. The manager is a facilitator who shows the way ahead and turns her employees into achievers in their own right.[27]

In influencing others to accept her direction and control, a new manager needs to project an image of confidence and competence. Gaining credibility, authority, and respect through appropriate dress and appearance is the subject of the next chapter on projecting your image.

ACTION GUIDELINES

Being accepted into the managerial ranks is only the first step. New managers need to demonstrate their competence in performing management functions and their ability to fit into the social milieu if they are going to stay there and continue to advance in their careers. Both seasoned male and female managers will be carefully watching the female newcomer's performance to see how well she learns and adapts. Several guidelines can be drawn to facilitate women's success in overcoming traditional barriers and developing managerial skills.

1. *Avoid traditional female roles.* New women managers may be tempted to yield to the pressures of male majorities and conform to their expectations of passive, dependent, or helpmate types of roles. It would be easier for everyone if tradition were confirmed. Being new in a management position, however, provides the opportunity to grow and to demonstrate creativity, assertiveness, decisiveness, and ability to take on responsibilities independently.

2. *Develop business acumen.* Women first entering management ranks must learn to relate to their superiors in a professional, not overly emotional manner.[28] Top executives tend to respect managers with a no-nonsense, bottom-line orientation, and a broad, strategic perspective.

3. *Clarify managerial role expectations.* In general, managers are responsible for making efficient and effective use of the organization's resources to accomplish the organization's goals. It

is important to clarify how this is expected to be done in any manager's particular situation. The new woman manager should find out by asking questions and talking to other managers about their experiences and techniques. She should find out what unwritten responsibilities must be accounted for, and ask such questions as: How are conflicts expected to be resolved? What managerial styles seem most effective? What alliances and coalitions exist, and how can they be used to facilitate the manager's job?

4. *Keep up to date on technological developments.* It is vital that women relate well to the versatility of computers and telecommunications, as well as other specific advancements in their area of special concentration. Keeping up to date on business developments in general will also add to their credibility and visibility.

5. *Become proficient in the functions of management.* Successful managers take the time necessary to adequately develop a plan for accomplishing objectives assigned to them. A few minutes of planning and organizing one's time and resources at the beginning of each day can save hours of confusion and anxiety for both the manager and those working for her. The same is true in even greater magnitude for long-term projects.

Finally, in order to assure goal implementation and accomplishment, the manager should do everything possible to build the understanding, commitment, and support she needs among those affected by her plans. It will also make the jobs of leading and controlling much easier because her subordinates will already understand and accept what they are doing as important and legitimate.

KEY TERMS

acceptance — a leader's ability to gain respect and win the confidence of others

communication — a leader's ability to get through to people at all levels

controlling — the management process of monitoring what is actually happening and correcting deviations from plans

decisiveness — a leader's ability to reach sound conclusions based on all of the evidence available in a decision situation

delegation — the process of assigning responsibility for duties and tasks, and granting authority to perform them

flexibility — a leader's ability to cope with change and adjust to the unexpected

initiative — a leader's ability to be a self-starter

lateral transfer — transfer from one position to another at the same level or to a different location

leading — the management process of linking planned objectives and their achievement

management — the process of planning, organizing, staffing, leading, and controlling the efforts of organizational members and using organizational resources to achieve stated organizational objectives

objectivity — a leader's ability to control personal feelings in an open-minded manner

organizing — the management process of deciding who is going to do what, and how people and activities will be related

performance — Task achieving behaviors

planning — the management process of determining goals and how they are to be achieved

relationship-related behavior — a leader's function which involves group maintenance to help the group operate more smoothly and feel good about its members

staffing — the management process of recruiting, placing, training, and developing organizational members

task-related behavior — a leader's function which is aimed at accomplishing the objectives of the work group

vertical transfer — promotion or demotion

DISCUSSION QUESTIONS

1. What are the barriers female managers face as controllers? What techniques should they implement to aid in this process?

2. Account for the barriers women face as organizers within as organization. What steps can be initiated to avoid these difficulties?

3. What are the three steps a female manager should take in order to overcome common leadership dilemmas and conflicting expectaions in the workplace?

4. What keeps women from moving into leadership positions?

5. What are some of the unique difficulties encountered by women in the planning process and what are some of the essential steps to formulate a successful managerial plan?

THE NEW DIRECTOR OF QUALITY INSPECTION

Before her promotion to Director of Quality Inspection, Tracy Elliot worked with the other seven inspectors at Turbo Products who all reported to the Director of Quality Inspection, Jim Evans. Everything seemed fine. Tracy had completed her college degree in Operations Management and worked as a manufacturing process controller before being promoted into Quality Inspection two years ago. Over the last three years she had proven an enthusiastic and competent colleague, always doing a quality job herself and serving as a valuable colleague to others when they needed help making their deadlines.

When Tracy joined Turbo Products she was already used to working with men in her college classes, and in her manufacturing control position. She felt accepted as a colleague by others who respected her statistical expertise. The same was true when she transferred to quality control, although she did notice little things in the way the other seven male inspectors treated her. They were overly polite and would avoid swearing in front of her; she was never invited to lunch or to drinks after work; jokes and non-work-oriented conversations stopped when she approached.

Tracy had always been totally committed to her job, and her performance earned her the promotion to Director of Quality Inspection when Jim Evans was promoted to Manufacturing Manager. But now, as a manager, superior technical performance just wasn't going to be enough to win over other inspectors. Now she was going to have to prove herself as someone worthy of their respect as a leader and manager. Tracy knew that working for a female manager was something new for these guys, but she was determined to demonstrate her managerial competence and win them over. The question was how.

The evening Tracy Elliot was named Director of Quality Inspection, seven male inspectors, her former colleagues, went to the local pub, got roaring drunk, and decided to quit *en masse*. When they arrived the next day, Tracy called them together, told them she had heard about this, and asked them to at least give her a chance at the Director's job. She made them a bet that if they stuck it out for one year under her supervision and at that time did not all agree that she was the best boss that they had ever had, she would buy all of them as many rounds of drinks as they wished at her resignation party.

QUESTIONS

1. What are the main managerial roles Tracy should concentrate on fulfilling? What difficulties do you anticipate she might encounter in these roles? How should she implement these roles to gain the acceptance of the quality inspectors?

2. What are some of the functions of management that Tracy now must assume? What can she do to enhance her effectiveness in each of these functions given the possible resistance of her male subordinates?

3. Which of the Action Guidelines for assuming managerial roles and functions will help Tracy the most? Why? What other guidelines can you suggest?

NOTE: *A year later the same seven inspectors sponsored a giant anniversary party for Tracy, and provided her with a bouquet of roses for winning the bet.*

ENDNOTES

[1] J. A. F. Stoner and R. E. Freeman, *Management*, 4th ed. (Englewood Cliffs, NJ: Prentice-Hall, 1989), 6-8.

[2] J. P. Kotter, "What Effective Managers Really Do," *Harvard Business Review* (November-December, 1982): 156-167.

[3] Nancy Schmidt and Barbara Schmidt, *Instructors' Film Guide for Women in Management: Threat or Opportunity?* (1973), 3.

[4] M. H. Mescon, M. Albert, and F. Khedouri, *Management: Individual and Organizational Effectiveness,* 2nd ed. (New York: Harper & Row, 1985), 4.

[5] W. Reif, J. Newstrom, and R. Monczka, "Exploding Some Myths About Women Managers," *California Management Review* (Summer, 1975): 72-79.

[6] D. McGregor, "An Uneasy Look at Performance Appraisal," *Harvard Business Review*, Vol. 35, No. 3 (May-June, 1975): 89-94.

[7] N. Stewart, *The Effective Woman Manager* (New York: John Wiley & Sons, 1978), 34-35.

[8] Hyler J. Bracy, Aubrey Sanford, and J. C. Quick, *Basic Management: An Experience Based Approach*, Rev. ed. (Dallas: Business Publications Inc., 1981): 126.

[9] Margaret Hennig and Anne Jardim, *The Managerial Woman* (New York: Pocket Books, 1978), 59-60.

[10] W. French, *The Personnel Management Process*, 6th ed. (Boston: Houghton Mifflin Company, 1987).

[11] *Employment and Earnings*, U.S. Department of Labor, Bureau of Labor Statistics, (January 1987).

[12] A. Johnson, "Women Managers: Old Stereotypes Die Hard," *Management Review* (December, 1987): 31-43.

[13] Leonard H. Chusmir and Victoria Franks, "Stress and the Woman Manager," *Training and Development Journal* (October, 1988): 66-72.

[14] K. Anundsen, "Keys to Developing Managerial Women," *Management Review* (February, 1979): 55-58.

[15] L. R. Gallese, "Corporate Women on the Move," *Business Month* (April, 1989): 31-36.

[16] Bracy, Sanford, and Quick, op. cit.

[17] A. M. Morrison, R. P. White, E. Van Velsor, "Executive Women: Substance Plus Style," *Psychology Today* (August, 1987): 18-26.

[18] Ibid.

[19] D. McGregor, *The Professional Manager* (New York: McGraw Hill, 1967), 23.

[20] D. Feuer, "How Women Manage," *Training* (August, 1988): 23-31.

[21] Stewart, op. cit. 8–9.

[22] Morrison, White, and Van Velsor, op. cit.

[23] Ibid.

[24] Henry Mintzberg, *The Nature of Managerial Work* (New York: Harper & Row, 1973), 30.

[25] F. Luthans, R. M. Hodgetts, and S. A. Rosenkrantz, *Real Managers* (Cambridge, MA: Ballinger Publishing Co., 1988).

[26] C. Pavett and A. W. Lau, "Managerial Work: The Influence of Hierarchical Level and Functional Specialty," *Academy of Management Journal* (March, 1983): 31-43.

27. P. Graham, "The Special Talents Women Bring to Participative Management," *International Management* (August, 1986): 60.

28. D. Feuer, op. cit.

ADDITIONAL RESOURCES

Colwill, Nina L. *The New Partnership: Women and Men in Organizations*, Palo Alto, CA: Mayfield Publishing Co., 1982.

Editors of *The Female Experience*. Del Mar, CA: CRM, Inc., 1973.

Fenn, Margaret. *Making It in Management: A Behavioral Approach for Women Executives.* Englewood Cliffs, NJ: Prentice-Hall, 1978.

Harrison, Barbara S. *Learning to Think Like a Manager.* New York: CRM/McGraw Hill Films, 1982.

Hunsaker, Phillip L. and Alessandra, Anthony J. *The Art of Managing People.* New York: Simon and Shuster, 1986

Josefowitz, Natasha. *Paths to Power.* Reading, MA: Addison-Wesley, 1980.

Kotter, John P. *The General Manager.* New York: Free Press, 1982.

Schmidt, Nancy and Schmidt, Barbara. *Women in Management: Threat or Opportunity?* New York: McGraw Hill Films, 1975.

Stewart, Nathaniel. *The Effective Woman Manager.* New York: John Wiley & Sons, 1978.

Stoner, James A. F. and Freeman, Edward. *Management.* 4th ed., Englewood Cliffs, NJ: Prentice-Hall, 1989.

Thompson, A. and Wood. M. *Management Strategies for Women or, Now That I'm Boss, How Do I Run This Place?* New York: Simon and Schuster, 1983.

Van Fleet, James K. *The 22 Biggest Mistakes Managers Make and How to Correct Them.* New York: Parker Publishing Co., Inc., 1973.

CHAPTER 3

PROJECTING
YOUR IMAGE

First Impressions Based on Appearance
   Decisions Made by Others
   Case Examples
   Specific Guidelines on Clothing
   Guidelines on the Use of Accessories
   Summary
Assertiveness
Proper Business Etiquette
Depth of Knowledge
Breadth of Knowledge
Versatility
Enthusiasm
Sincerity
Action Guidelines
Key Terms
Discussion Questions
Chapter Case: The Sally Henry Case
Endnotes
Additional Resources

Image is a term used to describe the picture a person projects to other people. A person's positive image can set the stage for success in business, while a negative image may set the stage for failure. In many respects the image a person projects is very much like a picture puzzle. The total image one projects to others is made up of several components. Among these are: (1) the first impressions based on appearance, (2) assertiveness, (3) proper business etiquette, (4) depth of knowledge, (5) breadth of knowledge, (6) versatility, (7) enthusiasm, and (8) sincerity. This chapter deals with these eight areas which the authors consider to be the critical components of one's image.

FIRST IMPRESSIONS BASED ON APPEARANCE

For the businesswoman in the 1990s, there is a move toward wearing a suit as a working uniform, and in the corporate world, the suit is the quickest signal of executive status. How do managers distinguish the female secretary from the female executive? *Dress is the easiest way to tell them apart*. The executive should *look* like an executive. Dressing in the corporate uniform is the first step. A 48-year-old female Director of Personnel states it as follows:

> *I personally have experimented with the "dress" issue. I found that when I dress conservatively, and especially in black, I immediately am treated with more authority, power, and respect than when I wear "trendy" or fashionable clothes. I believe that the conservative approach is more comfortable to executives— you somehow become more identifiable and are not "different" from them! "Differentness" seems to be a threat when you are female and they are male!*

If a woman manager is going to command the respect necessary to accomplish her objectives, *it is necessary for her to look like a manager and come across with an image that matches the expectations of those who are working for her and with her*. As irrational as it may seem, people do judge

Illus. 3.1
Managers who look and act like executives have a decided advantage over those who do not convey the appropriate image.

a book by its cover. It is important, then, for a new female manager to present positive first impressions so that others will continue to have an open mind and discover her genuine talents and skills.

Managers who look and act like executives do have a decided edge over those who do not convey the appropriate image. This is particularly important for new women managers. Positive first impressions can be long lasting and can provide a continuing effect for enhancing effectiveness. Negative initial impressions can create obstacles to being perceived as a competent manager. This tendency to preserve our initial impressions is called the **primacy effect** by social psychologists. According to Rubin, this general principle of first impressions establishes the mental framework in which a person is received. Later evidence is either ignored or reinterpreted to coincide with the framework.[1]

Discrimination on the basis of appearance is a fact of life in the working world.[2] The image a woman manager projects *can even be as important to job success as her skills*. Her ability to get a job and advance to a position of greater responsibility will often depend on the impression she makes on others. According to Carr-Ruffino, the people selected for higher level positions tend to look and act as if they fit the new role even *before* they're given the nod.[3]

Decisions Made by Others

Clothing is a powerful medium for projecting one's image. Clothing acts as a cue to those around a person. It helps strangers to identify that person and reinforces the image held by that person's acquaintances, friends, and business associates. What a female manager wears *immediately establishes her credibility and likeability*.[4] When she steps into a room, though no one in that room knows her or has seen her before, each will make at least ten decisions based solely on appearance.[5] They may make many more, but she can be assured that they will make these decisions about her:

1. Economic level

2. Educational level

3. Trustworthiness

4. Social position

5. Level of sophistication

6. Economic heritage

7. Social heritage

8. Educational heritage

9. Success

10. Moral character

It is important that a female manager make a favorable first impression so that the decisions made about her also will be favorable. Knowing how to use clothing to establish herself in whatever role she wants to play can help her win that role more quickly.

Case Examples

There are many women who are not sure what role they want to play. There are others who intentionally dress in a less professional manner and send out the wrong message, afraid that dressing well might detract from their intellectual profile. One senior partner in a law firm told us about a young woman who had entered the firm with high grades from law school and seemed to have a brilliant future ahead of her. The only problem was that no one in the firm wanted to introduce her to clients. "We were desperate," he said, "We wanted to retain her but she dressed so badly. We couldn't let any of our clients meet her." Fortunately for this young woman, some very good friends took her aside and taught her the rules of dress. Her appearance improved, and later the senior partner remarked, "She's now on her way to becoming a partner herself."

A woman's clothing immediately establishes her in a social order whether or not she is aware of it. One of the authors' brightest MBA students interviewed for a banking position. She was told that her record was excellent but that she obviously did not want a job in that field. Shocked, she went home and looked at herself in the mirror. Only then did she realize the kind of message she was sending out. She had dressed for the interview in the type of outfit she typically wore as a student: a full, printed dirndl skirt and a soft peasant blouse. The interviewer at the bank had suggested she might be more at home in journalism or the arts. In fact, she had not really wanted a job in banking and now holds a very responsible position with a graphic arts firm. She had revealed herself through her clothes without recognizing how much she told about herself.

Many women use clothing to help them become more assertive and professional. Because image is a powerful form of nonverbal communication, the right attire can help project the image that makes you feel good about yourself and sends a message that you are a competent professional. Morgan and Baker[6] recommend to women who feel shy several tactics for dress: Figure out what looks best on you; find out your best colors; if you don't know, ask your friends. When you dress assertively, you will start to feel more assertive and this can minimize or eliminate one source of apprehension.

If a woman knows what position she wants in a company, she can use clothing to help her get the job. The female secretary who wants to become a manager will get there faster if she starts dressing like the women managers in that company. The woman who wants to be chairperson of a group will have a better chance if she looks like a leader. A 28-year-old woman working her way up in the corporate ranks in the hotel industry vowed never again to wear pants to work. In her words:

> *When you're trying to get up the corporate ladder, there's a point when everybody has the same background. When you want to be recognized, a lot has to do with the way you project yourself. You have to play the part before you get it.*

Specific Guidelines on Clothing

As stated earlier, the suit is the accepted form of dress for the female executive. In other fields, there are other appropriate signals. In retailing, for instance, the hierarchy is established not only by the price of one's clothes but also the forwardness of their design. For the woman wanting to advance in the managerial ranks, the best advice is to dress as the people in these positions do. With skillful dressing, she can evoke a positive response and enhance her image as a successful manager.

To project authority and success, a woman should dress in a conservative manner in clothing made of natural fibers. This means that she probably will be spending more than she wants and possibly more money than she can afford at first, but such clothing will last longer and look much better. Fabrics like wool or cotton for suits, and silk for blouses, should be chosen. The female manager should wear apparel in colors and patterns that are conservative and in harmony with each other. She does not need many clothes, but the clothes she has should appear high quality.

Other more specific guidelines on appropriate dress developed by Molloy are as follows:[7]

1. Establish personal dress and grooming standards appropriate for the company where you wish to work. Before you apply for a job, try to find out what the workers there are wearing. If in doubt, dress conservatively. If you find out the dress code is more relaxed, you can adjust to it later. When you actually begin work, identify the most successful people in the organization and imitate their manner of dress.

2. Dress for the job you want, not the job you have. If you are currently a secretary and desire to become an executive, do not continue to dress like a secretary. Employees can communicate with their clothing that they are satisfied with their position. Some employers say they can walk into a company office and see who is ready for a promotion.

3. Avoid wearing the newest dress fad in a business setting. In most cases, the world of business is more conservative than the college environment, the arts, or the world of sports. If you are a "fashion setter," you might be viewed as unstable or lacking in sincerity. To be taken seriously, avoid clothing that is too flashy! There are exceptions to Molloy's *flashiness* rule. If your organization is one with an avant-garde image, like fashion or sales, this type of dress might be appropriate.

4. When you select a wardrobe, be sure to consider regional differences in dress and grooming standards. Geography is a major factor regarding how people should dress. What may be suitable business apparel for a receptionist working in Los Angeles may be too casual in Des Moines. Pay close attention to local customs and traditions when establishing your personal dress and grooming standards.

Although John Molloy put forth these guidelines in 1977, they are as sound today as when he first wrote them. Current thought on image management supports Molloy. Kripke[8] asserts the most sensible route is to buy work clothes that are industry appropriate and can be easily interchanged with each other. Concentrating on two or three key colors can give you a fuller wardrobe than a closet full of nothing that goes together.

These guidelines were supported by several successful women managers who responded to our own survey. A 35-year-old Regional Manager of Employees Communications at Atlantic Richfield Co. puts it this way:

On the subject of clothing . . . I feel that women should be flexible in their dress. For myself, if I am attending a meeting with all executives, I will dress conservatively (suit or dress).

However, if I go into the field (I work for an oil company), I will show up in jeans. This does not "ruin" my image. In fact, by dressing to fit the need, I can accomplish my goals better, and the (mostly) men I talk with there are more willing to work with me. If I showed up in a suit and low heels, I think many of them would freeze up around me.

In my job (I am an industrial editor), I must deal with all levels of employees and wish to be "approachable" to them (for story ideas). Therefore, I tend to wear fairly casual clothes in everyday situations around my office.

Another comment I have heard a number of times from the men I work with is—don't wear perfume in the office. That's a real turnoff!

The quality of a woman's wardrobe will influence the image she projects. Dressing for corporate credibility is important. The money she spends on career apparel should be viewed as an investment with each item carefully selected to look and fit well. A suit or dress purchased off the rack at a discount store may save dollars initially, but can cost her more if it does not help her get that promotion she wants. Clothes purchased at bargain prices often wear out quickly. The less money she has, the more important it is for her to buy quality clothing.

Guidelines on the Use of Accessories

Closely related to clothing area **accessories** such as jewelry, handbags, briefcases, and luggage. Any jewelry worn should be the real thing if the occasion or occupation is a formal, traditional one. Traditional business calls for subdued jewelry such as a pin, a gold bangle bracelet and non-dangling earrings. Trendier occupations such as retailing or public relations may allow more leeway. A watch is a must—and an attractive, good-quality watch can be purchased at a reasonable price. Again, because the woman manager wants to establish a conservative but high-quality image, she should be careful not to overkill even if she can afford it.

Luggage and briefcases make a definite statement. The woman manager's colleagues will note exactly what she claims at the baggage terminals. Like her clothes and shoes, accessories should look serious and professional. This means no pastels and no flowers, but preferably something made of leather with a conservative design. A good-quality briefcase costing between \$150 and \$300 will be money well spent. Also, both her briefcase and handbag should be kept highly organized. Rummaging around in them only makes her look like an "inefficient woman." She should make sure to include a very good pen and pencil set.

Summary

The overall image the woman manager strives for includes her made-up image: pulled together, manicured and pedicured, fashionable but not faddish, and every single hair in place! Of course, this is an extremely tough image to pull off especially when she is elbow-deep in work and hassled under pressure. Many current books give women detailed advice on image, ranging from the best colors to wear to ways of making the most of their body type.[9]

In short, the woman manager is trying to appear as a person of authority who is serious about her job and the results she is trying to obtain. This means that she needs to look self-assured and assertive. This look is conservative and expensive. She should not jeopardize it by looking too cute, too pretty, or too frilly—in other words, too feminine. Her clothes, voice, grooming, handshake, and body postures make a significant difference in the reception she receives from other people. First impressions count! If she does not present an appropriate image to create a positive impression on other people, that poor image will count against her. She should do the best to make her image work for her, not against her.

ASSERTIVENESS

An assertive person projects an image to others as confident, capable, and in charge. Some women, due to traditional socialization processes, have trouble being assertive and view assertiveness as a negative characteristic. The true goal of assertiveness helps an individual make a clear statement of what she wants, or how she feels in a given situation, without being abusive or obnoxious. An assertive person will avoid the passive mode of suppressing feelings and actions. A non-assertive or passive person is stepped on and taken advantage of, whereas the aggressive person steps on others. The ideal is the assertive woman who can deal with a problem in a mature and explicit way.

The following example illustrates the above point. Kathy Koop, project manager for a Fortune 500 company, opens her mail one morning and finds the following memo: "Congratulations, you have been appointed as division chair to collect money for the United Way Campaign. We are sure you will find it both an honor and a privilege to serve in this capacity for such a worthy cause. . . ." The memo is from an unknown volunteer. The task does not fit with Ms. Koop's long-term goals and she in no way ever indicated her interest in this position.

Ms. Koop is already heavily committed to both her work, family, and community activities. She can choose to respond in three different ways: passively, aggressively, or assertively.

> *Passive behavior*: Kathy does nothing and awaits further instructions. She tosses the memo away, simmering with anger and rage. She grits her teeth and hopes that the assignment will not be as time-consuming as she estimates.

> *Aggressive behavior*: Kathy grabs the phone, calls the person responsible for the memo and says, "Who do you think you are assigning me to your cockamamie committee? Don't you have any idea of the deadlines and pressure I have? I work twice as hard as anyone else around here. When I want to be on a committee, I'll volunteer." She complains to her co-workers about the outrage.

> *Assertive behavior*: Kathy calls the person who sent the memo and says, "I really appreciate your thinking of me in connection with your committee. However, I will not be able to accept the assignment. Perhaps I can assist you in finding another person."

The assertive woman manager is able to deal competently and in a straightforward manner, which greatly enhances her professional image. While the specific content and format of assertiveness training programs differ, the American Management Association courses concentrate on the development of the following types of skills:[10]

- The ability to make requests and state points of view in a confident, straightforward manner, without becoming pushy, annoyed, or angry.
- The ability to cooperate with others in solving problems in an adult manner, so that both parties are satisfied.

■ The ability to manage others without being aggressive or manipulative.

PROPER BUSINESS ETIQUETTE

Proper business etiquette is a key to managing your image. Many of the suggestions put forth so far in this chapter have been toward superficial aspects of the self, such as clothing and appearance. While an appropriate image is important, displaying good manners has received renewed attention as a key part of impression management.[11] Listed below are a few of the many suggestions offered by corporate etiquette consultant and author, Letitia Baldridge:[12]

1. The secret of good manners is to make other people feel comfortable.

2. When you are a host at a restaurant, remember to have the server take your guest's order before your own.

3. When you meet strangers at a business function, include the name of your organization with your name.

4. In making introductions, remember that a young person should be introduced to an older one, that the person of no rank should be introduced to a person of high rank.

DEPTH OF KNOWLEDGE

Depth of knowledge refers to how well a person knows his or her subject—or particular area of expertise. For a woman this is extremely important because people are watching her. For example, if she is a marketing manager, does she know what there is to know about the products she is responsible for, as well as the markets for them? If she is a personnel manager, does she know her personnel and is she thoroughly familiar with the employment policies and procedures of her organization, as well as with the laws that are applicable to them? Do other employees come to her because they respect her expertise, or do her subordinates,

Illus. 3.2
Keeping up with current trends and being an expert in one's company and industry can open doors to higher level positions.

peers, and superiors avoid her because of her shallow knowledge in her particular area of work? Does her depth of knowledge project credibility and command respect from her subordinates, or can she hear them saying the following about her? "I could do her job as well as she can."

In addition, how well does she know her company and industry? Is she up to date on her company's relative strengths and weaknesses compared to the competition? Being an expert in her specific line of work may help her retain her current managerial position, but *also* being an expert about her company and industry's overall status could mark her as a candidate for a higher level position. The woman manager should take advantage of any relevant training programs that her company may offer to improve herself.

A 46-year-old female president of a New York City mail-order marketing company added these thoughts:

Read the relevant business publications or trade papers—they are vital. Attending specific seminars and meeting people at trade associations, conventions, etc., are also important. When you increase your depth of knowledge, you will command respect

from your employees, peers, and superiors by projecting an image
of intelligence and credibility.

BREADTH OF KNOWLEDGE

The ability to converse with others on topics outside of one's particular area of expertise indicates that person's **breadth of knowledge**. For instance, does the woman manager know the latest developments in world events? Is she familiar with the latest books and movies that are popular? Does she know who won the football game on Saturday? In addition, can she converse with people about things that are of interest to *them*?

Many male managers assume that women are interested only in clothes, recipes, children, and looking for a husband. By increasing her breadth of knowledge, the woman manager will be able to develop rapport more easily. By not restricting the topic of conversation to something she alone desires to talk about, she will allow people to be more comfortable in conversing with her. When she is willing and able to talk to them, they will feel much more comfortable being in her presence. In fact, people will go out of their way to be in her presence and talk with her. They will feel that she shares something with them. The more people feel they share things in common, the better they like each other. So, by increasing her breadth of knowledge, the woman manager will increase her circle of influence with various types of people. Even if she is not up to date or knowledgeable about another person's topic of conversation, she should show interest in it by asking questions. This is one of the best ways to learn.

The responsibility for increasing one's breadth of knowledge falls totally on one's shoulders. There are a number of things that the woman manager can do today, regardless of her age or background, to increase her breadth of knowledge. She should read a local newspaper every day. If possible, she should read it from cover to cover. In addition to the daily newspaper, she might read one of the major weekly news magazines. This will give her a good background in national and international events as well as some additional knowledge in the areas of education, the arts, sports, books, movies, etc. She should make an effort to read at least two books per year outside her normal area of interest, and try to mix fiction and nonfiction.

Finally, the woman manager should make optimum use of typical nonproductive time spent on such activities as bathing, putting on makeup, driving to and from work, cooking, cleaning, and anything else she can think of. She can make use of this nonproductive time by watching a morning or evening television news show, listening to radio news programs anytime throughout the day, and listening to audio cassettes of books and/or educational materials. She should remember that increasing her breadth of knowledge comes most easily from reading, listening, and interacting with other people. *The Wall Street Journal*, *Business Week*, and *Working Woman* are a few examples of periodicals available.

VERSATILITY

Versatility refers to one's willingness and skill in adapting their behavior to best relate to other people. Very simply, it is good manners. It is where one steps out of one's comfort zone in order to communicate and interact effectively with other persons on their level.

Versatility is something one does to oneself, not to others. A woman manager practices versatility every time she slows down to interact with another person who does not feel comfortable moving as fast as she does. She is practicing versatility when she takes time to listen to another individual's personal story rather than getting right down to the task at hand. She is practicing versatility when she makes an effort to speak on the same level as the other person. She is practicing versatility when she covers a topic in much more detail than is typical of her style. She is practicing versatility when she is simply making an effort to meet the personal and professional needs of other people and make them feel comfortable.

Versatility is required because people are different and like to be treated differently. When the manager treats all people the same or treats them inappropriately, they feel uncomfortable with her and the tension level rises. This has an adverse effect on the trust relationship she is trying to establish with others.

ENTHUSIASM

Who is your favorite entertainer? Pretend that you are going to a benefit concert tonight to see your favorite entertainer whom we'll call Tammy Linn. The tickets cost $25 per person. An entertainer typically sings 12 to 15 songs during the course of a concert. As Tammy Linn comes on stage, the house thunders with applause. Then she walks up to the microphone and starts singing. She sings 15 songs as well as you have ever heard her sing them. But she sings them in succession, with no attempt to build rapport with the audience. At the end of the 15th song, Tammy thanks the audience for coming to see her and walks off the stage. How well do you think you and your date would have enjoyed that concert?

If you are like most people, you would feel you were cheated because the entertainer did not talk with the audience, did not build rapport, and showed no enthusiasm at all. Even though Tammy sang those 15 songs as well as you have ever heard them sung by anybody, you would still feel cheated. Would it improve your opinion of her if you knew that she did not feel very well because she stayed out late the night before and had a hangover at the time of the concert? Would it improve your attitude any if you knew that, just prior to coming out on stage, she had an argument with her business manager about an advertising contract? Again, if you are like most people, these revelations would not in any way change your feeling that you had been cheated by the concert. If Tammy Linn had just shown a bit more enthusiasm and warmth to the audience, you would probably feel much differently. You might even feel enthused or elated.

When you show lack of enthusiasm for your job or your company, do you think your peers really know or even care why you are not acting enthused? Shouldn't they have the same feelings toward you as you had toward Tammy Linn? Wouldn't they feel cheated by a manager who lacked enthusiasm, much as you would feel cheated by an entertainer who lacked enthusiasm?

Most managers like to see enthusiasm in their employees. Enthusiastic employees seem to work better. If a manager wants her employees to have enthusiasm, she must project enthusiasm herself! It doesn't just happen. Enthusiasm is like a contagious disease—it's catching. When the manager outwardly shows enthusiasm about herself, her job, and her company, the same attitude will rub off on her employees.

SINCERITY

Being sincere means being genuine and not faking it. The manager should make a concerted and genuine effort if she is going to change her image with respect to the critical components we have discussed in this chapter. As with any change of behavior, initially it will feel a little bit uncomfortable. But if the woman manager does it long enough and is sincere, it will become a part of her. This sincerity, or lack thereof, will be projected to other people, and it becomes part of the total image she projects to others. If she comes across as insincere to other people, it will have a more damaging effect on her relationships than if she had violated all the other components of her image. So, above all else, the manager should be sincere in her interactions with other people and project that sincerity to them.

ACTION GUIDELINES

The image a manager projects to others will help to maximize or minimize her interpersonal success. The response she receives from the world around her is a measure of her success in interpersonal relations. From the beginning to the end of every transaction with another person, she is on stage. Every word, gesture, expression, and impression that she projects will be seen and evaluated, consciously or subconsciously, by that other person. Therefore, she should go through great pains to make sure that the image she projects to other people, in each and every transaction, is an image that helps facilitate communication and build productive relationships.

KEY TERMS

assertiveness — the ability to make a clear statement of needs and feelings without being abusive

breadth of knowledge — a term referring to a person's ability to converse with others on topics outside of his or her particular area of expertise

depth of knowledge — a term referring to how well a person knows his or her particular area of expertise

image — a term used to describe the picture a person projects to other people

primacy effect — the tendency of initial impressions to be preserved

versatility — a term referring to a person's willingness and skill in adapting his or her behavior to best relate to other people

DISCUSSION QUESTIONS

1. What are the steps a woman manager can take to appear as a person of authority who is serious about her job?

2 What are the practical steps a female manager may take to increase both the breadth and depth of her knowledge?

3. How does a woman's measure of versatility affect her managerial performance?

4. How does enthusiasm help a female manager to motivate subordinates and satisfy superiors?

5. How can a woman's clothing and her overall image projection figure into her success as a manager?

CHAPTER CASE

THE SALLY HENRY CASE

Sally Henry is a trainee at the First National Bank of Coronado. At present she handles a variety of customer transactions such as receiving installment payments, selling cashier's checks and traveler's checks, and handling savings account deposits and withdrawals. The bank is a busy one as it is located in a business area adjacent to a residential neighborhood. Sally's short-range goal is to acquire as much experience as possible to obtain a position in the commercial loan department.

Sally is an expressive person. She displays self-confidence and gets along well with people. In the area of dress, she tends to favor the "in" look. She spends a lot of her free time shopping and prides herself on finding bargains. She likes to keep up with the latest hairstyles and thinks of herself as a style setter in the area of apparel. When she shops for clothes she likes to buy items that serve a dual purpose: items that can be worn to work and still be suitable for social occasions. She does not earn a great deal of money at this point and feels that new purchases must serve a dual purpose.

Recently Sally came to work wearing a pantsuit that reminded people of a rock star. The vibrant jacket featured a button front and a shirttail bottom. The jacket was studded with silver stones on the shoulders and cuff. The contrasting pants were a solid color and were extremely form-fitting. Most of the employees made positive comments about the new outfit, but the bank manager was not favorably impressed. At one point during the day he said to Sally, "I know you have hopes of moving into commercial lending, but you haven't got a chance in a get-up like that." Sally replied, "Well, everyone else likes it." The bank manager just shrugged and said, "It's a little too casual," as he walked away.

QUESTIONS

1. Assume you are a wardrobe consultant hired by the First National Bank of Coronado. What advice would you give Sally Henry?
2. Will Sally Henry need to change her wardrobe in order to achieve her long-range career objective?

3. Should everyone associated with First National Bank of Coronado wear the same type of clothing to work? Explain.

ENDNOTES

[1] Zick Rubin, "The Rise and Fall of First Impressions—How People Are Perceived," in B. Patton and K. Tiffen, II, eds., *Interpersonal Communication in Action* (New York: Harper & Row, 1977), 150.

[2] Egon Von Ferstenberg, *The Power Look* (New York: Holt-Rinehart-Winston, 1978); also Pamela Kripke, "From Corporate to Creative Managing Your Image," *Working Woman* (February, 1988): 98.

[3] Norma Carr-Ruffino, *The Promotable Woman* (Belmont, CA: Wadsworth Publishing Co., 1985), 85.

[4] John T. Molloy, *The Woman's Dress for Success Book* (New York: Warner Books, 1977).

[5] William Thourlby, *You Are What You Wear—The Key to Business Success* (Kansas City: Sheed Andrews and McMeel, 1978), 1.

[6] Philip Morgan and H. Kent Baker, "Developing a Professional Image: Learning Assertiveness," *Supervisory Management* (August, 1985): 16-19.

[7] Molloy, op. cit.

[8] Kripke, op. cit.

[9] C. Jackson, *Color Me Beautiful* (New York: Ballantine Books, 1980). See also B. August, *The Complete Bonnie August Dress Thin System* (New York: Rawson, Wade Publishers, 1984).

[10] *American Management Association Course Catalog* (August, 1986 - April, 1987), 30.

[11] Andrew Du Brin, *Human Relations: A Job Oriented Approach* (Englewood Cliffs, NJ: Prentice-Hall, 1988), 283.

[12] Letitia Baldridge, "A Guide to Executive Etiquette," *Business Week Careers* (October, 1986): 60-63; also *Letitia Baldridge's Complete Guide to Executive Manners*. Sandi-Gelles-Cole, ed. (New York: Rausen Associates, 1985).

ADDITIONAL RESOURCES

Morrison, Ann, White, Randall, and Van Velsor, Ellen. "Executive Women: Substance Plus Style." *Psychology Today* (August, 1987): 18-24.

Pante, Robert, *Dressing to Win: How to Have More Money, Romance, and Power in Your Life*. New York: Doubleday, 1984.

Srivasta, Suresh, *Executive Power: How Executives Influence People and Organizations*. San Francisco: Jassey-Bass, 1986.

Working Woman magazine regularly features articles on dress and corporate image.

CHAPTER 4

CAREER DEVELOPMENT

Career Management
    Meanings of Career
    Career Concepts
    Planning Your Career
            Know Yourself
            Set Specific Goals
Barriers to Career Development
    Low Initial Challenge
    Low Self-Actualization Satisfaction
    Lack of Regular Performance Appraisal
    Unrealistically High Aspirations
    Low-Visibility, or "Safe" Positions
    Threat to Supervisors
    The Glass Ceiling
    Problems of and Strategies for Reentry Women
            Competition with Younger Women
            Relating to Younger Supervisors
Strategies for Career Advancement
    Realistic Job Previews
    Basic Everyday Tactics

Mentors

   What is a Mentor?

   Is a Mentor Really Necessary?

   What Can a Mentor Do for the Woman Manager

   How to Find a Mentor

      Make Your Goals Known

      Seek High Visibility and Document Your Accomplishments

      Use the Networking System

      Remain Professional

   Problems Encountered in the Mentor Relationship

      Traditional Cultural Conditioning

      Sexual Attraction

      The Servant Trap

      Difficulty in Letting Go

   Can Women Be Mentors?

Career Dilemmas

   Dual Career Couples

   The "Mommy Track"

   Linear Career Crises

Alternative Career Paths

   Women as Entrepreneurs

   Working Out of the Home

   Job Sharing

Action Guidelines

Key Terms

Discussion Questions

Chapter Case: Parent and Professional

Endnotes

Additional Resources

Everything that has happened in my career has been planned. I set goals in college and at each job. My goals were not narrow or restrictive; I developed alternatives for advancement at each level. For example, in one mid-level managerial position, my alternatives were (1) to get promoted to the vice-president's position within five years, or (2) to get a comparable promotion in another department within five years, or (3) to get a position with a higher salary and responsibility in another organization. I always had options, and I was constantly working on them. I believe a woman can make her own breaks in life. It is hard work, but we do have some control over our destinies.

The above approach to career development is almost textbook perfect! This 36-year-old vice-president of a large utilities company was prepared, was flexible, and assessed multiple options. Unfortunately, many women tend to focus on their present jobs with little long-term career planning. They think, "If I just do my job, the company will take care of my career." This does not always happen!

Career women today have more freedom of choice than any generation of women before. Yet with the large influx of women entering the ranks of management, old rules of corporate America are no longer appropriate and new rules have come into play.[1] What are these new rules and what are the needs of women in terms of career planning, development, and advancement? This chapter will address these questions and show how the woman manager can achieve career success and satisfaction if she has the appropriate information on career opportunities and follows through with a planned development effort. This takes training, skills, and an awareness of job requirements and opportunities.

Meanings of "Career"

The concept of career has many meanings. A commonly accepted definition of career is "the individually perceived sequence of attitudes and behaviors associated with work-related experiences and activities over the span of a person's life."[2] The career consists of both attitudes and behaviors and is an ongoing sequence of work-related activities.

Career Concepts

In recent years, relatively slow growth in the economy has combined with the large number of Baby Boomers entering mid-career to limit severely the opportunities for promotion into upper-level management. This has resulted in the need for alternatives to the definition of success based solely on upward mobility in the organization. Michael J. Driver has identified four alternative career concepts that serve as models for the "ideal career."[3]

1. **Linear Career Concept.** This is most similar to the stereotypical view of careers, in which an individual decides on a field early in life, develops a plan for upward mobility, and executes it. The linear career concept is often linked to a need for achievement and power.

2. **Steady-State Career Concept.** Here an individual also selects a specific field of work, and may continue to improve professionally and financially. Yet the steady-state career-driven person does not necessarily strive to move up the corporate hierarchy. This career concept is motivated by a need for security and to maintain a role in society.

3. **Spiral Career Concept.** These individuals are motivated by a need for personal growth. They view their careers as a series of infrequent but major shifts into different fields of work. Within each occupation they work hard and excel in status and rank, before moving on for new opportunities and challenges.

4. **Transitory Career Concept.** Driven by a need for independence and identity, this individual drifts from one occupation to another with no particular pattern. Often, a transitory person is exploring alternatives while seeking to find a career identity. Other transitory people are trouble shooters who are driven by the novelty and challenge of problem solving. Once things are stabilized, they feel a need to find another challenge.

Planning Your Career

Before the female manager can formulate a career plan, it is necessary for her to be in touch with her personal interests and abilities. If these are not obvious to her, a variety of assessment services are available through governmental, educational, and private services.[4] These same organizations can help her determine the types of occupations that match her talents and interests, as well as the specific opportunities and entrance requirements.

Another key ingredient for career success and satisfaction is to formulate a career plan. This involves taking the initiative and responsibility to set both short-range and long-range goals, and to lay out specific steps to be taken to achieve those goals. However, before goals can be set, the female manager must take a careful look at her needs and desire for career growth.

Know Yourself. The first step in career planning requires the manager to know herself. This means having an appreciation of her strengths, accomplishments, and desires. To get to know herself better, she should think about herself, her goals and aspirations, and her work life. She should write out several separate answers to the question: "Who am I?" Then she should write several separate statements about "Things I would like to accomplish." These statements

FIGURE 4-1

EXERCISE 1—KNOW YOURSELF

Who Am I?	Things I Would Like To Accomplish
I am	I would like to . . . .
I am	I would like to . . . .
I am	I would like to . . . .

should be as specific and concise as possible, and finally should be ranked in the order of their importance to her (see Figure 4-1).

This self-perception exercise can generate data for self-assessment of the manager's skills, accomplishments, weaknesses, aspirations, satisfactions, and values. It provides a starting point for developing her vision of the future—which is necessary for goal setting—and taking action to achieve her goals.

Set Specific Goals. The next step in career planning is to set specific goals. Goal setting clarifies the situation and focuses on specific issues. A manager's chances of finding career satisfaction increase if she establishes clear-cut goals. *Occupational floundering* is the result of *not* setting realistic goals. This occurs when an individual enters the labor force without a firm commitment to an occupational goal.

One aid for setting realistic goals is for the woman manager to talk to someone she respects such as her boss, colleagues, knowledgeable friends, a mentor, her husband, her siblings, or her parents. Two purposes can be achieved by this: (a) goals become clearer even to oneself when verbalized to another; (b) different perspectives are gained by talking to different people and more realistic goals can be set.

Another aid to help focus on setting specific career goals is for the manager to write out different responses to the following statement: "Five years from now I will be satisfied if . . ." Then, for each goal she has just listed, she should complete this statement: "To accomplish this goal, I will . . ." (see Figure 5-2).

FIGURE 5-2

EXERCISE 2—SET SPECIFIC GOALS

Five Years From Now I Will Be Satisfied If	To Accomplish This Goal, I Will
. . . .	. . . . ,
. . . .	. . . .
. . . .	. . . .
. . . .	. . . .
. . . .	. . . .

After following this procedure to set five-year goals, the manager should repeat the exercise using ten- and fifteen-year time periods. As difficult as it may seem to project that far into the future, it will help the manager to look beyond her short-run career plans. Remember, these goals are not laid in concrete and can be adjusted over time.

The results of a manager's work in the preceding career planning exercises are a set of prioritized goals and strategies for achieving them based on realistic self-assessment. Conceptualizing life goals that project future alternatives is something many women traditionally have not done. Goal setting is a crucial prerequisite for career development. The lack of it is a barrier to effective career development.

BARRIERS TO CAREER DEVELOPMENT

From the moment new employees enter the organization, they are given cues about the quality of performance that is expected and rewarded. Most new employees want to be accepted into this new social system and they are highly receptive to cues from their environment. However, many new employees—both men and women—suffer from the **reality shock syndrome**: the disparity between initial job expectations and the hard realities of what the job actually entails. This reality shock can be unpleasant, disconcerting, and depressing.[5] Following is a list of significant barriers to career development encountered by women entering management positions today.

Low Initial Challenge

Both the job search and the recruitment process are selling jobs in many ways. The female applicant presents her best side and emphasizes her strong points, but so does the company. Recruiters often overstate the promise and challenge of the first job in order to attract the most desirable and promising candidates. In reality, most organizations start employees out on a relatively easy project and only gradually increase the difficulty of the projects as the employees gain experience.

Low Self-Actualization Satisfaction

Overzealous recruiters often promise growth and self-fulfillment on the job. More often than not, however, an organization rewards conformity to its customs and standard operating procedures. Very few organizations reward creativity in entry-level jobs, resulting in feelings of frustration and discontent among new women managers. However, it is important to recognize that a job, in and of itself, should not be relied upon as the sole source of fulfillment. Women who have been able to view their current job as merely a means to an end, in terms of their broader career objectives, have been able to look beyond the initial discontent.[6]

In addition, the new employee can take the initiative to create challenges on her own by taking a more active role in personally defining her job, and by asking for challenges—for more difficult and complex tasks—as she gains some experience in her position.

Lack of Regular Performance Appraisal

Most people feel that performance appraisal is necessary to motivate and train new employees. Thus, regular feedback on performance is promised to most new personnel, yet many managers perform this appraisal poorly with new employees or neglect it altogether. Their performance appraisal may simply consist of, "You're doing a fine job; keep it up." This leaves new people in the organization in a state of confusion as to how well they are really doing and how they can improve.

Unrealistically High Aspirations

Many new employees begin work eager to apply the modern skills and techniques that they have been taught. They feel that they already have the ability to perform at levels well above their entry-level position. This can be particularly true of recent graduates with higher level degrees. However, these new employees are generally unskilled in practical applications and realities of the work world, and their high aspirations and classroom theories are often not sufficient alone to replace years of experience in the field. Says Martha Miller, a social psychologist and former Associate Dean of the Yale School of Management: "We expect to be water-walkers, and it is a rude awakening to find ourselves slogging through the mud."[7]

Low-Visibility, or "Safe" Positions

Many studies[8] have shown that women are often placed into low-status, low-visibility departments of their companies, such as personnel or public relations, with little opportunity to make decisions relating to corporate policy or affecting the bottom line. This can lead to feelings of isolation and lack of control over a still very male-oriented organizational network. These "safe" jobs hold little real power or opportunity for visibility. As a result, male managers will often bypass women for promotion to more influential positions.

Threat to Superiors

A newcomer fresh out of technical school, college, or graduate school may bring more expertise to a job than her superior possesses. In addition, the newcomer may be paid more than the superior's initial salary. The supervisor/subordinate relationship may be particularly strained when a young, bright, and highly motivated female employee has more knowledge in a particular area than her male supervisor. It may be best for her long-term career success to act humble and not come on too strong at first.

The Glass Ceiling

For most women who strive to rise above the level of general manager, there is yet another harsh reality—the **glass ceiling**—a barrier of stereotype and subtle discrimination that is apparently still blocking promotion to senior management.[9] With less than two percent of Fortune 500's top corporate executives being female, the prognosis for the near future is not bright, and it is expected that over the next two decades only a small handful of women will break the glass ceiling and reach the upper echelons of management.

The reasons for this invisible barrier to the top appear to be a combination of both internal and external factors. First, there still exists a certain amount of sexism and ingrained corporate thinking among male executives. This is complemented by self-doubt and negative expectations by women hoping to move past the barrier.[10]

Since there is a limited amount of room at the top, women managers need to recognize that their careers will likely plateau at a certain level. They can either stick with it, in hopes of eventually breaking past the ceiling, or they can consider other career alternatives or a career change.

Problems of and Strategies for Reentry Women

The midlife woman faces a major organizational adjustment when she reenters the work force after a substantial time of child rearing, especially if she has never been a full-time manager. The number of midlife women reentering management has steadily increased in recent years. One reason for the opening of management opportunities has been the women's movement. Second, the increased divorce rate has made it necessary for many women to take over primary financial support of their families in more responsible jobs. Third, many families with professionally qualified spouses require two incomes just to keep pace with inflation and their desired lifestyle.

The reentry woman faces problems in management that do not apply to the young female who has just graduated from college: (1) competition with more recently educated, younger women, and (2) difficulty taking orders from younger superiors. The woman manager should be sensitive to this unique position, whether she fills it herself or must relate to those who do.

Competition with Younger Women. Midlife women are often overly concerned that they are unequal competition to their younger counterparts. Very often the younger woman has more recent and more advanced education in business management or a related field, whereas the midlife woman may have been out of both college and the work force for several years. Younger women are often thought more physically attractive by some male decision makers and, therefore, may have a non-performance related advantage. More mature women, on the other hand, often are stereotyped as having a better record of attendance and punctuality, representing a lower turnover risk, and being a more credible authority figure in management.

Neither of these commonly held views is particularly true, of course, and the final outcome of career competition is usually based on competence and performance.

What can be done to help a midlife woman ease her reentry into management? First, women can pursue additional education to expand their current level of skill and knowledge, through MBA or certificate programs. Many aspiring female managers are liberal arts graduates who need additional financial and management training. This can be accomplished through a full-time program, or through part-time or night school classes while working. Many companies will sponsor promising candidates in such programs as the Smith Management Program at Smith College or the Program for Developing Managers in the Graduate School of Management at Simmons College.[11] Secondly, the midlife woman can often use her age to her benefit by networking through acquaintances made over the years. Finally, she can consider starting in an assistant-to capacity, working for a higher-level manager. Through her association with key individuals in the organization, she will begin to develop a base of power from which she can build.

Relating to Younger Supervisors. Many midlife women find it difficult to be supervised by males or females who are young enough to be their children. Young supervisors sometimes feel awkward supervising women old enough to be their mothers. Adjustments have to be made in both directions. Exposure to the situation seems to be the best cure for such feelings of awkwardness.

Another helpful approach to bridging the age gap in such relationships may require midlife women to recognize that today technical qualifications and job experience determine the balance of authority. In a work setting, age is a weak source of authority compared to experience and job competence.

STRATEGIES FOR CAREER ADVANCEMENT

There are numerous strategies for advancing the woman manager's career. A point made earlier in this chapter bears repeating here: *A well-conceived career plan that incorporates a step-by-step strategy for reaching goals is vital to the female manager's career success.* The manager needs to establish clear-cut goals, set a timetable, and reevaluate her goals as time progresses. In addition, the following strategies have been recommended by Schoonmaker[12] and others:

1. Accept that there are some inescapable and irreconcilable conflicts between the woman manager and the organization. Personal goals enter heavily into the formulation of career goals. Ideally, there is an integration of career and personal goals, but things don't always work out ideally. What is good for the organization is not always good for the manager. She must recognize the need to watch out for herself, and modify her goals where necessary.

2. Accept that the boss may be essentially indifferent to her career objectives. Though it is ideal to have a mentor who cares about her and her career, the woman manager should be prepared for the fact that this may not occur. She should be prepared to practice self-nomination. She should have the courage and assertiveness to ask for what she wants—a promotion, a raise, or a transfer—because her boss may not be aware that she is actually seeking more responsibility.

3. Analyze her assets and liabilities. What can the manager do well? What does she enjoy doing? One of the most vital ingredients in her successful career planning is to have an accurate picture of her strengths, weaknesses, and preferences. Realistic career goals should enable her to operate from a position of strength.

4. Learn the rules or company policies. Recognizing that she has to deal with the informal as well as the formal organization means being sensitive to and aware of the customs and informal rules of conduct. Developing good political skills is a very important element of conscious career planning.

    Questions such as "Who is really in charge?" and "Who influences the people who make big decisions?" deal with sensitive material. The woman manager who asks superiors such questions may be perceived as aggressive or naive. It is more tactful to rephrase these questions in a procedural fashion and address them to knowledgeable co-workers or sympathetic secretaries. A mentor is the obvious person to confide in.

    Another tactic is for the manager to balance social behavior with her work. Some personally-oriented, social interaction may build necessary rapport and help her get the cooperation she needs from co-workers to accomplish her job. If she is intent on career advancement, a minimum amount of social interaction is necessary to keep her on good terms with her peers.

5. Don't hesitate to invest in further education. It would be wise to incorporate this into the manager's career planning. For women in particular, education results directly to increased salary. An advanced degree also may help a female manager move up within her current company and field.[13]

6. Carry out her plan. It is useless for the manager to have a plan unless she carries it out. If her plan calls for going to school, changing jobs, or requesting a raise, she should do it.

7. Chart her progress. Rarely will the manager's career progress as she expects. She should be prepared and be flexible enough to change. The entire career planning process is an ongoing, dynamic process.

8. Stay flexible! For a woman manager in today's fast-paced corporate climate, flexibility is the key to maneuvering herself into progressively better positions. This includes flexibility to take on new jobs or tasks, to work with varying managers and subordinates, and to roll with the punches and move on to the next project if one goes bad.[14]

Realistic Job Previews

To create more realistic expectations and to combat the high turnover rate caused by reality shock, many organizations are giving their applicants and new employees realistic job previews. It's not fair to the individual or to the organization to sell something that simply is not there in the first job. By asking for and receiving realistic job previews, aspiring new managers can be informed about both the positive and negative aspects of the job for which they have applied. This allows applicants to form realistic initial expectations, make better decisions, and avoid high dissatisfaction with the actual situations they encounter.

Several studies[15] have shown that realistic job expectations lead to decreased employee turnover. Job acceptance rates were not found to be lower for applicants exposed to unfavorable information about the job than they are for recruits exposed only to positive job information.

Two aspects of the individual's early job experiences appear especially critical: the match of expectations with initial job assignment and the supportive behavior of the individual's first supervisor. Thus, a female employee's early job experiences and the type of supervisory behavior received are quite important in influencing her adjustment to the organization and subsequent career success.

Basic Everyday Tactics

Once the manager is in the midst of her career, there are many things she can do to enhance it. To succeed in business she not only needs to be competent and to work hard, but she also needs to play sensible office politics. She should not underestimate the role that politics plays in organizational life. Some specific tactics are discussed below.

1. Do excellent work. High performance and excellent work are foundations of a career strategy. Great political ability alone can sometimes cause a mediocre individual to rise above others, but this doesn't happen often. Generally, the better the manager works, the greater her chances for success and recognition. It is only when she and her colleagues are at the same level of performance that political savvy causes her to stand out. Doing excellent work then is a prerequisite to every other tactic for advancing her career.

2. Be visible. If the manager wants to be rewarded for her performance, she has to be sure her superiors know about it. She should remember that she is her own greatest fan! One woman manager gave the following advice: "The method of putting it down on paper . . . becoming visible . . . it's effective. People know . . . it's your idea. Instead of just calling somebody up, you send a memo . . . . Get something back."
   There are several ways for a manager to advertise her actions without being viewed as a braggart or as too self-interested. Some of these ways are shown in Figure 4-3.

3. Create a network of supporters. The female manager should take every opportunity to pass on and share power with her subordinates and peers. People tend to acquire and expand their own

FIGURE 4-3

STRATEGIES FOR BEING VISIBLE

- Send memos to her superiors when projects have been completed

- Actively solicit feedback

- Submit periodic progress reports

- Get assigned to special projects and task forces

- Volunteer for different assignments

- Pay honest compliments to people

power only when others become empowered by virtue of their connection with that person.[16] By developing a group of supporters and increasing her base of power, the female manager will have a better chance of meeting her career goals.

4. Present the right image. The manager wants to make sure that as she becomes more visible she is also presenting the right image. Specific strategies for projecting the right image were discussed in Chapter 3.

5. Help her boss succeed. The more the manager helps her boss, the more valuable she will be. Strategies to accomplish this include those shown in Figure 4-4.

FIGURE 4-4

STRATEGIES FOR HELPING A BOSS SUCCEED

- Display loyalty

- Do good work

- Suggest new approaches to problems

- Keep her boss informed

- Contribute to her boss's objectives

6. Find a sponsor. The manager should find a high-level person to serve as an organizational ally. This is such a key career determinant that strategies for finding and maintaining a sponsor, or mentor, will be elaborated on in the next section.

MENTORS

Mentor mania has swept across business organizations today. It is generally agreed that, whether that individual is male or female, a mentor can be a key player in the career of a female manager. When successful women executives talk about their luck or the various forces that helped them get where they are, many of them mention another significant person. Although the names have been changed, one exceptional, but true, example is what happened to Betty Fisher.

After graduating from college, with a degree in Business Administration, Betty Fisher worked four years in a large savings and loan organization as a financial officer before returning to college for her MBA. Betty obtained her MBA at twenty-nine, joined General Hydraulics Corporation as executive assistant to James Burns, the company's 43-year-old chairman and chief executive officer. A year later, Burns gave Betty a bigger title and additional responsibilities as vice-president for corporate and public affairs. Three months after that she was promoted to fill the vacancy of vice-president for strategic planning. Fisher's rapid rise in the corporation was facilitated by her ability and relationship with Burns.

Burns exposed Fisher to the General Hydraulics world. She called herself his "alter ego" and "most trusted confidante." He agreed that she was his best friend. Their friendship was built on trust. Burns provided valuable information concerning company politics and provided contacts both inside and outside the organization. He used his influence to speed Fisher's entry and advancement into top management of the corporation. He acted as teacher, counselor, and guide. He also offered moral support during emotionally difficult times. Burns enhanced Fisher's skills and intellectual development. In short, Burns was Fisher's mentor.

This example leads to several interesting questions. What exactly is a mentor? Is a mentor really necessary? What can a mentor do for the woman manager? How can she find a mentor? What problems can she encounter in the mentor relationship? Can women be mentors?

Illus. 4.1
A mentor—who acts as a teacher, counselor, and coach—can be a key player in the career of the female manager.

What is a Mentor?

The dictionary defines a mentor as a wise and trusted teacher. Ever since the poet Homer's faithful and wise Mentor first advised Odysseus, wise individuals have counseled, taught, coached, and sponsored the young. The mentor acts as a teacher, counselor, and coach to the younger, inexperienced person in the matter of the latter's career, just as Burns acted toward Fisher. The mentor can be within the protégé's organization or outside of it. The mentor can be a supervisor, company executive, associate, husband, wife, friend, or professor.

The roles of a mentor can be divided into two broad categories: psychosocial functions and career functions. **Psychosocial functions** consist of those aspects of the mentor relationship that improve the new manager's sense of competence, identity, and effectiveness. **Career functions** are those aspects that help the woman manager learn the ropes and prepare for advancement. There are seven specific functions a mentor performs for a protégé:[17]

1. *Sponsorship*—nominating the female manager for key promotions in the organization

2. *Exposure and Visibility*—providing new opportunities for the protégée to demonstrate her unique talents and abilities

3. *Coaching*—assisting the new manager in developing strategies to achieve her work objectives

4. *Protection*—minimizing the woman manager's risk in controversial or difficult situations

5. *Psychological Support*—help to enhance the protégée's sense of competence and identity

6. *Acceptance and Confirmation*—providing feedback to the new manager on her work performance

7. *Counseling*—providing a confidential outlet for the protégée to discuss her concerns and fears, and facilitating informal exchanges of information about both work and non-work experiences

Effective mentoring behavior conforms very closely to these definitions. A director of training and development for a leading soft drink company described the importance of her mentor as follows:

> *This is a very political place and my mentor is a very political person. He watches out for me and talks me up to other people. Many of the men I work for find me threatening because I work too hard. They try to lock me out of knowing what's going on around here. It's important to me to have at least as much information as the people who are trying to stab me in the back. My mentor is my key to the men's room.*

Other responses to our survey highlighted the same political role played by other mentors. A television production executive stated, "A mentor is a person who opens doors for you and who has such confidence in you that you have confidence in yourself. By the time you're trying to climb the corporate ladder, if you don't have a mentor, others do."

Is a Mentor Really Necessary?

Most people seem to think that mentors are necessary, although a few believe otherwise. Below are some reasons for and against the use of mentors, followed by results of recent research on the subject.

A mentor may be necessary at two crucial stages of a woman's climb to the upper levels of management. The first period of need occurs during the early phase when a woman first embarks upon her career. At this early stage of development, a personal and parental sort of mentoring is common. The protégée not only learns more about the job but is also initiated into game playing, political techniques, image building, and becoming a team member.

The second crucial stage during which a woman needs a mentor comes when it's time for a final push to the top rungs of the ladder. The mentor's function at this stage is to provide a seal of approval.[18] This enables the protégée to gain the respect of others above and below on the ladder of command, as well as that of those outside the organization. Being adopted by a senior person is perhaps the only sure way for a woman to move beyond middle management into positions of real power.[19]

Helen D. Nolan, president of The Magnificent Doll, a New York City retail store specializing in antique and imported dolls and a partner and creative director of Della Temina, Travisano and Partners ad agency, told us she didn't believe in mentors! She wrote: "The concept of mentors as necessary opposes the idea that women learn to become self-sufficient and self-reliant entities. Until they do, I don't think they should expect to be respected in business."

Research results show that Ms. Nolan most definitely holds a minority opinion. Our survey found that the vast majority of successful female managers believe that mentors are essential.[20] This contention is supported by an abundance of research findings for both men and women. In fact, it has been found that the lack of a mentor may be a major developmental handicap.[21] Most executives who have had a mentor earn more money at an earlier age, are better educated, and are more likely to follow a successful career path than those without one.[22]

What Can a Mentor Do for the Woman Manager?

Our survey responses from 85 successful middle- and upper-middle-level women managers contained answers that were strikingly similar. When asked what their mentors did for them, they replied:

My mentor was most helpful to me in the area of . . .

- learning how to deal with my male counterparts.
- developing my knowledge of the industry and recommending me for promotion.
- encouraging me to shoot for higher goals.
- introducing me to the ins and outs of corporate politics, criticizing me constructively, and advising me as to my worth to give me self-confidence.
- overcoming others' resentment and objections to my being a woman manager.
- pointing out what I had to offer to those less observant.
- sticking his neck out to promote me—before it was fashionable.
- overcoming discouragement.
- inspiring me to be more creative.
- keeping me and my performance visible to senior management and always giving credit for my work.

How to Find a Mentor

Women starting out in their careers often ask, "How do I find a mentor?" It is more difficult for a woman than it is for a man to find a mentor in most large organizations. The characteristics the woman needs to succeed—enthusiasm, the right image, and working well with others—are also the same characteristics necessary to attract a suitable mentor. Men actively seek mentors and go where they are likely to be found. Women in similar situations simply cannot afford to wait to be chosen. A new woman manager should actively seek a mentor, preferably an older individual in the generativity stage of their own career. She should look for the people who are in a position to help her and let them know she respects

their ability and seeks their support. Ultimately the mentor selects individuals to sponsor. However, by practicing the career development strategies discussed below, a woman will increase her chances of finding a
suitable mentor.

Make Your Goals Known. People do not assume automatically
that women want to get ahead. One way to overcome barriers women
face when finding a mentor is to convince potential mentors that they
are committed to a permanent career. A mentor may not want to
invest time in training a woman who may only be a temporary asset.
Consequently, a mentor may see women as assistants, not successors.
A woman needs to deal with this stereotype by confirming her
seriousness about her career.

Seek High Visibility and Document Your Accomplishments.
It is important for a woman manager to keep an accurate record of
her accomplishments for performance reviews and career discussions. She should let people know her achievements in tactful ways
such as writing "for your information" notes or asking advice on the
follow-up strategy for her completed project. High-visibility assignments and projects in which she will be seen by the "right" people are
the best ones to seek out. By using these techniques, a manager will
get the recognition she deserves.

Use the Networking System. For many years men have comfortably and naturally helped each other get ahead in the business world.
In recent years, women have also adopted the network route to career
advancement (see Figure 4-5). Women who have previously relied
almost exclusively on males to be mentors are now looking to influential women for support, guidance, and role modeling.[23] Most cities
have groups of women who meet monthly in the evening, during lunch
hours, and even for breakfast. These networking groups can be a
source of encouragement and support for the woman who takes risks
in her professional setting.

Remain Professional. In relationships with male superiors who
may be potential mentors, a woman should at all times remain totally
professional. It may be fun sometimes to be cute or flirtatious in
relaxed situations, such as at lunchtime, but this image may carry on
and detract from her effectiveness at work. Her boss may have a

FIGURE 4-5

EXAMPLES OF NETWORKING SYSTEMS

**Business & Professional
Women's Foundation**
2012 Massachusetts Ave., NW
Washington, D. C.   20036
(202) 293-1200

**Federation of Organizations
for Professional Women**
2437 15th St., NW
Suite 309
Washington, D. C.   20009
(202) 328-1415

**The International Alliance,
an Assn. of Executive and
Professional Women**
8600 LaSalle Rd., Suite 308
Baltimore, MD   21204
(215) 321-6699

**National Association for
Female Executives**
127 W 24th St.
New York, NY   10021
(202) 645-0770

**American Society of
Professional and
Executive Women**
1429 Walnut St., 4th floor
Philadelphia, PA   19102
(215) 563-4415

**American Business Women's
Association**
9100 Ward Parkway
P. O. Box 8728
Kansas City, MO   64114
(816) 361-6621

**National Council of
Career Women**
P. O. Box 3731
Washington, D. C.   20007
(202) 333-8578

**National Council of Women
of the United States**
777 U.N. Plaza
New York, NY   10017
(202) 697-1278

**NOW (National Organization
for Women)**
1401 New York Avenue, NW
Suite 800
Washington, D. C.   20005
(202) 331-0066

**Women's Equity Action
League**
1250 Eye Street, NW
Suite 305
Washington, D. C.   20005
(202) 898-1588

**Women's Workforce
c/o Wider Opportunities
for Women**
1325 G. Street, NW
Lower Level
Washington, D. C.   20005
(202) 638-3143

Catalyst
250 Park Avenue, S.
New York, NY   10003
(212) 777-8900

**National Federation of
Business & Professional
Women's Clubs**
2012 Massachusetts Ave., NW
Washington, D. C.   20036
(202) 293-1100

difficult time viewing her as a competent professional when she is presenting a marketing plan to him later. She should not send mixed messages about the image she is trying to project.

Problems Encountered in the Mentor Relationship

Must a woman's mentor be male? Since there are more male managers, and they hold the more influential positions in organizations, most mentors are male. A male mentor with significant power and prestige can be very effective in enhancing the prestige of a protégée. This type of "man's stamp of approval" makes a woman a more acceptable colleague or team member to her mostly male colleagues.

Being a mentor is an important cycle in men's lives.[24] Successful men express a sense of responsibility for putting back into life what you get out, and many find satisfaction in being role models and developing talent.[25] However, some potential problems exist in the female/male mentor relationship that are absent from the male/male or the female/female mentor relationships.

Traditional Cultural Conditioning. Their traditional cultural conditioning causes many senior male executives to view women as wives, mothers, and sweethearts, but not as executive peers. Such men do not consider women to be appropriate subjects for the intensive time and effort required to bring them along in the executive ranks. They view other men as safe investments with a higher probability of success than women. Fortunately, as more and more women enter the managerial ranks, this stereotype is slowly changing.

Sexual Attraction. As more and more women move into higher levels of management in organizations, the number of male/female mentor relationships is on the rise. Many special problems result, including sexual attraction, marital disruption, and damaging gossip.[26] Romantic or sexual interests confound the mentor relationship and may create conflicts and power struggles where there were none before.

In view of the closeness of the mentor/protégée relationship, it is easy to see how romances develop. Since mutual respect and admiration are an integral part of the mentor relationship, the natural consequence is often sexual attraction. In addition, lunches, meetings, out-of-town business trips, and other social occasions which are a part of the mentor relationship, can further heighten the romantic significance of the relationship.[27]

Even if the mentor/protégée interaction is purely professional, the appearance of romantic favoritism can cause damaging rumors and resentment by co-workers. When a woman is on the inside track as a result of having a male mentor, her peers and competitors probably will assume that sex is a part of the picture.[28] Whether by a real attraction between the mentor and protégée, or merely through rumors in the organization, another unfavorable outcome is often disruption of either or both marriages of the two individuals involved.

What can be done to avoid this serious pitfall of cross-gender mentorships? The following guidelines may help the woman manager in dealing appropriately with the mentor relationship.[29] These guidelines apply whether the woman is in the role of protégée, or that of mentor.

1. Keep the relationship strictly business. Avoid conversations regarding family or personal subjects, and never use pet names or nicknames.

2. Avoid the appearance of romantic involvement. Leave your office door open during meetings, hold meetings during regular business hours, and use the same language and tone of voice with all co-workers.

3. Know your values, and carefully consider the impact that romantic involvement would have on yourselves and others. Try to take an objective look at the total picture before leaping into an affair. Look at the impact on your careers, your co-workers, spouses, and families.

4. Assume a parental role. If you become attracted to your protégé, but do not want to become involved, assume the role of parent to the protégé to help ward off sexual attraction.

If you do fall in love with your mentor or protégé, a new mentor should take over the coaching and development job. The usual outcome of sexual involvement is for one of the individuals to transfer departments or change jobs altogether.

The Servant Trap. If female protégées successfully avoid the sexual trap, they still have to watch out for the **servant trap**.[30] Because men are used to having women serve them they may ask a woman manager to do all kinds of work that is more fitting for someone in a lower position. It is sometimes difficult to refuse a demeaning task without seeming to reject one's superior. However, there are times when it may be necessary for a woman to sit down with her mentor and clarify her role and career expectations. It may be appropriate at this time to suggest that whatever tasks he has been asking her to do can be delegated to someone else in a more appropriate position.

As more women move into management positions and work side by side with men, men will no longer view them as sex objects and servants but as friends and colleagues.

Difficulty in Letting Go. Another potential problem with a mentor-protégée relationship is the mentor's difficulty in letting go. Some women have felt that mentors behave like overprotective fathers holding them back instead of enhancing their careers. In these cases there is a need for the protégée to break away, become independent, and function on her own. Even the best of mentors must eventually be abandoned if the protégée is to become fully mature.[31]

Can Women Be Mentors?

Although the number of females entering the upper ranks of management is increasing, female mentors are still difficult to find. If a woman is lucky enough to find a female mentor, the latter will have two additional qualities over those of a male mentor. She can be a role model for the protégée, and she will understand what it is like to be a woman in the protégée's position because she has probably been there herself.

In the past, many women in the upper ranks of organizations felt their positions were too precarious to permit them to help anyone else. Others were Queen Bees who, "in the face of all odds and without the aid of affirmative action, have made it to the top." Many of these women feel that "No one helped me, so why should I help others?" [32]

All organizations have rites of passage or an initiation period that every newcomer has to go through. However, these need not be the same rites experienced by women who entered years ago and fought all the odds. The problems faced by women beginning managerial careers today are different, but they are still difficult. Many people recognize this. As the growing number of women in high-ranking corporate posts pushes other women closer to equity with male colleagues, female mentors have begun to appear in more abundance. Many executive women now make being a mentor to younger women part of their goals. Organized networking groups of professional women have grown by leaps and bounds in the past five years. These groups work like males' old boys' networks by providing professional information, support, references, information about job openings, and emotional nurturance.

CAREER DILEMMAS

As the demographics of the work force and the priorities and expectations of both female and male managers shift, several new problems arise for organizations. The rising cost of living increases the need for dual career couples. Women must constantly face a difficult decision between staying on the fast track or raising children and relegating themselves to the **mommy track**. In addition, as the baby-boom generation enters mid-career, a linear career crisis is occurring—with only a limited number of top management positions available and many individuals competing for them.

All of these career dilemmas are faced by women in the corporate sector today. These problems are giving rise to a whole array of alternative career tracks, as well as many new options being offered by employers to meet the changing needs of an increasingly female work force.

Dual Career Couples

According to recent government statistics, husband-and-wife wage earners make up 56% of marriages in the United States.[33] As the number of dual career couples increases, men and women must learn to balance not only two separate careers, but also child care, housework, and entertaining. Mutual accommodation, flexibility, and willingness to compromise are imperative for both the career and the relationship.[34]

The changing role of women in the work force and the family is also bringing about changes in a couple's willingness to relocate for one spouse's job. Corporations are beginning to recognize that relocation decisions are the result of two careers being considered. Programs such as job-finding assistance for the spouse are surfacing throughout many organizations across the country. Companies are also reducing or eliminating their regulation of nepotism within the organization.[35] Most corporations are playing an increasingly active role in assisting families with relocation. Others are reducing the frequency and need to relocate their key managers and personnel.

An interesting alternative to relocation for many couples is the **commuter marriage**. Currently over 700,000 couples in the United States have opted for this type of arrangement, and studies have shown that it can be surprisingly successful.[36]

Dual career families do not exist, however, without considerable strain for both parties. Many women experience stress from multiple roles, which is exacerbated as the number of children she has increases.[37] Despite attempts by working couples to equalize the burdens of running the household, raising the family, and taking care of children's needs, it is more stressful for women than men because women usually do not let go of primary responsibility.[38] This may change with the next generation of dual career women who are being exposed to different values and lifestyles and experience different relationships.

To ease some of these burdens, companies like Hewlett-Packard, IBM, and Levi Strauss are offering child care facilities, flexible work time, and even a flexible work place.[39] These options are especially beneficial for managerial women who are single parents. It has also been found that as men share more equally in home roles, two positive things occur: (1) communication and interaction between spouses become more positive, and (2) job satisfaction and mental health of women increase.[40]

The Mommy Track

Across the country, women managers are leaving the fast track, at least temporarily, and opting for career-and-family arrangements. They are seeking a better balance between career goals and mothering, and at the same time are forcing corporations to take a closer look, become more flexible, and change their policies so as to keep many bright young women in the organization.

Should women have to choose between career and family? Should their upward mobility be stifled simply because they choose to have children? The issue is still hotly debated. Many women, with the help of their organizations, have very successfully combined both while barely losing a step in their career path. Others have been happy opting for lesser positions, part-time work, or working out of their home during child-rearing years. Still others are gaining strong support from their husbands, who are spending more time caring for their children and less time in the corporate fast lane.[41] Although few men are willing to take on the "daddy track," their number is gradually increasing as many women become the primary wage earners of the family.

How are corporations responding to the increasing number of women managers opting to raise children? Many are recognizing the need to accommodate working mothers in order to keep them as valuable resources for the organization. Corporations are providing alternative career paths, extended leave of absence, flexible scheduling, flextime working, job sharing, and telecommuting as options for working mothers.[42] The trend toward accommodating, not penalizing, these women is apparent. With so many corporations providing flexible alternatives, not to do so would almost guarantee that an organization would lose its most valuable women managers to a company that does provide alternatives.

Linear Career Crises

As mentioned earlier in this chapter, the number of people entering the ranks of management today is very high. These Baby Boomers are facing a linear career crisis, because the limited number of executive positions available is not nearly enough to absorb the large number of highly qualified, achievement-motivated individuals striving to achieve in management.

Women, in particular, have had a difficult time penetrating senior management levels in organizations.[43] Many women find their careers plateauing at middle management, and feel disillusioned as their high-flying expectations are not being met. Many corporations have contributed to these heightened expectations by promoting women beyond their competency, giving them fancy titles and offices but very little responsibility. This action only served to raise hopes, as people reporting to these women soon realized they had no real power.[44]

As a result of these types of career dilemmas, many women managers are beginning to rethink their career paths and priorities. They are asking themselves: What is right for me? What are my strengths and weaknesses? What kind of rewards do I want and what am I willing to do to get them?

ALTERNATIVE CAREER PATHS

As a result of the linear career crises and a growing desire for more fulfillment from work, many women managers are stepping out of the fast track and taking alternate career paths. The number of women starting up their own businesses, working out of the home, and job sharing has increased significantly in recent years, while another large group has chosen to make a radical career change to improve their work situation.

Women as Entrepreneurs

Paralleling the movement of women into the work force is an increase in the number of female entrepreneurs.[45] There are great risks in starting up a business of your own; many women who have tried and not succeeded find loneliness, overwork, and less money to be the key problems. However, many successful women entrepreneurs have enjoyed the freedom, excitement, and opportunity for financial gain which made the hard work worth their while.[46] Many successful women entrepreneurs, in fact, were once in fairly high level and secure positions in corporations but left because they could not break the glass ceiling.[47]

Working Out of the Home

Women who want to combine career and family have a number of options to work in their home. These include: (1) Arrange a deal with their current employers whereby part or all of their work can be done at home and over the phone; (2) Start their own business by setting up their office

Illus. 4.2
Many women enjoy the
freedom, excitement, and
opportunity for financial gain
that accompany owning.
their own business.

in their home; (3) Free-lance or contract work done primarily out of the home; for example, artists, writers, consultants, and accountants.

Child care is actually a must for most working women whose work demands their full and undivided attention. Working at home does, nevertheless, eliminate hours spent commuting and allows a working mother to spend more time with her children.

Job Sharing

Many corporations are allowing two employees to share job title, work load, salary, health benefits, and vacation time.[48] Job sharing can be arranged in a variety of ways; for example, one employee can work the morning hours and the other work in the afternoon five days a week. Another commonly used method is to work alternating days or weeks. Unfortunately, job sharing is rarely available to managers.

ACTION GUIDELINES

1. The woman manager needs to take time to plan her career carefully. This involves a careful look at her strengths, weaknesses, accomplishments, and both work and family aspirations. It is important to set specific goals for 5-, 10-, and 15-year time frames and map out strategies to achieve these goals. She should set a timetable for her goals and reevaluate them as her career progresses.

2. The woman manager should take the initiative to create challenges in her work, let her goals and accomplishments be known, and look at her current job in terms of the broader picture of the organization and her own career development. A part of this strategy is to deliberately seek successive success experiences through assignments to projects that build her sense of competence. This helps enhance her self-image and self-esteem as well as others' regard for her.

3. Avoid low-visibility positions. The female manager should steer away from peripheral staff functions, and seek out more visible line functions where she will make decisions that affect the bottom line.

4. Reentry women should consider continuing education, using their network of acquaintances, and starting in an administrative capacity to get in the door.

5. Day-to-day strategies for the female manager include: doing consistently outstanding work, making herself visible, creating a network of supporters, presenting a professional image, and helping her boss to succeed.

6. Women should seek out and develop a mentor relationship with either a male or female executive in the organization. As women move up in the corporate ranks, they should make being a mentor to younger women part of their goals. They also can join networking groups of women nationwide to learn from and contribute to the careers of other women.

7. Women managers should consider following alternate career paths such as starting up their own business, working out of their homes, or job sharing.

KEY TERMS

career — the individually perceived sequence of attitudes and behaviors associated with work-related experiences and activities over the span of a person's life

career concepts — according to Driver, four basic career patterns—linear, steady state, spiral, and transitory—by which people perceive their careers

comparable worth — the concept that jobs requiring comparable knowledge, skills, and abilities should pay at comparable levels

glass ceiling — a barrier of stereotype and subtle discrimination that is blocking the promotion of women into senior management

job sharing — an arrangement in which two employees share title, workload, salary, health benefits, and vacation time for a single position

linear career concept — according to Driver, career concept by which an individual chooses a field, develops a plan for advancement, and executes it

mentor — a senior person who undertakes to guide a junior person's career development

networking — looking to other influential individuals for support, guidance, and role modeling in business

psychosocial functions — according to Kram, those aspects of a mentor relationship that improve one's sense of competence, identity, and effectiveness

reality shock syndrome — a barrier to career development consisting of the disparity between initial job expectations and the hard realities of what the job actually entails

realistic job preview — description provided by an organization to applicants and new employees that summarizes both the positive and negative aspects of the job

servant trap — the situation in which a woman finds herself when her mentor asks her to do work that is more fitting for someone in a lower position

spiral career concept — according to Driver, career concept by which individuals motivated by personal growth perform well enough to advance in status and rank

steady state career concept — according to Driver, career concept by which an individual chooses a field but, though improving professionally and financially, does not seek to move up the organizational hierarchy

transitory career concept — according to Driver, career concept by which an individual moves from one job to another with no apparent pattern or progress

DISCUSSION QUESTIONS

1. Discuss the key ingredients in planning a successful career.

2. Describe and discuss at least four barriers to career development.

3. "The concept of mentors as necessary opposes the idea that women learn to become self-sufficient and self-reliant entities. Until they do, I don't think they should expect to be respected in business." What potential problems do you see with a female manager espousing this belief? What attitude does this sound reminiscent of?

4. What are some of the potential problems a female manager may encounter in a mentor relationship and how can they be avoided?

5. Describe some common career dilemmas and list some alternative career paths to combat these dilemmas.

CHAPTER CASE

KATHRYN HILL: PARENT AND PROFESSIONAL

When Courtney screamed, Kathryn Hill jumped out of bed and grabbed her robe, glancing at the clock. It was 3:00 a.m., and her husband, Blake, was still sound asleep, not having been awakened by the piercing screams of their 18-month-old child. Courtney continued to cry as Kathryn held her closely and tried to comfort her. Kathryn suspected it was another ear infection—the second one this month.

As she stood there rocking the child, Kathryn's thoughts turned abruptly to practicalities. She knew she needed to take Courtney to the doctor first thing in the morning, but she also had an important meeting scheduled for 9:00 a.m. Kathryn and a senior partner in her law firm were to represent a client in discussions about the terms of a $20 million lawsuit brought against the client and five other defendants. Because of the number of defendants, the meeting had been difficult to arrange. Kathryn had prepared memoranda for the senior partner in charge and was to make a presentation to all the defendants concerning the costs if a prompt settlement were not reached.

Kathryn knew she could not possibly take Courtney to the doctor and make it to work in time for her meeting. She hoped that Blake would be able to stay home in the morning to take Courtney to the doctor. If he couldn't, what would she do? She didn't want to challenge Blake about which commitment—his or hers—was more important. A confrontation would only lead to bigger questions: Whose career was more important? Whose contribution to the family was more valuable?

It was half past five, and Courtney had dozed off. Kathryn was starting to grow weary of her own thoughts—she had been through them so many times before. She felt that the difficulties she faced while the children were young could be somewhat eased if her husband were more flexible about his work and committed more energy to child care and household tasks. She couldn't tell if his job was really as demanding as he claimed, but she suspected it wasn't. Blake believed women are fully as capable as men in every aspect of the modern working world, but in Kathryn's view, he didn't fully appreciate the demands of parenthood. Sometimes Kathryn wondered if she should just quit her job.

QUESTIONS

1. What are the career dilemmas faced by Kathryn?

2. Do you feel Kathryn should quit her job? Why or why not?

3. What are some of the alternate career paths available to working mothers like Kathryn? Which, if any, do you think would apply in this situation? Explain.

   Source: Adapted from Lynda Sharp Paine, a case prepared for the Center for the Study of Applied Ethics, The Colgate Darden Graduate School of Business Administration, University of Virginia, 1984.

ENDNOTES

[1] J. Ciabattari, "Career Turning Points," *Working Woman* (October, 1987): 87-94, 164-167.

[2] Douglas T. Hall, *Careers in Organizations* (Santa Monica, CA: Goodyear Publishing Co., 1976), 1-5.

[3] M. J. Driver, "Career Concepts and Career Management in Organizations," in C. L. Cooper, ed. *Behavioral Problems in Organizations* (Englewood Cliffs, NJ: Prentice-Hall, 1979), 79-139.

[4] These assessment sources are listed in Daniel C. Feldman, *Managing Careers in Organizations* (Glenview, Il.: Scott, Foresman and Company, 1988), 55-60 and 199-209.

[5] Douglas T. Hall, op cit.

[6] L. J. Nonkin, "Catch-28," *Working Woman* (May, 1987): 118-120, 142-143.

[7] Ibid.

[8] L. H. Chusmir and V. Franks, "Stress and the Woman Manager," *Training & Development Journal* (October, 1988): 66-70.

[9] K. A. Bunker, "Cinderella Doesn't Live Here Anymore," *Issues & Observations* (Spring, 1988): 1-6.

[10] K. W. Wiley, "Up Against the Ceiling," *Savvy* (June, 1987): 51-52, 71.

[11] Monci Jo Williams, "Women Beat the Corporate Game," *Fortune* (September 12, 1988): 128-138.

[12] Alan N. Schoonmaker, *Executive Career Strategy* (New York: American Management Associations, 1971), 150-160.

[13] J. Ciabattari, op. cit.

[14] Ibid.

[15] S. L. Premack and J. P. Wanous, "A Meta-Analysis of Realistic Job Preview Experiments," *Journal of Applied Psychology* (1985): 706-719.

[16] D. Feuer, "How Women Manage," *Training* (August, 1988): 23-31.

[17] K. E. Kram, *Mentoring at Work: Developmental Relationships in Organizational Life* (Glenview, IL: Scott, Foresman, 1985), Chapters 2 and 3.

[18] Ruth Halcomb, "Mentors and the Successful Woman," *Across the Board* (February, 1980): 13-18.

[19] L. A. Westoff, "Mentor or Lover?" *Working Woman* (October, 1986): 116-119.

[20] Johanna S. Hunsaker, "The Mentor Relationship: Fact or Fiction" (From a paper presented at the annual meeting of the Academy of Management, New York, August 16, 1982).

[21] Daniel J. Levinson, *The Seasons of a Man's Life* (New York: Knopf, 1978), 40-63.

[22] Gerald R. Roche, "Much Ado About Mentors," *Harvard Business Review* (January-February, 1979): 14-15, 20-28. See also C. Borman and S. Colson, "Mentoring: An Effective Career Guidance Technique," *The Vocational Guidance Journal*, Vol. 3 (1984): 192-197.

[23] Philomena D. Wauchay, "The Climb to the Top: Is the Network the Route for Women?" *Personnel Administrator* (April, 1980): 72-80.

[24] Daniel J. Levinson, op. cit., 40-63.

[25] Lawton Fitt and Derek Newton, "When the Mentor is a Man and the Protégée a Woman," *Harvard Business Review* (March-April, 1981): 56-60.

[26] J. G. Clawson and K. E. Kram, "Managing Cross-Gender Mentoring," *Business Horizons* (May-June, 1984): 22-32.

[27] L. H. Chusmir and V. Franks, op. cit.

[28] L. A. Westoff, op. cit.

[29] Ibid.

[30] Natasha Josefowitz, *Paths to Power: A Woman's Guide from First Job to Top Executive* (Reading, MA: Addison-Wesley Publishing Company, 1980), 93-95.

[31] Gail Sheehy, *Passages: Predictable Crises of Adult Life* (New York: E. P. Dutton and Company, 1974), 151.

[32] Natasha Josefowitz, op. cit., 98.

[33] Anastasia Toufexis, "Dual Careers, Doleful Dilemmas," *Time* (November 16, 1987): 90-91.

[34] James A. F. Stoner and R. Edward Freeman, *Management* (Englewood Cliffs, NJ: Prentice Hall, 1989), 756.

[35] Maria H. Sekas, "Dual-Career Couples—A Corporate Challenge," *Personnel Administrator* (April, 1984): 36-38, 40-46.

[36] Anastasia Toufexis, op. cit.

[37] Una Sekaran, "The Paths to Mental Health: An Exploratory Study of Husbands and Wives in Dual-Career Families," *Journal of Occupational Psychology* (1985): 129-137.

[38] Una Sekaran, "Factors Influencing the Quality of Life in Dual-Career Families," *Journal of Occupational Psychology* (1983): 161-174.

[39] Una Sekaran, "Understanding the Dynamics of Self-Concept of Members in Dual-Career Families," *Human Relations* (1989): 97-116.

[40] J. H. Pleck and G. L. Staines, "Work Schedules and Work-Family Conflicts in Two-Career Couples," in J. Aldons (ed.), *Two Paychecks* (California: Sage, 1982).

[41] Elizabeth Ehrlich, "The Mommy Track," *Business Week* (March 20, 1989): 126-134.

[42] Ibid.

[43] M. A. Von Glinow and A. K. Mercer, "Women in Corporate America," *New Management* (Summer, 1988): 36-42.

[44] L. J. Nonkin, op. cit.

[45] Donald D. Bowen and Robert D. Hisrich, "The Female Entrepreneur: A Career Development Perspective," *Academy of Management Review* (1986): 393-407.

[46] J. Ciabattari, op. cit.

[47] Sharon Nelton and Karen Berney, "Women: The Second Wave," *Nation's Business* (May, 1987): 18-22.

[48] Elizabeth Ehrlich, op. cit.

ADDITIONAL RESOURCES

Bolles, Richard N. *What Color Is Your Parachute? A Practical Manual for Job Hunters and Career Changers.* Berkeley, CA: Ten Speed Press, 1980.

Bowen, Donald D. "The Role of Identification in Mentoring Female Protégées." *Group & Organization Studies* (March-June, 1986): 61-74.

Bruce, Calvin E. "Counselor, Coach and Cheerleader." *Managing Your Career*, insert to *The Wall Street Journal* (Spring, 1989): 21-24.

Burack, E., Albrecht, M., and Seitler, H. Growing: *A Woman's Guide to Career Satisfaction.* Belmont, CA: Lifetime Learning Publications, 1980.

Byrne, John. "No Time to Waste." *Forbes* (May 6, 1985): 110-114.

Castro, Janice. "Rolling Along the Mommy Track." *Time* (March 27, 1989): 72.

Ciabattari, J. "Managerial Courage." *Working Woman* (September, 1988): 105-108, 220-221.

Cunningham, Mary. *Powerplay: What Really Happened at Bendix.* New York: Simon & Schuster, 1984.

Ekstrom, Ruth. "Women in Management: Factors Affecting Career Entrance and Advancement." *Selections*, Vol. II, No. 1 (1985): 28-32.

Fitt, L. and Newton, D. "When the Mentor Is a Man and the Protégée a Woman." *Harvard Business Review*, Vol. 59 (March-April, 1981) 56.

Kram, Kathy E. "Mentoring in the Workplace." in Douglas T. Hall and Associates, *Career Development in Organizations*. San Francisco: Jossey/Bass, 1986, 160-201.

Moore, Lynda L.,(ed). *Not as Far as You Think: The Realities of Working Women*. Lexington, MA: Lexington Books, 1986.

Morrison, A. M., White, R. P., and Van Velsor, E. "Executive Women: Substance Plus Style." *Psychology Today* (August, 1987). 18-26.

Noe, Raymond A. "Women and Mentoring: A Review and Research Agenda." *Academy of Management Review* (1988). 65-78.

Schwartz, Felice N. "Management Women and the New Facts of Life." *Harvard Business Review* (January-February, 1989): 65-76.

Sekaran, Una. *Dual Career Families: Contemporary Organizational and Counseling Issues*. San Francisco: Jossey/Bass, 1986.

Sheehy, Gail. "The Mentor Connection: The Secret Link in Successful Women's Life." *New York Magazine* (April, 1976). 14-23.

Von Glinow, M. A., Driver, M. J., Brousseau, K., Prince, J. B. "The Design of a Career Oriented Human Resource System." *Academy of Management Review* (1983): 23-32.

Williams, Monci Jo. "Women Beat the Corporate Game." *Fortune* (September 12, 1988): 128-138.

CHAPTER 5

SELF-MANAGEMENT

Stress Management
   Sources of Stress
            Uncertainty
            Lack of Control
            Pressure
            Work Overload or Underload
            Confusing Directions and Conflicting Demands
   Methods of Dealing with Stress
            Coping Techniques
            Adaptation Techniques
Time Management
   Time-Management Techniques
            Establish Priorities
            Control Time Wasters
            Avoid Perfectionism
            Learn to Say NO
   Other Timesaving Ideas
Action Guidelines
Key Terms
Discussion Questions
Chapter Case: The Overwhelmed Real-Estate Salesperson
Endnotes
Additional Resources

I can put the wash on the line, feed the kids, get dressed, pass out the kisses, and get to work by 5 of 9:00—cause I'm a wo-man.

So went the TV jingle for Enjoli, the "8-hour perfume for the 24-hour woman." Today's career woman, however, often finds herself trapped by the superwoman squeeze. She experiences constant pressure attempting to juggle her career with her personal life, family life, and social life (if she has one). Unlike the career woman portrayed in the Enjoli perfume commercial, today's career woman often finds herself hardly able to catch her breath as she tries to fulfill her multiple obligations.

The women who pursue careers in management must constantly be on the alert, scouting the territory for potential problems. The basic self-management skills that can help women managers cope more effectively with their multiple responsibilities pertain to the areas of (1) stress management and (2) time management.

STRESS MANAGEMENT

Several definitions of stress have been offered over the years, but the most direct way of defining it is, "In its medical sense, **stress** is essentially the rate of wear and tear on the body."[1] Stress represents a physiological, biological, and psychological response to a situation that evokes the stress reaction. For some people this can be manifested by sweating hands, anxiety, or tense shoulders.

Whether a person experiences a stress response depends on how the person perceives and responds to the demands of the environment. Not all events produce stress for everyone, but those events that are perceived as threatening will elicit this stress reaction. These events are called **stressors.**

Nelson and Quick classify stressors as caused either by role demands, job demands, environmental demands, interpersonal demands, or extra-organizational demands.[2]

1. A **role demand** would be something expected of a woman through the role she occupies. In most families, the mother is expected to carry primary responsibility for childrearing simply because her role is mother (i.e., a nurturer).

2. **Job demands** are those requirements that are expected through the job occupied. Research has indicated that managerial work itself is stressful. Managers are vulnerable to demands of work load, both in quality or difficulty of the work itself and in terms of simply having too much to do.[3]

3. The physical setting in which work takes place may increase the experience of stress. Noise levels, temperature, a fast pace, long hours, office politics, and poor communication procedures are all examples of **environmental demands**.

4. **Interpersonal demands** include relationships with supervisors, responsibility for subordinates, as well as peer relationships.

5. **Extraorganizational demands** are responsibilities outside of the job that can detract from job performance. Relationships with spouse, children, friends, and parents would be in this category. For most women, extraorganizational demands are closely tied with role demands.

Many women accept stress as inevitable; it is the price paid for having a career. Other women do not anticipate stress, and they learn the hard way that managing a career and a personal life is an extremely demanding job. Only after being pushed to the brink of collapse do they recognize the need to manage their lives in ways that minimize stress and maximize performance and satisfaction. This is what **stress management** is all about—the ability to manage the forces in one's life rather than being controlled by them.

All people need some stress in their lives. Stress can be *functional* by activating and enhancing one's performance. For example, a dry mouth and a tight stomach before an important presentation often help a manager to do a good job, but too much stress can become *dysfunctional*. Too many tight stomachs may cause the manager to develop a bleeding ulcer. Beyond a certain point, too much stress overloads the body's system and performance decreases. The female body is warned of too much stress through such symptoms as chest pain, menstrual disorder, sore neck or back, headache, bad breath, insomnia, excessive sleep, or stomach pain.

The managerial woman deals with stressors experienced by all managers. However, she faces a unique set of stressors rarely encountered by her male counterpart: discrimination, stereotyping, conflicting role demands of marriage and/or a family and career, and social isolation.[4] These demands, combined with the normal stresses experienced by managers, can produce abnormal reactions.

When people make too many demands on themselves, they experience physiological, emotional, and psychological changes called the "stress response." The body reacts to a stressor by pumping hormones into the blood stream where they go into action. The body's response is essentially the same whether the stress results from playing tennis, surviving a frightening accident on the freeway, going to an important meeting, or running a race.

Different situations can be more or less stress-producing for different people. People also differ in terms of their ability to tolerate stress; an individual's stress tolerance varies over time.

Maddi and Kosaba have investigated the factors that cause some people to be exhausted and drained by stressful events while others are stimulated and challenged.[5] They reported ability to handle stress was a function of four characteristics: (1) personal style and personality, how one tended to perceive, interpret, and respond to stressful events; (2) social supports, the extent to which family, friends, co-workers, and others provided encouragement and emotional support during stressful events; (3) constitutional predisposition or how robust and healthy one's body seemed in terms of inborn physical construction, and (4) health practices, the extent to which one stayed in good physical condition through exercise and avoided destructive behavior such as smoking.

By far the most important personality dimension identified in their research was a concept they called **hardiness**. A woman manager high in hardiness would be committed to her work and her life, would have a sense of control rather than powerlessness, and view change and problems as challenges.

Next, the issue of energy and health should not be overlooked by women managers. In the rush to establish a career in a man's world, a woman manager should not ignore the important parts of her private life such as recreation and health maintenance. Much has been written recently about heart attacks and ulcers which male managers commonly suffer. It is dangerous for managerial women to assume that they are somehow immune to the wear and tear that similar careers may have on their health. Women who work full time are subject to the same stressors and strain as men. Women workers also have to get up in the morning, fight traffic, climb on subways, worry about deadlines, work for promotions, and like men, they sometimes go home and take out their frustrations on their families. Working women are subject to the same illnesses as men: heart disease, high blood pressure, ulcers, and increasing rates of alcoholism.

Stress appears inevitable for all managers and especially women managers. The women the authors interviewed suffered from stress, and they revealed their symptoms in the following responses:

- "I've had a constant nervous stomach since I took this senior vice-presidency."
- "I eat like a big pig when I am under stress at work. Pressures and deadlines on me mean ten extra pounds."
- "I get very tired. I go to bed early, but then I wake up in the middle of the night and think of all the work I need to do."

Sources of Stress

Uncertainty, lack of control, and pressure are common sources of stress for all managers. Middle-management women may be gulping Alka-Seltzer as much as middle-management men do.

Uncertainty. *New* women managers, in particular, experience much stress because they live with perpetual ambiguity and uncertainty. Often they are one of a few women in their positions, and their jobs lack clear definitions of responsibilities or expectations of performance.

Many working women who have children bear a double burden. They have problems associated with the reliability of their baby-sitters, the health of their children, and baking cookies for the PTA. In each instance, there is the constant fear that at any time something may happen to upset the status quo.

Lack of Control. Another source of stress related to uncertainty is lack of control, and often people have no control over the stress-inducing quality of uncertain or unpredictable events. At other times, even when people know what might happen, they cannot take the appropriate steps to meet the demands. They may know the proper solution but they are powerless to control other people and/or the events necessary to bring about the desired outcome. For example, it can be extremely stressful working for a supervisor who changes plans abruptly or springs last-minute rush assignments on a subordinate.

Pressure. Pressure is a source of stress involving how a person evaluates and feels about an event. Consider the difference between meeting a deadline on a project important to a manager's career—one that may result in a promotion—and meeting a deadline on a routine project. Although the real pressure of each project may be the same and may cause just as many disruptions in her work or home life, the woman manager is likely to experience them in very different ways. The first project has more riding on it, but the pressure is a turn-on. It is as exciting as it is stressful! The second project lacks excitement and value and is purely stress producing.

Work Overload or Underload. Having too much or too little to do can create job stress. A burdensome work load can create stress in two ways. Fatigue can reduce tolerance for minor annoyances and irritations, and make everything seem to be a big deal. Secondly, a person under the burden of too much work feels perpetually behind schedule and racing to catch up. Sarah, a manager of a chain of small specialty stores, describes her experience with an overwhelming job:

I took over as manager of the chain because it represented an opportunity for me to make some real money, the profit sharing package was terrific. It quickly dawned on me that this job was no picnic. The owner tried to squeeze all of the costs he could out of the place. That meant he tried to get by with the minimum amount of help possible. The stores really were busy during weekends, and the sales associates could hardly manage the load and give the kind of service people expect in small specialty stores. The owner wanted the sales associates to push accessories and expensive add-ons on the customers. This led to a lot of hassles that the sales associates didn't bargain for. As the manager, I have to bear pressure from the owner as well as keep my staff happy. I really am caught in the middle. When I tried to talk to the owner, he said to quit if I couldn't handle the pressure and do my job. So I quit.

A disruptive amount of stress also can occur when people experience role underload, or too little to do. Role underload is frustrating because it is a normal human reaction to want to work toward self-fulfillment. People who do not have enough to do face boredom and monotony.

Confusing Directions and Conflicting Demands. "I'm not really sure what I am supposed to be doing," said a woman manager of her new managerial responsibilities. "No one wants to let me in on any of the policies or procedures." People in many different places of work find that when work expectations are sloppily defined either by intent or neglect it is a frustrating and stressful experience. Additionally, many managers receive conflicting demands from two or more superiors. When the demands of superiors conflict, loyalty dilemmas and stress are the consequences.

Methods of Dealing with Stress

How can one manage stress in a productive way and avoid its negative outcomes? There are several stress-reducing techniques that have been proven to be useful, but first it helps to recognize a difference between coping techniques and adaptation techniques.[6] **Coping techniques** help a person to live with the problem, while **adaptation techniques** solve the problem by modifying either the sources of stress or the person's reactions to them. In order to manage stress, the manager has to find ways to modify the situations that cause stress, as well as her ways of responding to stress.

Coping Techniques. Coping techniques generally involve things that seem to help people get through a stressful time. One common coping technique involves the use of drugs or alcohol. One study found that 40 percent of the sample of senior female executives had been or were still taking tranquilizers, antidepressants, and sleeping pills to relieve tension.[7] At the middle level of management, the number of women on Valium and related drugs was about 30 percent. Because of the stresses of a dual career and their own inner achievement pressure, some women managers found themselves thinking about work during their "own" time. One of them said, "I find very often my brain ticking over like mad at night and I can't sleep . . . I take Valium then, but never during the day."

Female managers in the United States smoke more than women in other job classifications.[8] Another way some managers cope with stress is to drink alcohol. However, alcohol, cigarettes, or drugs, do not relieve stress. They may temporarily mask the feelings a person experiences, but they do not change the stress-producing event or the person's feelings about it. In many cases, the use of drugs or alcohol only compounds problems and leads to dependence, addiction, poorer performance, and physical deterioration. Smoking has been linked to cancer as well as various cardiovascular diseases.[9]

Adaptation Techniques. Adaptation techniques have more positive effects, although they still do not eliminate dysfunctional stress on a permanent basis.

Regular physical exercise is one such method of adapting to stress and much evidence exists proving regular exercise has multiple benefits for physical and mental health. Unfortunately, many women do not find the time for physical exercise. It is not a priority. Many females were not socialized as children to incorporate exercise as a regular part of their life-style. This is unfortunate because it has long been recognized by medical authorities that certain types of pent-up frustration, anxiety, and stress may be released through physical exertion. The rapid rise in heart attacks and strokes among young Americans has been an instrumental factor in bringing about a significant increase in physical activity such as jogging, bicycle riding, aerobic dancing, jazz exercising, and walking. The female manager can use exercise as a way of building physical strength, as well as releasing tension and anxiety. Comments from women who incorporate exercise in their lives reflect the exercise-stress link:

■ A high ranking executive of a utility company comments, "On weekends there is nothing I like to do better than really heavy yardwork. Hauling off bushes and strenuous weed pulling really helps me to unwind."

■ A petite MBA student reports, "When I am uptight nothing helps me like pounding at the punching bag. It feels great, and I calm down."

■ A stockbroker: "I'm on the racquetball court three nights every week. It's about the only way I can handle the phone jangling all day long. In this business it's either you take care of your tensions, or drink and smoke too much and wind up in the hospital. The choice seems straightforward to me."

Recreation is another method for escaping from situations that bring about stress. Taking vacations, going to the movies, or doing whatever the manager really likes to do provides a chance to relax and renew her system for dealing with the stressful situation again.

Relaxation exercises are other ways of giving the manager some positive time out. There are a wide variety of techniques, methods,

Illus. 5.1
Regular physical exercise is one method of adapting to stress.

and approaches to becoming more in touch with oneself at different levels of consciousness. Techniques include Transcendental Meditation (TM), biofeedback, general relaxation, meditation, and yoga.[10] These techniques can be extremely valuable in teaching the manager how to remove herself temporarily from a tension-producing environment or to relieve frustration and anxiety. One telephone company supervisor who meditates every afternoon stated, "When I get back from meditation, I am not only more effective, but I get along better with people and myself too. I am much more productive." This is an example of how spending time creates time! Spending some time to relax or exercise revitalizes the manager, allowing her to become more productive than she would be if she had continued to perform under stress.

There are many other strategies that the manager can employ to help reduce the level of regularly experienced stress or, at the very least, to help cope with continuing high stress. A few further examples are given below:

1. Increase her *self-awareness* of how she behaves on the job. She can find out what are her limits and recognize signs of potential trouble. Learning when to withdraw from a situation and when to seek help from others on the job are often effective strategies to relieve stress.

2. Develop *outside interests* to take her mind off work. This solution is particularly important for high-achieving, hard-driving people whose physical health may depend on toning down their relentless drive for success.

3. Try to find a variety of personal or *unique solutions* for coping with stress. One savings and loan executive described how she reacts to stressful situations. "I walk into my office, close the door, and pound the hell out of my typewriter, saying all of the things on paper that I want to say. It works every time. Then I rip up and shred the paper and throw it in the trash can."

4. Identify what specific things cause stress in her life. In order to do something about stress, she first has to *identify its source*. Then it may be possible to eliminate or modify it.

5. Schedule her life so that *conflicting demands* can be avoided. This is important on both a lifetime and a day-to-day basis.

6. *Plan* her career. She shouldn't just assume that things will work out. Often they don't; if they do, they won't always be in directions she prefers.

7. Try to *reduce uncertainty* as much as possible by establishing a regular routine for those things within her control. Then she will not have to worry about when to do what.

TIME MANAGEMENT

A major contribution to stress for managerial women is the lack of sufficient time to get everything done in their lives. **Overload** (too much to do in the time available) and **multiple roles** (being responsible for many different kinds of activities) are usually to blame. These are inherent in managerial positions and can be overwhelming at times. In a study conducted for the Department of Health, Education and Welfare,[11] the Occupational Safety and Health Administration (OSHA) listed the job of **manager** as the number one high-stress job. Using time effectively, then, can be a major step in handling the stress and multiple demands of the managerial role.

Many matters reaching a manager's desk demand substantial blocks of time, and seldom is there enough time to do everything fully or effectively. Time is a scarce, precious, and irretrievable resource. Unlike money, human resources, or raw materials, time cannot be accumulated. People are forced to spend time, whether they choose to or not. They can, however, determine the way in which they spend it. As are other resources, time is either mismanaged or it is handled effectively.

Many managers do not use their time wisely. They fail to match their time with their most important responsibilities, and they will not acknowledge the fact that they need to take control and learn to utilize time more effectively. While a manager cannot manufacture more time, she can learn to make better use of the time she has. As is often said, managing time does not mean working harder—it just means working smarter!

For the woman manager this problem is especially crucial. She not only faces the overwhelming demands of her managerial assignments, but also often has multiple commitments. Women in management often have the responsibility of a job and a family (another full-time job) simultaneously, whereas men in comparable positions often have wives who assume the traditional role of caring for the family. Employed women generally get little help with the housework from their husbands.[12] Culture has conditioned most people to believe that the home is the woman's responsibility. Unless she has a husband who shares equally in family responsibilities, she has two jobs in contrast to a male peer's one. Whoever asked a man how he manages to combine marriage and family with a career? How many career women have expressed the wish that they had a "wife?" How many times could the woman manager have used one herself?

To combine two time-consuming careers, a woman has to become an expert manager of her time. If she wants to compete successfully with her male counterparts, she needs to seek efficient ways to juggle her office and home routines.

The women managers in our survey tended to manage their time well. One successful woman in the savings and loan industry pointed out that "managing my time is important not only for controlling my stress level, but also because others are watching me, making sure I'm not wasting my time on frivolous conversations and gossip!"

Some male managers are conditioned by the myth that women waste time pursuing frivolous activities. The woman manager must work to overcome this myth. Effective management of time is a potent demonstration of competence,which can dispel the foundation of this negative stereotype.

Time-Management Techniques

One of the most useful approaches to effective time management is described by Alan Lakein in his book, *How to Get Control of Your Time and Your Life*.[13] Basic to his system is learning how to plan what one wants to do and then organizing one's use of time to get it done. "Time is a constant that cannot be altered. . . . We cannot manage time itself. We can only manage our activities with respect to it." In other words, managing time, like managing stress, involves learning to manage one's own behavior.

Two of Lakein's time-management techniques are (1) to establish priorities and (2) to control time wasters.

Establish Priorities. Whether the manager is planning for today or next year, she needs to establish her priorities. She has to identify and concentrate on the tasks of the highest priority and eliminate low-priority activities.

Lakein suggests using the simple *ABC Priority System*.[14] It works like this: The manager should plan her daily work by listing everything she needs to do today. She should write a capital "A" next to those items on the list that have a high value (the things that are really important), a "B" for those with medium value, and a "C" for those with low value. She gets the most out of her time by doing the A's first, and saving the B's and C's for later. When she has a sense of what her A goals are, she can begin to plan her time to accomplish them.

ABC's are relative, depending on one's point of view. The A tasks generally will stand out in contrast to B and C tasks. A person's ABC's may change over time. Today's A may become tomorrow's C, while today's C may become tomorrow's A. The manager needs to set priorities continually, always considering the *best use of her time right now*. When she begins to feel overwhelmed and frustrated, she should

Illus. 5.2   Effective time management includes planning what needs to be done and then setting aside the time to do it.

remind herself that there is always enough time for the important things. After all, what difference does it really make if a C task does not get done? She should ask herself, "Would anything terrible happen if I didn't do this item?" If the answer is no, then she shouldn't do it.

Control Time Wasters. A **time waster** is an event, incident, or situation that eats into one's time if repeated often. Although a time waster is not necessarily always wasteful or undesirable, the manager may wish that it did not take so much of her managerial time—time that she could use more profitably on more significant aspects of her job. Some common situations that *can* become time wasters are: meetings, correspondence, visitors, reports, questionnaires, committee work, complaints, employee grievances, lost materials or records, "emergency" situations, telephone calls, overinvolvement in a subordinate's personal problems, community activities, appointments, late arrivals, lack of delegation, interruptions, and pet projects.

The manager should take several minutes to consider what her time wasters are. After listing them, she should take a closer look and ask herself some questions. Which of her time wasters are generated internally by her? Which are generated externally by events or other people? Which could she control or eliminate? What has she done, attempted to do, or what does she plan to do about these time wasters?

In addition to the above strategies suggested by Lakein, there are other time management techniques a woman manager could practice.

Avoid Perfectionism. Women have long been rewarded for crossing all the t's and dotting all the i's. Thoroughness and attention to detail can be a virtue, but excessive striving for perfection in all areas is often self-defeating behavior. Time management consultants Turla and Hawkins advise:[15]

1. Don't run all over town looking for a particular folder when second-best will do.

2. Don't have letters retyped to be perfect; the recipients will either file them or throw them away.

3. Realize that below average to a perfectionist often is perfectly acceptable to others.

Learn to Say NO. Many women have a notoriously hard time saying no to requests. An effective time manager learns to tactfully decline requests that interfere with her work priorities. A boss is more difficult to turn down than a co-worker. When this happens, it may be helpful to point out how the new task will interfere with higher-priority ones.[16] When a boss recognizes a motivated worker, chances are this will be rewarded and the worker may avoid being saddled with less-important tasks. Learning to say no may require practice, even rehearsal!

Other Timesaving Ideas

By sharpening her awareness of her use of time, the manager can control and create more time for herself. Some further timesaving ideas for her include the following:

1. Keeping a daily THINGS TO DO TODAY list and reviewing it each morning.

2. Blocking off time for priority activities—either save a time slot in each day or set a day aside each week.

3. Not letting anything interfere with priority time.

4. Assigning priorities based on value/time ratios.

5. Scheduling appointments, but always reserving at least one hour a day of uncommitted time.

6. Handling paper only once; don't keep reshuffling it.

7. Not procrastinating—if something has to be done, do it immediately.

8. Delegating as much as possible to others. Unless the manager absolutely has to do something herself, she should assign it to someone else. Management means getting things accomplished through other people.

9. Learning to know her "prime time." When does she work best? She should save her prime time for priority projects.

10. Trying to be flexible. The manager should always leave time in her schedule for emergencies or catching up.

11. Planning time to relax. If she is exhausted, she will not be able to work effectively or efficiently.

12. Learning to use transition time to get things done. For example, does she read, catch the news on radio, or discuss matters with her husband and family while she dresses, does her nails, or eats breakfast? How does she use her time spent in commuting, coffee breaks, lunch hour, or waiting in offices? Does she carry her list with her so that she can use time to plan? Does she carry paper and pencil for writing or does she have something to read?

13. Turning C activities into things that can be put off indefinitely. How many C activities are unimportant? A woman manager should learn to discriminate and put them aside.

By taking a hard, close look at how she is presently using her time, the manager may surprise herself. She may find that she does not have to do it all. She may be able to delegate other things, thus leaving herself free for all those activities which only she can handle.

Beyond the strategies already mentioned for managing time well, there is another essential guideline for the manager. She must invest time in order to make time, and considerable time must be invested in herself. The solution does not lie in forfeiting a rich and complex life. As Baruch, Barnett, and Rivers point out in their book *Lifeprints: New Patterns of Love and Work for Today's Woman*, multiple roles and demands benefit women. Those women with both careers and families have a greater sense of well-being than women who have only one or neither.[17] Research from the Wellesley College Center for Research on Women supports the idea that significant mental and physical health differences exist which *favor* employed women over nonemployed women.[18] Moreover, contrary to the stereotypical belief that a high-powered career is dangerous to one's health, in fact, the advantages are great for a woman in a high-status occupation! Being employed is beneficial. One key to a successful work experience is effectively managing stress and time with the ability to create balance.

ACTION GUIDELINES

No one chapter in a book can change a woman's life, tell her how to get rid of stress entirely, or how to manage her time completely. However, there does seem to be a basic principle underlying much of what is known about managing stress and time. Demands associated with valued and rewarding activities are consistently less stressful and more energizing than are demands associated with activities not personally meaningful.

The bottom line, then, is not *how much* the manager is doing, but *what* she is doing and *why*. Women who manage their goals and priorities will have a head start on self-management. They can keep stress within optimal limits and use it to energize their efforts toward valued goals.

KEY TERMS

adaptation techniques — methods of dealing with stress that solve a problem by modifying either the sources of stress or one's reactions to them

coping techniques — methods of dealing with stress that involve helping a person put up with the problem

multiple roles — a contributor to stress that consists of being responsible for many different kinds of activities

overload — a contributor to stress that consists of having too much to do in the time available

stress — the rate of wear and tear on the body

stress management — the ability to manage the forces in a person's life rather than having these forces control the person

stressors — events or environments that are perceived as threatening and therefore produce stress

time waster — an oft-repeated event, incident, or situation that tends to eat into one's time

DISCUSSION QUESTIONS

1. What are some of the typical sources of stress for female managers and what are the strategies that can be employed to help cope or adapt to continuing stress?

2. What are the special time-management concerns that face a woman and how can they be dealt with?

3. Discuss ways a woman can achieve balance in her life.

4. What are your most prevalent time-wasters? List positive ways you can control them.

5. What multiple roles do you currently hold and how do you balance these roles?

CHAPTER CASE

THE OVERWHELMED REAL-ESTATE SALES-PERSON

Kathy Cooper looked at herself in the bathroom mirror and thought to herself, "You're looking bad, kid. Somehow you have got to get your life straightened out. You're on a treadmill, and you don't know how to get off. But it's a bad time to be thinking about myself right now. It's time to meet with a client, and if I sell this one, it's really a peach of a deal. I have to keep working hard while I can, because you never know when the market will dry up. But first, I have to meet with my broker, Bonnie Leebon. I wonder what she wants."

Bonnie Leebon began the meeting with Kathy Cooper in her usual open manner: "Kathy, I'm concerned about you. For a long time you have been one of the best salespeople in our firm. You received compliments from me and from all of the other brokers in town. Everyone wanted to work on deals with you. Now you are hardly making it. You don't return phone calls, you've become irritable, you are lacking in enthusiasm. A lot of your paper work contains glaring errors, the escrow officers are complaining. Your work is late, we had to delay six escrows last month because you didn't have your paperwork in, and no one could find you. This has got to stop. What is your problem?"

"I wish it were only one problem, Bonnie. I feel like the world is caving in on me. I work about sixty hours a week. I am really trying to perform well, to earn commissions for my family. I am also studying for my broker's license two nights a week. If I can keep up the pace, I'll be done by next fall. But it is getting to be a real grind."

"How are things at home, Kathy?"

"Much worse than they are here. My husband, Rob, travels a lot, and he is getting fed up with never seeing me when he *is* home. It seems like I'm either working late, at class, or at dinner with a client. My daughter Ashley isn't very happy either. She's 13 and you know how exhausting teenagers can be! She used to be such a sweet little girl, but now I hardly know who she is. She asked me the other day if Daddy and I were getting divorced. She doesn't see us together very much, and when she does, she can feel the tension between us."

"So, you're under pressure at home and at work," said Bonnie.

"And at school, I am having a real hard time with all of the math necessary. If I don't study really hard, I'll never pass the broker's exam."

"Do the best you can, Kathy. I'm sympathetic, but I do need better performance from you."

As Kathy left Bonnie Leebon's office, she said: "Thanks for being up front with me. My problem is that my boss, my husband, my child, and my teachers all want better performance from me. I wish I knew how to give it."

QUESTIONS

1. What suggestions can you offer Kathy for working out her problems?

2. Why is this case included in a chapter on stress and time management?

3. What stress symptoms is Kathy experiencing?

ENDNOTES

[1] H. Selye, *The Stress of Life* (New York: McGraw-Hill, 1976), 1.

[2] D. Nelson and J. Quick, "Professional Women: Are Distress and Disease Inevitable? *Academy of Management Review* (April, 1985): 206-218.

[3] "Stress on the Job," *Newsweek* (April 25, 1988): 40-44; and Gibles, Nancy, "How America Has Run Out of Time," *Time* (April 24, 1989): 58-67.

[4] Nelson and Quick, op. cit., 209.

[5] S. Maddi and S. Kosaba, *The Hardy Executive: Health Under Stress* (Homewood, IL: Dow-Jones, Irwin), 62.

[6] Robert Kreitner, "Managing the Two Faces of Stress," *Arizona Business* (October, 1977): 2-14.

[7] Gary L. Cooper and Marilyn J. Davidson, "The High Cost of Stress on Women Managers," *Organizational Dynamics* (Spring, 1982): 44-53.

[8] B. Jacobson, *The Ladykillers: Why Smoking is a Feminist Issue* (New York: Pluto Press, 1981).

[9] J. C. Quick and J. D. Quick, *Organization Stress and Preventative Management* (New York: McGraw-Hill, 1984).

[10] Roger Allen, *Relaxation Exercises for Controlling Stress and Tension* (College Park, MD: Autumn Wind, 1979). See also B. B. Brown, *Stress and the Art of Biofeedback* (New York: Harper & Row, 1977).

[11] "Stress on the Job," *Newsweek* (April 25, 1988): 40-44.

[12] Douglas Hall and Judith Richter, "Balancing Work Life and Home Life: What Can Organizations Do to Help?" *Academy of Management Executive* (August, 1988): 213-223.

[13] Alan Lakein, *How to Get Control of Your Time and Your Life* (New York: Peter H. Wyden, 1973), 73.

[14] Ibid., 25-27.

[15] P. Turla and K. Hawkins, "The Flaws of Perfectionism," *Success* (December, 1982): 23.

[16] E. Bliss, "Give Yourself the Luxury of Time," *Mainliner* (December, 1986): 56.

[17] G. Baruch, R. Barnett, and C. Rivers, *Lifeprints: New Patterns of Love and Work for Today's Woman* (New York: McGraw-Hill, 1983), 150.

[18] G. Baruch, L. Biener, and R. Barnett, "Women and Gender in Research on Work and Family Stress," *American Psychologist* (February, 1987): 130-136.

ADDITIONAL RESOURCES

Braiker, Harriet. *The Type E Woman: How to Overcome the Stress of Being.* Los Angeles: Dodd, Mead Co., 1986.

Ciabattari, Jane. "The Kind of Stress Managers Know Best." *Working Woman* (September, 1987): 125-130.

Davidson, Marilyn and Cooper, Gary. *Stress and the Woman Manager.* New York: St. Martin Press, 1983.

Hall, Douglas and Richter, Judith. "Balancing Work Life and Home Life: What Can Organizations Do to Help?" *Academy of Management Executive* (August, 1988): 213-223.

Mackoff, Barbara. *Leaving the Office Behind.* New York: Dell Publishing Co., 1986.

CHAPTER 6

COMMUNICATING EFFECTIVELY

Need for Effective Communication
Special Communication Problems for Women
    Characteristics of Women's Speech Patterns
    Reverting to Inappropriate Family-Socialized
    Behaviors
    Ways to Overcome Weak Speech Patterns
Roadblocks to Effective Two-Way Communication
    Hidden Intentions
    Preoccupation with Tasks
    Emotional Involvement
    Distortions to Match One's Expectations
    Misperceptions
    Distrust
Listening
    Poor Listening Habits
        Doing All the Talking
        Interrupting
        Avoiding Eye Contact
        Showing Boredom
        Allowing Telephone Interruptions

Listening (Cont'd)
    Active Listening
Ways to Overcome Sender Barriers to the Communication Process
    Use Redundancy
    Be Complete and Specific
    Claim the Message As Your Own
    Ensure That Your Messages Are Congruent
    Develop Credibility
Developing Persuasiveness in Communication—Twelve Guidelines
The Need for Adequate Feedback
    Types of Feedback
            Verbal Feedback
            Nonverbal Feedback
            Fact Feedback
            Feeling-Feedback
    Effective Use of Feedback
Action Guidelines
Key Terms
Discussion Questions
Chapter Case: Kathy Adams: Accounting Department Manager
Endnotes
Additional Resources

Seldom are managers alone at their desks thinking or contemplating alternatives by themselves. They spend between 50 and 90 percent of their time in interpersonal communication. Of that time, 10 percent is spent communicating with superiors, 40 percent with subordinates, and 50 percent with peers.[1] When they are not talking to their superiors, peers, or subordinates face-to-face, managers are on the telephone or writing memos and letters. Even then it is unusual for a manager to work uninterrupted for more than a half hour without having to stop and verbally communicate with others.

The **communication process** begins when one person sends a message—oral or written—to another with the intent of evoking a response (see Figure 6-1). *Effective communication* occurs when the receiver's interpretation of the message matches the sender's intended meaning.

How well do you communicate with others? If the people working for you were to rate your communication effectiveness on a scale of 1 to 10, how would you score? Have you ever had a breakdown in communication where you were misunderstood by the other person or where you misunderstood the other person's message? What were the consequences? These things happen to everyone at one time or another. Most of these barriers can be overcome, however, by mastering the skills presented in this chapter on effective communication.

FIGURE 6-1

THE COMMUNICATION PROCESS

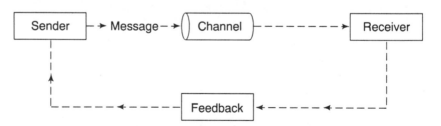

Source: Donald C. Mosley, Leon C. Megginson, and Paul H. Pietri, Jr., *Supervisory Management: The Art of Working With and Through People* (Cincinnati, OH: South-Western Publishing Co., 1985), 169.

NEED FOR EFFECTIVE COMMUNICATION

An effective manager must be an effective communicator. This truism is suggested by the very definition of managing, which is getting things done through other people. If a manager does not effectively communicate what needs to be done, how can she expect to get things accomplished? Even if the manager accurately communicates directives, problems often occur if instructions are given in ways that cause misunderstandings with other people. The result can be an incompletely or incorrectly executed job.

Effective communication is also necessary to accomplish the management functions of **planning**, **organizing**, **staffing**, **directing**, and **controlling**. Plans must be communicated if they are expected to be carried out. **Organizing** involves communicating to others their responsibilities and job assignments. **Staffing** involves the solicitation of accurate information from job applicants through written, verbal, and nonverbal communication to determine effective person-job matches. **Directing** and **controlling** require interpersonal communication in order to motivate employees to strive for organizational goals and to stay on track.

Effective communication is more than simply speaking and writing well. It means choosing words carefully and knowing when to talk and when to listen. It includes anything that communicates your intentions to another person. Communication is going on all the time in many different ways through a variety of verbal and nonverbal channels.

Women do have some advantages over men when communicating in groups. Research has shown, for example, that when a group of men are talking, part of the process is gaining the floor—a competition in which the winner is the one who speaks. Women, on the other hand, tend to take turns in group discussion and are more cooperative. This is important in terms of consultative and democratic decision making processes that should lead to high morale and commitment from people in the organization.[2]

SPECIAL COMMUNICATION PROBLEMS FOR WOMEN

Early social conditioning teaches women to speak like ladies, which may partially translate into developing speech patterns that are more submissive and less incisive than men's. The first step for enhancing

Illus. 6.1   Effective communication includes choosing words carefully and knowing when to talk and when to listen.

communication effectiveness is awareness of how women's unique speech and language patterns sometimes inhibit their effectiveness in communicating.

Characteristics of Women's Speech Patterns

Research on speech and language patterns indicates that fear and insecurity very often shape the way some women talk.[3] Their choice of words, voice intonation, general tone of hesitancy, and high pitch are often interpreted as uncertainty or even an appeal for help. The following characteristics have been found to be generally consistent in women's speech. It is important to correct these deficiencies, because they can detract from a woman's influence and credibility.

1. The use of **empty adjectives** that connote little meaning and have a fluffing effect. For example, "marvelous," "divine," "terri-

ble," are empty adjectives. People whose speech is filled with empty adjectives are usually not taken very seriously.

2. The use of **tag questions** after a declarative statement that automatically defer and pass the ball to the other court. For example, "It's really time for a break now, right?" By itself, the statement shows confidence and conviction. By adding the tag question, however, the speaker gives the impression of being unsure of herself. Tag questions avoid conflicts but they also surrender the speaker's decision-making power.

3. The **questioning intonation** at the end of a statement that neutralizes or eliminates the intended assertiveness of the statement. This has the same effect as a tag question. "Time for a break," for example, can be stated as a question, or asserted as an order.

4. The use of **hedging or modifying phrases** which detract from the impact of a statement. Phrases such as "sort of" and "I guess" give speech a tentative and uncommitted quality. "I guess we should probably sign with Turbo Products," is not as convincing as a more assertive statement such as, "Turbo Products is the best choice because of their track record and price."

5. The use of **hypercorrect or excessively polite speech** which may be misinterpreted. Some examples are not using contractions (i.e., don't) or being overly cautious about using slang or swearing. Instead of building respect and status, hypercorrect or excessively polite speech can give the speaker an uptight image, which is often described behind her back with the very words or adjectives that she so carefully avoids. Communication effectiveness may actually be decreased if the speaker concentrates so much on the correctness of speech that the intended meaning is not conveyed.

6. The use of **disclaimers** that preface an opinion to protect the speaker from losing face if she's wrong. For example, "I'm probably misinformed, but" or "I'm not really sure, but." Disclaimers decrease the level of the speaker's influence. In fact, disclaimers almost invite listeners to disagree and try to prove that the speaker is wrong. They should not be used when the speaker is sure of her position and being challenged by someone who is trying to intimidate her. On the other hand, if trying to increase the comfort level of subordinates and help them improve without

becoming defensive, disclaimers can help them accept your advice without losing face.

7. The use of **fillers** such as um and uh signal uncertainty and lack of preparation. Fillers also open the door for interruption and allow others to take away the speaker's right to speak.

8. The use of **apologies** that rob the speaker's requests or declarations of their focus and authority is seen in statements such as, "I really hate to bother you now because I know that you are really busy, but I'd like to ask you to take a minute and edit this memo for me." Apologies clutter and lengthen a request. They detract from the speaker's stature and influence. Compare the above lengthy request with "Please take a minute to edit this memo."

9. The *overuse* of the word *try*, which signals weakness. For example, "I'll try to get the report done on time." The word *try* in this response makes the manager sound frail and incompetent. Compare this response with "You've got it!"

Most of the above examples describe women's tendency to back off from strong assertions. This type of speech pattern may reflect perceived power differences that already exist or, even more important, they may actually help to create them.[4]

Finally, women have been found to use *smiles and nods* more than men in business conversations. In studies of low- and high-status language behaviors, women were perceived to have greater power when they smiled less and held their heads relatively still.[5]

These ineffective behaviors are partially based on past cultural conditioning, which inhibits many women from stating directly what they want, especially if it means overriding the opinions of others. The temptation exists to revert to the ingenue role, the seductive role, or the little girl role which worked so well as a child, and a simple glance or gesture is often all that is required.[6]

Reverting to Inappropriate Family-Socialized Behaviors

The goal of effective communication is an adult-adult, problem-solving type of interaction.[7] When women revert to the more passive speech patterns just described, the father-daughter, mother-son, or mother-daughter relationship develops, which are manifestations of inappropriate family socialization in the workplace. Take the following negative examples:[8]

■ A woman manager defers to a male peer on a policymaking issue (father-daughter pattern).

■ Although a male manager may be angry at a female manager for an error she made, he still acts in such a way as to protect her (father-daughter pattern).

■ Male and female managers use sex to play out power and control issues (father-daughter or mother-son patterns).

■ Men use female managers as mothers by telling them about personal problems, but not treating them as real colleagues with whom they also share professional problems and per form tasks (mother-son pattern).

■ In emotional situations, a male manager may defer to a female manager if he needs sympathy or support (mother-son pattern). For example, a male manager might step aside after a confrontation with a secretary who bursts into tears and call for a female manager to comfort her.

■ There might even be rare instances of women managers not sharing their competence with each other, especially if a negative, competitive mother-daughter pattern develops.

Ways to Overcome Weak Speech Patterns

In the above examples, women managers allow themselves to lose communication effectiveness by reverting to the role of a parent or a child. To be more effective in communicating, women managers should combine the adult problem-solving mode with their strengths as nurturing parents and with their creativity as spontaneous children. By acting as adults, they can avoid communication problems and be able to love, assert, express anger and fear, be caring, and solve problems with an image of strength and confidence. In addition, the following guidelines are suggested to help women managers overcome any weak speech patterns they might be using:[9]

1. It sometimes helps the manager to *monitor her speech*. She can tape-record and listen to her conversations for a few days to detect undesirable speech patterns. She can plan how she might phrase her statements more powerfully and practice doing so in role-playing sessions by herself or with an understanding friend.

2. The manager should avoid apologizing for her thoughts and feelings. She should *talk in terms of herself* and begin by using "I, my, I want, I need," etc. These are clear statements of what she wants, feels, or thinks. They connote power and decisiveness.

3. The manager should *talk in specifics, not generalities*. It is not always wise or necessary to use euphemisms in order to be tactful or polite. Often it is better to state directly what's on one's mind. "We aren't getting it together" is not nearly as effective as "Your late report cost us that contract."

4. When interrupted by men, reply with something like, "Let me first complete what I was saying."

5. If your idea is ignored in a meeting, but later offered by a man and taken up, discussed, and accepted, ask, "How is this different from what I said just a few minutes ago?"

ROADBLOCKS TO EFFECTIVE TWO-WAY COMMUNICATION

The most basic and recurring consequence of poor communication is that the receiver of a message interprets it differently from the way the sender intended. Miscommunication can annoy a superior, cause someone to be stereotyped, promote defensive and hostile attitudes, and produce negative evaluations that can result in reprimand or even dismissal. Some common roadblocks to effective two-way communication are described below.

Hidden Intentions

The sender's intentions are private and exist only in the mind. These intentions are not always made clear, especially if they concern feelings of liking or disliking. Such feelings are usually not directly stated but implied either verbally or nonverbally. The ambiguous statement, "This is not a bad job. Do you want more of these assignments?" is a good example of this. For clear communication to occur, the receiver in a situation like this must accurately decipher the true intentions behind the stated message.

The manager's use of hypercorrect speech, tag questions, and questioning intonation are good examples of acting on hidden intentions. In general, however, women have less difficulty with this roadblock than men because they are usually more open and willing to reveal their attitudes, beliefs, and concerns than males.[10] Women managers are known to be better self-disclosers than their male counterparts who more often portray the stereotypical "strong, silent type."

Preoccupation with Tasks

Oftentimes managers are so preoccupied with tasks that, when someone approaches to talk with them, they are not able to detach themselves from the tasks to listen effectively. When this happens, not only do they fail to receive the message the sender intends, but they also may communicate a feeling of not caring. This in turn may cause the sender to have negative feelings, which could make future communication even more difficult.

Preoccupation, which interferes with feeling perception and consideration, is probably a greater problem for male managers, who are more singularly task-oriented than female managers.[11] Female managers are generally more socially oriented and are usually more willing to take a break from tasks to help or affiliate with others, through awareness of their needs for nurturance.

Emotional Involvement

Many males are very concerned with dominance and contentiousness, which makes it difficult to pay attention and listen to others when they are emotionally involved in a discussion. They often listen to the other person only to find an opening to say what's on their mind and may miss entirely the meaning of the other person's message in their haste to get their point across. Females are generally even more emotional than males. Although female managers have been found to be more receptive than male managers when communicating with subordinates about their feelings, when they are angry or upset they, too, can miss important points in another's message.[12]

Distortions to Match One's Expectations

Sometimes managers listen to evaluate and to make judgments about a subordinate. If subordinates are aware of this evaluative listening, it can cause them to become guarded and defensive. Very often the result is that the subordinate tends to cover up inadequacies to insure a positive reaction from the manager rather than expressing the real concerns that cause problem solving and personal growth to be thwarted.

Women managers should be especially aware of this evaluation when communicating with male superiors, who may have negative stereotypes of them to begin with. This is particularly crucial during the female manager's initial stages on a new job, when males typically seek to test her competencies and ability to act like a manager. Female managers need to avoid the use of empty adjectives, tag questions, and hedging phrases. These may be interpreted by males as signs of insecurity or dependence, which are often seen as evidence of incompetence in managerial positions.

Misperceptions

It is much easier to hear the words being spoken than to understand their intended meaning. For example, the words "it's a nice day" might be intended to be taken literally or the speaker could be using these words as an excuse to change the subject to something more relevant. A misperception on the part of the receiver of such a message might cause inappropriate responses.

Female managers should use their sensitivity to read the underlying intentions of their male counterparts before accepting at face value what is said. Female managers' strengths in sensitivity, affiliation, and promoting positive relations might hinder effective communication if they fail to consider the subtle, subsurface gamesmanship typical of male interactions from adolescence through adulthood. Males tend to compete and challenge, often through subtle innuendos. Such gamesmanship usually occurs when males are interacting among themselves in clearly defined competitive situations. If female managers do not make distinctions in accordance with specific situations, inappropriate distrust can develop.[13]

Distrust

Lack of trust causes a decrease in the amount of information shared and an increase in suspiciousness regarding the validity of the information. The restricted communication that results from distrust often originates from many of the problem areas previously discussed. A fair degree of paranoia may be functional for new women managers because, initially, their competence and ability are tested. Existing managers, especially males, will try to determine if a new woman manager can take a joke, if she is up to date on relevant technical areas, and if she understands departmental acronyms, etc. After women managers have proven themselves and been accepted, they can fall back to normal discretion.

While males may be confused by their own emotional ambiguity when working with females in positions of authority, most women have a plus in the area of perceived trustworthiness through their relatively higher degree of self-disclosure, openness, and sociability. Women should be careful, however, to disclose only appropriate information about themselves and not to be too open. The criterion is **strategic openness**: disclosure appropriate to the situation. Excesses in these behaviors can promote the feminine stereotype and "mother role."

Although the above is a formidable list of communication barriers which most people have experienced, there are things managers can do to overcome these barriers. **Active listening**, for example, is so important that the entire next section is devoted to this topic.

LISTENING

Listening is not the same as hearing. People usually hear the entire message, but too often its meaning is lost or distorted. **Listening** is an intellectual and emotional process in which one integrates physical, emotional, and intellectual inputs in search of meaning. In order to be good listeners, managers should try to be objective and understand the sender's viewpoint. This requires a conscious attempt to understand the speaker without letting personal opinions influence the content of the speaker's message. Managers should concentrate on understanding what the speaker wants to communicate, not what they want to hear.

The normal untrained listener is likely to understand and retain only about 50 percent of a conversation. After another two days, this relatively low percentage drops even lower to a less impressive 25 percent retention rate.[14] This means that recall of a conversation from more than a couple of days prior will almost always be incomplete and usually inaccurate. This is one reason why people often disagree about what has been discussed!

Listening to employees can help them feel understood and accepted by their manager. Listening builds rapport and helps accurately determine the employees' problems, feelings, and goals. With active listening, the solutions that managers propose will become more meaningful, more relevant, and more fully supported by employees. In addition, the employees will usually reciprocate by really listening in return when the managers speak.

Female managers are usually better listeners than male managers because females typically show more concern, encouragement, attentiveness, and receptiveness than males.[15] Even when they are listening effectively, however, managers need to demonstrate this to others by communicating their attentiveness through alert eye contact and body posture. It is also important to avoid poor listening habits, which can subtly develop over time and interfere with listening effectiveness.

Poor Listening Habits

There are a number of poor listening habits that often inhibit a manager's ability to listen effectively. While reading about the habits described below, try to determine objectively if you are guilty of any of them. If so, you will know where to begin your program for improvement in the art of listening.

Doing All the Talking. Many managers, especially males, believe that speech is power, which causes them to attempt to monopolize the conversation by doing all the talking, telling their employees what their problems are, and dictating how to solve them. This macho need to always be dominating throughout a conversation is not shared by most female managers, who are more likely to ask questions, while men are more likely to answer them.[16] Although the manager needs to be assertive to make suggestions and correct misunderstandings, this male need to do all the talking is not a trait to be emulated. A manager cannot learn anything if she is the one doing all the talking, and it is also difficult to build rapport and get the information needed for problem solving and decision making.

Interrupting. How do you feel when somebody finishes your statements for you, or tells you "I know what you mean," before you have even finished your message? A manager should allow her subordinates the courtesy of completing their train of thought also, because it might be very different from what she was assuming when the tendency to interrupt began. Although men have been found to interrupt mixed-sex conversations more often than females,[17] this is another behavior to be avoided. The feelings of being smart, dominating, and important, which may accompany interruption, can result in misunderstanding and resentment from subordinates who may consider the interruption as just the opposite.

Avoiding Eye Contact. Have you ever been talking to someone who constantly looked out the window or was continually distracted by passersby? If you have, you probably felt pretty frustrated and wondered if your message was getting through, and if the listener even cared. Although people listen with their ears, they are judged to be listening through eye contact. Maintaining a gentle, intermittent eye contact is an integral skill of an effective listener. It demonstrates that a manager is concentrating and concerned. She must be careful, however, not to combine prolonged eye contact with other nonverbal behaviors, such as fixing her hair, overly relaxed posture, or sitting too close, which combined, can be mistaken by a man to indicate that she is interested in him as a romantic person.

Showing Boredom. Instead of truly listening, some managers communicate their boredom while someone is talking by toying with a pencil, fixing their hair, doodling, shuffling through papers, wiping glasses, or playing with objects. Another classic example of showing boredom occurs when a manager frequently looks at her watch while the other person is speaking, or continues what she is doing as the other person talks. Managers also show boredom when they act rushed and make comments about their busy day when a subordinate is trying to explain a problem. Such behaviors communicate to the other person that the manager really does not care about what they are saying, and can cause them to avoid sharing information she might really need to know.

Allowing Telephone Interruptions. Managers frequently ignore their subordinates by taking incoming phone calls or by making outgoing phone calls while subordinates are in the office to have a serious conversation. The effect is to make the subordinate feel unimportant. A manager should hold all incoming calls while employees are in the office, or at least take the phone off the hook. This will help demonstrate the respect and sincere interest needed for open communications between a manager and subordinates.

Overcoming these barriers requires **active listening**. This takes great concentration and attention, but it is essential for effective communication.

Active Listening

The active listener is skilled at sensing, attending, and responding.[18] **Sensing** is the ability to recognize the silent messages (i.e., vocal intonation, body language, facial expressions) that the speaker is sending. **Attending** refers to the verbal, vocal, and visual messages that the active listener sends to the speaker. This includes appropriate eye contact, open body language, affirmative head nods, and appropriate facial and verbal expressions. **Responding** refers to the active listener's giving feedback on the accuracy of the speaker's message and feelings, keeping the speaker talking, gathering more information, making the speaker feel understood, and getting the speaker to better understand the problems or concerns being discussed.

Active listening is one-half of the effective communication equation. On the other side is sending effective messages to others. Several guidelines for being a better communicator are discussed next.

WAYS TO OVERCOME SENDER BARRIERS TO THE COMMUNICATION PROCESS

From the sender's viewpoint, perhaps the most crucial difficulty in effective communication is getting the receiver of a message to understand the message as the sender intended. To increase the likelihood of a message being correctly understood, managers can employ the strategies explained below.

Use Redundancy

Redundancy means using more than one channel of communication. For example, when speaking with her employees, the manager might use the appropriate facial and body gestures, diagram what she is talking about, and summarize her message on a piece of paper. This ensures that the receiver has the opportunity to receive the sender's message through more than one of the senses.

Be Complete and Specific

Another way to ensure that a message will be understood is to make it *complete* and *specific*. Here it is important to give all the background information necessary for the receiver to understand the manager's frame of reference and intentions. Then the manager should refer to concrete deadlines and examples, leaving no room for misunderstanding by the receiver.

Claim the Message as Your Own

The manager claims a message as her *own* by using personal pronouns such as "I" and "mine." By doing so, she takes responsibility for her ideas and feelings. This idea and feeling claiming mindset helps counter tendencies to abdicate responsibility through tag questions and hedging phrases. "I'm a little concerned that I won't be able to meet the deadline for the new project you assigned to me," is better understood than, "Don't you think you're asking for a bit much?"

Ensure That Your Messages Are Congruent

The manager should make sure her verbal and nonverbal messages are *congruent*. If she tells subordinates she is available to help them but, when they come in with problems, acts in a frustrated and condescending way, she is really communicating an attitude nonverbally that is quite different from her verbal message.

Develop Credibility

A manager's **credibility** as a sender is probably the single most important element in effective interpersonal communication. A sender's credibility concerns the belief on the part of subordinates that the sender knows what she is talking about and will be able to help them do their jobs better. Several factors that can affect sender credibility are described below.

It is important that the sender of a message be perceived by the receiver as an *expert* on the topic under discussion. A subordinate will be more apt to listen to the manager's opinions on how to complete a work-related project that the manager has much experience with than the manager's opinion regarding how the subordinate should express religious preferences. Although formal education and degrees help managers to be perceived as experts, their track records and on-the-job experience are more relevant indicators. Women managers' credibility is enhanced significantly once they have proven themselves on the job, but it is often a never-ending battle. Women managers are expected to demonstrate extreme competence, often more so than their male counterparts, even though they are equivalent in all respects.[19]

The receiver of a message is also concerned with the sender's *motives*. Does the subordinate perceive a manager's motives for sending a message as selfish or as helpful to the subordinate? Managers should be open, but tactful, about their motives because it is very difficult to hide them. Owning up to motives tactfully will allow the employees to accept the manager's intentions in a more positive way. It also will save the employees unnecessary anxiety and energy that otherwise would be wasted trying to discover what the manager's underlying motives really are. For example, if a manager told her subordinate that the reason he was being sent to a university certificate program was to advance his career as a quality

Illus. 6.2
A cordial manner helps
establish credibility and
promote positive relations
with subordinates.

facilitator, the subordinate would not have to worry if he was sent because the manager wanted him out of the way, thought he was incompetent, or was preparing him for a transfer.

Managers are an important information source to their subordinates. *Reliability* as an information source is evidenced by the employees' perceptions that a manager is dependable, predictable, and consistent. Being up to date on new developments affecting the work group's productivity also increases perceptions of the manager's expertise and competence. Some important questions that managers should ask themselves in this regard are: Am I always prepared to provide the information subordinates require? Will I be consistent in my applications of criteria for success? Can all subordinates count on me to treat them equally?

A manager who is *warm and friendly* is more apt to be well received by her subordinates than one who walks around in a hostile manner with a chip on her shoulder. Whom would you approach with work or personal problems? With whom would you be more likely to communicate about your uncertainties or hesitancies in implementing a new procedure for solving a difficult problem?

This factor in establishing credibility is especially important for women managers, probably more so than for males, as illustrated by a study of 150 people in three large organizations. The research showed that successful female managers exceeded males in promoting positive relations and showing concern for subordinates.[20] If subordinates did not perceive their female supervisors as being warm and friendly, the subordinates rated them lower in supervisory effectiveness. This was not the case for male supervisors, who were expected to be more task-oriented and quick to challenge but not necessarily warm and friendly.

A *dynamic* manager who is assertive, emphatic, and forceful sends more credible messages than one who appears passive, withdrawn, and unsure of herself. If a manager expects people to pay attention and act on her messages, she needs to put the necessary energy into asserting herself and making sure the importance of her request is understood.

If friends or other staff members tell a new subordinate that the manager is trustworthy, the new subordinate will tend to believe it. If, on the other hand, a manager's image has been tarnished through a negative reputation, the others probably will be suspicious of whatever she says until proven otherwise. This is the phenomenon known as the *self-fulfilling prophecy*: expectations are usually acted upon and confirmed. For example, subordinates have heard that the manager is not competent. They may not put 100% effort into a suggestion from the manager, which causes it to fail and confirms the prophecy, but because of lack of effort, not incompetency.

No evidence indicates that any one of the above factors is more important than the others. A high-credibility sender scores high on all, but a low-credibility sender needs to be low on only one to negatively tarnish her reputation. A manager needs emphasis on all factors to avoid having subordinates discount her message and communicate effectively.

DEVELOPING PERSUASIVENESS IN COMMUNICATION

More effective communicators use persuasiveness where appropriate to gain the support of others in pushing their ideas forward. **Persuasiveness** combines commitment, eloquence, honesty, integrity, enthusiasm, and humor. Following are twelve guidelines that a manager can use to develop a more persuasive style of communication.[21]

Know exactly what you want. A manager is far more likely to gain the support of others if she has clearly defined the idea in her own mind. Clarification and commitment to a plan will help foster the same feelings in others. It is usually more productive, for example, to present a game plan for solving a problem when presenting the problem itself. That way there is a much better chance of immediate action being taken.

Develop fallback positions. A manager should have carefully thought out in advance several alternates to her original plan. This will help keep the ball rolling if the first idea is defeated. If someone raises an insurmountable objection to her strategy, she should have another one on backup, instead of simply succumbing in a stalemate.

Send up a trial balloon. By presenting her idea as a question or speculation, a manager can better assess the opposition, and subsequently pursue, modify, or abandon the proposal as appropriate. Phrases such as, "I wonder what would happen if we did X, Y, and Z" can be used to try out an idea and learn the extent of your opposition.

Make your idea their idea. It is always easier to get people to adopt an idea that they feel is their own. By using trial balloons and skillfully making suggestions, a manager can get others to adopt her idea as their own and, in doing so, help them to develop and improve upon their expertise.

Phrase it in terms of their interests. People are far more likely to support ideas if they can clearly see how they will benefit. Show them, for example, how increasing quality and productivity will not only make more money for the company but also save their jobs and earn them a larger bonus.

Ask for more than you want. A manager should build slack concessions into her budget, deadlines, and other critical areas. After negotiations, she will have a better chance that the final plan accepted will be close to what was had originally hoped, than if she had just laid the bottom line figure on the table. If by chance she ends up getting more than needed, she will look even better coming in under budget or ahead of time.

Get a yes early on. By starting her discussion with an easily agreeable item, a manager can start off with a positive, upbeat first impression. By asking a question, no matter how simple, where the answer is yes, she has established a positive frame of mind— the "yes pattern."

Draw out a no early on. Once people have been allowed to demonstrate their power to disagree, they are usually much more open to agreement. Most people want to be thought of as players, not just pawns. By letting them "win one," even though it may be insignificant, others will be more willing to let a manager have her way on subsequent issues.

Anchor it in writing. By putting her ideas in writing, a manager adds more weight to them. Written statements also force her to organize more carefully and think through each detail. Limit each proposal to one page and make only the key points. Ask for a response within a specified period, and send copies to other significant parties.

Answer objections with benefits. It is important to accept and respect both the objections and the objector's needs. Rather than trying to overcome their logic, a manager should simply point out how her proposal benefits them. She also can consider raising and solving the objections herself, before her opponents do. In doing so, she eliminates their element of surprise and shows that she has nothing to hide.

Go higher. If she is truly committed to an idea that is being stifled at one level, a manager should consider going up the hierarchy to someone more supportive. This is a risky move to make, but if she tells her boss that she wants another opinion and why, and then invites him/her to go along with her to explore the possibilities, she stands a much better chance of succeeding without alienation. It is always better to put things in a win-win, team perspective than a win-lose confrontation.

Show your appreciation. Nothing works better than a simple thank you note to the person or people with whom a manager has just negotiated a deal. It can help eliminate any bad feelings from a tough negotiation, while at the same time setting the pace for smooth implementation.

THE NEED FOR ADEQUATE FEEDBACK

One of the best ways to insure a receiver's accuracy in understanding the message is to provide adequate feedback to the sender. **Feedback** refers to the process by which the receiver tells the sender exactly what the receiver heard and what the receiver thinks the message means. In the feedback process, the sender receives information from the receiver about how the message was decoded and interpreted. The sender can then modify the original message if necessary.

If the manager is not able to obtain feedback on how her message is being decoded, inaccuracies may occur that may never be corrected. The main way to correct inaccuracies in communication is verification of common understanding through the process of feedback. For example, when a boss says, "Call me later and we'll discuss it," does the boss mean 15 minutes from now, one hour from now, tomorrow, or next week? When a memo states, "All employees should dress in businesslike attire," does that mean only suits, or just no jeans and t-shirts, or what? These statements, like countless others, can have unlimited meanings. They create a high probability of misunderstanding in communication. Unless statements are clarified, a great likelihood exists they will be misunderstood. This means directions or instructions will not be implemented accurately, and the relationship between both parties may be strained. Through the application of feedback skills, these highly ambiguous statements can be transformed into very specific effective communication.

Like listening, the use of feedback is very often taken for granted. Feedback may, however, be the most important aspect of interpersonal communication. Without feedback, how can one person *really* know if the other person truly comprehends what is being said? In conversations with subordinates, fellow managers, and superiors, how often have you felt like saying to them, "I know you think you understand what I said, but I'm not so sure that what you heard is what I meant." The effective use of feedback skills helps reduce the probability of this type of misunderstanding and misinterpretation.

Types of Feedback

Feedback can be given verbally or nonverbally. Its purpose can be to verify facts or feelings.

Verbal Feedback. People most frequently use verbal feedback through speaking and asking questions. The manager can use verbal feedback to clarify her employees' messages, or she can use it to give positive and/or negative strokes to others.

By asking employees simple questions, the manager can determine whether her instructions are effective or whether she should modify her approach. For example, a question such as, "Let me know if I've explained myself clearly. Exactly what do we need to do here?" allows her to determine if a subordinate understands exactly what is required. Asking for feedback can avoid capriciously cutting the topic too short or dragging on too long. Another example of a feedback question is, "Would you like to get right into the details of this job, or do you have some other questions that you'd like to ask me first?" This question allows the manager to determine the employee's present state of mind and level of receptivity to the information she is about to give. Without asking this question, she might have continued with more details of the job when the employee actually had a number of questions.

Verbal feedback can be used by managers to give positive and negative strokes to their employees as well. Simple statements such as, "You did a really good job," "I really trust you," and "I appreciate your error-free report," show the employees specifically that the manager recognizes and appreciates what they are doing. This type of feedback prompts them to continue to perform in a positive manner.

When an employee's behavior gets out of line, negative feedback can be given to correct the deviation. It is often dysfunctional just to ignore an employee's deviant personal or work behavior. Silence may be construed by the employee as tacit approval. Comments to the employee such as, "I've avoided assigning you to our new projects because you've missed a lot of work lately," or "You didn't complete the job by the 10:00 a.m. deadline" provide the employee with the type of verbal feedback required to correct the deviant behavior.

During a conversation, managers also need to make sure that they understand completely what the employees are trying to communicate. Managers need to paraphrase back employees' words to make sure they have not misinterpreted the real issues or ignored subtle concerns the subordinate may be hesitant to state emphatically. It can be beneficial for the manager to then ask if the manager's restatement is an accurate interpretation of the subordinate's message.

Most clarifying feedback typically begins and ends with statements such as those shown in Figure 6-2.

FIGURE 6-2

CLARIFYING FEEDBACK STATEMENTS

Begin with:

"Let me be sure I understand what you have said."

"Let me see if I can summarize the key points we've discussed."

"I hear you saying . . ."

"I think I hear you saying that your central concern is . . ."

"As I understand it, your major objectives are . . ."

End with:

"Did I understand you properly?"

"Did I hear you correctly?"

"Was I on target with what you meant?"

"Were those your major concerns?"

"Can you add anything to my summary?"

Nonverbal Feedback. The body, eyes, face, and posture can communicate a variety of positive or negative attitudes, feelings, or opinions. Continuous nonverbal feedback occurs consciously and unconsciously in communication between supervisors and subordinates. Perceptive communicators utilize nonverbal feedback from their receivers to assess the degree of understanding, agreement, and interest, and then to structure the content and direction of their messages accordingly.

The manager's reaction to nonverbal feedback is often more important than the amount of nonverbal feedback she receives. When she perceives she is losing the employee's interest, for example, the manager can react to that nonverbal feedback by changing her pace, topic, or tone of voice.

In addition, the manager has to be careful about sending **mixed signals** to employees. This means saying one thing, but communicating something totally different through body language. Picture a manager who shuffles into a meeting with her sales staff, stands slumping at the front of the room, and while staring at the floor says in a dull, lifeless tone of voice, "I am extremely pleased with the January sales figures." While her message is very positive, her nonverbal cues create the opposite effect. These mixed signals force the employee to choose between the verbal and the visual aspects of her message. Most often, they choose the nonverbal aspect of the message.

Mixed signals also create a level of tension and distrust. Right or wrong, receivers feel the senders are hiding something or else they are less than candid. Tones of hesitancy and tentative speech styles (e.g., "sort of") are typical examples of nonverbal feedback sent by female managers through mixed signals.[22]

Fact Feedback. A manager can use fact-finding questions to elicit specific data and information. If the facts she receives are ambiguous or incomplete, it is important to clarify them with feedback indicating her concern. Then the other person will know that she is confused and needs more or better information.

Fact feedback is also important when managers are relating important factual information to employees. When employees depend on the manager's facts, it is critically important that they have complete and clear information. To guarantee that they do, a manager should ask employees to summarize what they have heard her say and if they need any more information.

Fact feedback is useful when managers want clarification, agreement, correction, translation of messages, or interpretation of words and phrases. The following messages are perfect candidates for fact-feedback statements because they contain words or phrases that are quite unclear.

- "Due to recent layoffs, all employees are expected to work harder from now on."

- "Don't spend too much time on that job."

- "We will be visiting Philadelphia and New York City. We expect to open our first unit there."

When there is a chance for misunderstanding to occur, the chances are that it will. Fact-feedback helps make messages clearer and can avoid misunderstandings.

Feeling-Feedback. The best **feeling-feedback** is two-directional: The receiver makes a concerted effort to understand the feelings, emotions, and attitudes that underlie the sender's message and vice-versa. The receiver also should provide feeling-feedback by letting the sender know that the messages have gotten through—at the gut level. In contrast to fact feedback aimed at a meeting of the minds, feeling-feedback facilitates a meeting of the hearts.

Feeling-feedback is enhanced through the effective use of **empathy**, which is putting yourself into another's shoes so that you can see things from the other person's point of view. When the manager understands where the employee is coming from and can identify with the employee's true feelings, it is appropriate to project this emotional awareness in order to reinforce rapport, build common understanding, and increase trust.

Effective Use of Feedback

Can you recall times where you could have smoothed over some communication problems simply by using some of the forms of feedback discussed above? Effective communication between two people is never easy, and the manager has the primary responsibility to make it work. The following guidelines are designed to facilitate the use of feedback.

Give and get definitions. The interpretations of words or phrases may vary from males to females, supervisors to subordinates, or from one group to another. When people believe words have one, and only one, meaning, they may assume others also assign the same meaning to them, when they actually have different interpretations. This can lead to subsequent misunderstandings, breakdowns in communication, and decreased trust. To avoid such situations, the manager should give and get clear definitions of dubious words or phrases. For example, instead of assuming that a subordinate knows what the manager means when she tells a subordinate to "Take your time and do it right," the manager should define exactly what time she means by saying, "Take another day to make sure the project meets the exact specifications." Otherwise, the manager may end up not hearing from the subordinate for a month and running into deadline problems because the subordinate interpreted "take your time" as an indefinite period.

Avoid making assumptions. Making assumptions invariably causes misunderstanding because most of the time assumptions are not entirely accurate. Other people may have frames of reference that are totally different from the manager's. Consequently, it is wise not to assume that others are on the same wave length until common understanding is clarified through feedback. The same is true about words and phrases that may mean different things to each communicator. To illustrate, a manager who assumes that an employee is as concerned about meeting a deadline as the manager is, and will work late to make it, can be in for a disappointment when the employee automatically departs at the standard time and the project is not completed.

The classic phrase uttered by people who make assumptions is "I know exactly what you mean." Many people use that statement without ever using the necessary feedback skills to determine exactly what the other person means. By using more feedback and making fewer assumptions, the accuracy of interpersonal communication can be greatly enhanced.

Ask questions. A good rule of thumb is, "when in doubt, check it out," and one way to check it out is through asking questions. The manager should ask clarifying questions, key questions, fact-finding questions, and feeling-finding questions freely during conversation to get feedback. Another good time to ask questions is when you need to seek feedback from individuals to make sure they have understood their assignments.

Simplify language. The manager should abstain from using words that can be easily misinterpreted or mistranslated, especially technical terms and company jargon. Some terms familiar to the manager may be totally foreign to others. A good strategy is to simplify language and technical terms so that everyone can understand and feed back to the manager the correct information.

Keep tuned in. In a conversation, the manager should observe the other person, be sensitive to the other person's feelings, and respond to those feelings appropriately. The receiver's nonverbal feedback may mean that the manager should change his or her approach or message accordingly. If a subordinate agrees to take on some extra work over the weekend, but the manager senses from the subordinate's facial expressions and tone of voice a lack of commitment, the manager should probe a little deeper to determine what the employee needs to insure achievement of the task.

Give feedback on the behavior, not the person. When employees do something especially well, the manager should give them positive feedback and relate it specifically to the action or behavior that was performed. This reinforces excellent performance. When employees do not perform well, the manager should give them constructive negative feedback directed specifically toward the action or behavior that needs to be corrected.

Under no circumstance should the manager criticize an employee as a person because of an inappropriate action. This is not only degrading but also counterproductive. Many ineffective managers, upon learning that one of their employees did something wrong, criticize that employee personally by saying, "You're an idiot, that was really stupid," or "You can't do anything right, can you?" These statements constitute inappropriate feedback. In fact, they are not feedback at all, but inappropriate value judgments. If the employees believe these statements, a negative self-fulfilling prophecy may occur; "If we are really stupid, we cannot be expected to perform adequately." In any case, a manager cannot expect an employee to improve performance on a particular task or behavior unless the employee knows specifically which behavior or action must be corrected?

Know when to withhold feedback. There are times when it is best not to give feedback at all. Sometimes the manager should bite her tongue, and even restrain her body language and facial expressions. Examples are situations where the employee cannot effectively cope with any more negative feedback, or the feedback concerns something the employee cannot do anything about anyway.

Give more positive than negative feedback. Most people have difficulty "hearing" and accepting negative feedback. If you are attempting to improve behavior, it helps to start by complimenting the employee on something done well, and only then following with problems and constructive ideas on how to improve.

ACTION GUIDELINES

Effective managers must be effective communicators. Getting things accomplished through other people requires that they understand exactly what needs to be done, when, and how. This will not happen without accurate and effective communication. These guidelines can help to enhance communication effectiveness.

1. Be on the lookout for traditional female communication problems, such as *empty adjectives*, *tag questions*, *hedging phrases*, and excessively polite speech. Listening to your speech via a tape recorder may help detect some of these power-robbing flaws of which you are unaware. Also, avoid communication idiosyncrasies by using adult-adult and problem-solving types of interactions versus parent or childlike responses.

2. Be aware of and avoid common roadblocks to communication like hidden intentions, preoccupation, emotional involvement, distorting to match expectations, misperceptions, and distrust. The techniques discussed in this chapter can be used to get around these roadblocks.

3. Avoid poor listening habits like doing all the talking, interrupting, lack of eye contact, showing boredom, allowing telephone interruptions, and being easily distracted. Enhance active listening skills through sensing, attending, responding, and empathizing.

4. Use redundancy, being complete and specific, claiming the message as your own, making sure your messages are congruent, and developing credibility to enhance your understandability.

5. Work to develop persuasiveness in your communication style in order to obtain support and commitment from others.

6. Use feedback effectively by giving or getting definitions, not making assumptions, asking questions, simplifying language, being aware of the speaker's feelings, giving feedback on the behavior and not the person, and knowing when to withhold feedback.

KEY TERMS

apologies — words that clutter or lengthen the speaker's requests or declarations and rob them of their focus and authority

attending — a term referring to the verbal, vocal, and visual messages that the active listener sends to the speaker

communication process — a cycle that begins when one person sends a message to another with the intent of evoking a response and ends with the other person's response

credibility — an important element in interpersonal communication evidenced by the belief of the receiver that the sender of a message is trustworthy

disclaimers — words or phrases that preface an opinion to protect the speaker from losing face but decrease the level of the speaker's influence

empathy — the process of putting oneself into another's shoes so that one can understand matters from the other person's point of view

empty adjectives — words that connote little meaning and have a "fluffing" effect

fact feedback — a type of feedback consisting of fact-finding questions that are meant to elicit specific data and information

feedback — the process of a receiver's telling the sender exactly what it is that the receiver heard being said and what the receiver thinks the meaning of the message is

feeling-feedback — a two-directional feedback by which the receiver makes a concerted effort to understand the feelings, emotions, and attitudes underlying the sender's message and projects to the sender that the message has gotten through

fillers — vocal sounds that signal the speaker's uncertainty and lack of preparation

hedging or modifying phrases — phrases that detract from the impact of a statement

hypercorrect or excessively polite speech — speech that can give the sender an uptight image and that may be misinterpreted by the receiver

listening — an intellectual and emotional process in which one integrates physical, emotional, and intellectual inputs in search of meaning

mixed signals — the act of saying one thing while communicating something totally different through vocal intonation and body language

questioning intonation — the tone at the end of a statement that neutralizes or eliminates the intended assertiveness of the statement

redundancy — a way to overcome communication barriers by using more than one channel of communication

responding — a term referring to the active listener's giving feedback on the accuracy of the speaker's message and feelings, keeping the speaker talking, gathering more information, making the speaker feel understood, and getting the speaker to better understand the problems or concerns being discussed

self-fulfilling prophecy — the phenomenon occurring when expectations are usually acted upon and confirmed

sensing —the ability to recognize the "silent" messages that a speaker is sending

strategic openness — disclosure of information when appropriate

tag question — question used after a declarative statement, which automatically "passes the ball" from the sender of the message to the receiver

transactional analysis — a method of explaining the interactions and communication between individuals based on the roles they assume

DISCUSSION QUESTIONS

1. What are some of the characteristically female speech patterns that inhibit effective managerial communication?

2. Account for the barriers to clear two-way communication. How can one overcome these roadblocks?

3. How can a female manager consciously improve her communication effectiveness to achieve sender clarity?

4. How can a manager make effective use of communication feedback?

5. What are some overall guidelines for enhancing communication effectiveness?

CHAPTER CASE

KATHY ADAMS: ACCOUNTING DEPARTMENT MANAGER

Kathy Adams had graduated four years ago with an accounting degree from a major midwestern university. Since then she had worked for a large retail clothing chain originally as a payroll accountant, and since her promotion earlier this year, as Payroll Department Manager.

Kathy had earned her first managerial assignment through demonstrated commitment and excellent performance. Since she was only in her mid-twenties, she was much younger than many of the other employees that she supervised. She was also the only female manager in the finance area.

During the first several months as manager, Kathy seemed to get along well with most of the other employees and her ideas for improvement were generally accepted and proved beneficial. Recently, however, she had noticed that several of the male accountants seemed to avoid her and resist her ideas for better cooperation and operating procedures between payroll and accounting departments.

Last month, the payroll department had been a little late printing paychecks, which had irritated a majority of the employees. Kathy's investigation turned up that the accounting department had not given the payroll department the needed figures until two days past the required deadline. Further exploring indicated that accounting had no procedures for insuring that data was collected and ready on time.

Kathy analyzed the accounting system and devised a simple way to make sure that all information was collected by accounting and processed in time for payroll to make out monthly checks by the end of each month. She arranged for a meeting the next day with the accounting department manager, Robert Gray, and the chief payroll accountant, Mike Donovan, to discuss her new proposal. The following conversation took place at the meeting:

> **Kathy:** "I know you two are really busy, and I hate to bother you, but I think I might have come up with a terrific idea that we could use to, uh, . . . maybe make the payroll system a little more efficient."

Mike: "Are you suggesting that we're not doing our job in getting payroll out on time? I think the current system is just fine!"

Robert: "I agree with Mike, and furthermore I feel that . . ."

Kathy: *(interrupting)* "Oh, no—it's not that you're not working hard. It's just that this new suggestion might be able to speed things up a little, and that's what you guys want, right?"

Robert: *(getting angry)* "See? You just said it again—you don't think our procedure is fast enough in payroll accounting. If we weren't interrupted with meetings like this, you bet we'd be a lot more efficient!"

Kathy: "You aren't understanding me at all. I guess that means you don't want to hear my idea."

The two men shrug their shoulders and give each other knowing glances. All three leave the meeting, not really understanding what the other has actually meant. Kathy sat in her office later that day and wondered why Robert and Mike had reacted so defensively to her suggestion for improvement. It did not as though they had even heard it, let alone understood what she meant and why it was needed. She just was not getting through to them.

QUESTIONS

1. What did Kathy do wrong in introducing her new idea to her accountants?

2. What were some of the roadblocks to effective communication, and what could Kathy have done to eliminate some of these barriers?

3. How could Kathy have used more persuasiveness in her communication to obtain the support of her two subordinates?

ENDNOTES

[1] A. G. Sargent, "The Androgynous Blend: Best of Both Worlds," *Management Review* (October, 1978): 60-65.

[2] Jan Grant, "Women as Managers: What They Can Offer to Organizations," *Organizational Dynamics* (Winter, 1988): 56-63.

[3] R. Lakoff, "Language and Women's Place," *Language in Society*, 2 (1973): 45-79.

[4] M. B. Parlee, "Conversational Politics," *Psychology Today* (May, 1979): 28-38.

[5] R. Key, *Male/Female Language* (Metuchen, NJ: Scarecrow Press, 1981).

[6] G. Sassen, "Success Anxiety in Women: A Constructivist Interpretation of Its Source and Its Significance," *Harvard Educational Review*, Vol. 50, No. 1 (February, 1980): 21-22.

[7] For a detailed discussion in terms of transactional analysis, see D. Jongeward, *Everybody Wins: Transactional Analysis Applied to Organizations* (Reading, Mass.: Addison-Wesley, 1973).

[8] A. G. Sargent, op. cit., 65.

[9] S. H. Vogler, "Talking Tough—It's Not What You Say, But How You Say It," *Working Woman*, 8 (April, 1983): 34-35.

[10] J. E. Baird, Jr. and P. H. Bradley, "Styles of Management and Communication: A Comparative Study of Men and Women," *Communication Monographs*, 46 (June, 1979): 101-111.

[11] E. F. Borgetta and J. Stimson, "Sex Differences in Interaction Characteristics," *Journal of Social Psychology*, 60 (1963): 89-100.

[12] Baird and Bradley, op. cit., 101-111.

[13] J. Pfeiffer, "Girl Talk-Boy Talk," *Science*, 85 (January-February, 1985): 58-63.

[14] R. G. Nichols, "Listening is a Ten-Part Skill," *Nation's Business*, Vol. 45 (July, 1957): 56-60.

[15] Baird and Bradley, op. cit., 101-111.

[16] A. Johnson, "Women Managers: Old Stereotypes Die Hard," *Management Review* (December, 1987): 31-43.

[17] Ibid.

[18] P. L. Hunsaker and A. J. Alessandra, *The Art of Managing People* (New York: Simon & Schuster, 1986), 130-131.

[19] A. M. Morrison, R. P. White, E. Van Velsor, "Executive Women: Substance Plus Style," *Psychology Today* (August, 1987): 18-26.

[20] Baird and Bradley, op. cit., 101-111.

[21] J. Calano and J. Salzman, "Persuasiveness: Make It Your Power Booster," *Working Woman* (October, 1988): 124-125, 160.

[22] Key, op. cit.

ADDITIONAL RESOURCES

Bonville, Thomas G. *How to Listen—How to Be Heard*. Chicago: Nelson-Hall, Inc., 1978.

Bull, Peter. *Body Movement and Interpersonal Communication*. New York: John Wiley & Sons, 1983.

Hall, Judith A. *Nonverbal Sex Differences: Communication Accuracy and Expressive Style*. Baltimore: Johns Hopkins University Press, 1984.

Hunsaker, P. L. and Alessandra, Anthony J. *The Art of Managing People*. New York: Simon & Schuster, 1986.

Level, Dale E. and Galle, William P., Jr. *Managerial Communications*. Plano, Texas: Business Publications, Inc., 1988.

Rasberry, Robert W. and Lemoive, Laura Fletcher. *Effective Managerial Communication*. Boston: Kent Publishing, 1986.

CHAPTER 7

POWER AND POLITICS

Traditional Power Failures of Women Managers
Sources of Power for Women Managers
    Legitimate Power
    Reward Power
    Coercive Power
    Referent Power
    Expert Power
    Information Power
    Association Power
Power and the Woman Manager's Career
    Using Feminine Characteristics to Advantage
    Adopting a Masculine Style of Behavior
    Seeking Entry into Old Boys' Network
Strategies for Enhancing Interpersonal Power
    Be Assertive
    Be Courteous
    Direct Your Thinking
    Neutralize Resistance
    Inoculate the Key Decision Makers
    Use the Media
    Build Support Groups
    Gatekeep
    Hold Out
    Go Around
    Threaten to Resign
Sex as a Power Tactic
    Flirtation
    Dating
    Flings
    Affairs
Action Guidelines
Key Terms
Discussion Questions
Chapter Case: Patricia Hill: King of the Mountain?
Endnotes
Additional Resources

When women move into managerial roles in organizations, they need to exercise power and authority. Some women believe that a woman manager can easily accept these new role requirements and exercise new behaviors necessary to deal with power and politics. A few even feel that women who gain power can be tougher infighters than the men they deal with by appropriately using their sexuality to get what they want. In quoting Michael Korda's article on "Sexual Office Politics," Horn and Horn share Korda's conviction that "a woman who knows her business and has a position of power can refuse to accept sexual put-downs and even chop a man off at the knees if the situation warrants it."[1] This can help to establish power, respect, and a no-nonsense work environment.

One woman executive said, "The competition is going to get a lot hotter. . . . Women have always used sex as a substitute for power, a way of fighting back; men have thought of sex as a way of keeping women in their place." This female executive views the issue of sex in office politics as shifting in favor of the woman, and a tool for managerial and career effectiveness.[2]

The other extreme is sentiments voiced by new women managers who say they want no involvement in organizational politics whatsoever. They just want to do their job and stay out of "all that other stuff." Unfortunately, this is not possible. Managers are involved in politics the minute they start to work for an organization. People are different. There are differences in backgrounds, values, aspirations, and objectives, and all these elements affect the performance and feelings of everyone in the organization.

Office politics means getting all the different human elements to work *for* a person rather than *against*. A woman manager needs to do her job effectively, and she needs to have others like and respect her, especially those whose opinions count in rewarding her managerial competence.

Understanding the uses of **power**, the potential to influence others, is integral to understanding office politics. Power influences a manager's effectiveness—whether the manager is dealing with one or two people or with an entire organization. Many women, unfortunately, prefer not to think of their jobs in terms of power. When asked how power oriented are they, many modestly reply, "Not at all." This response may be based more on cultural conditioning than on true feelings. Everyone has attitudes toward power, and it is the exercise of power that determines how well individuals perform in their roles.

TRADITIONAL POWER FAILURES OF WOMEN MANAGERS [3]

Most businesswomen, even those in management, usually find themselves occupying the more routine and low-profile types of jobs. Examples are certain staff positions where they serve in support capacities to line managers and have no direct managerial responsibilities of their own, or in supervisory jobs managing periphery activities that do not allow them to develop credibility or to influence subordinates. A 1989 *Wall Street Journal* tally indicated, for example, that 40 percent of the women holding the title "section chief" do not have any staff to manage.[4] Since these types of positions are often routine and highly standardized, they offer women minimal visibility and require little discretionary decision making.[5] This non-critical capacity tends to keep women managers out of the mainstream of organizational politics. Their corresponding lack of clout and their exclusion from information and support networks make women in these positions structurally powerless.

Another problem stems from good intentions on the part of male superiors who actually are trying to give their female subordinates every chance to succeed. Well-intentioned male managers may try to protect female managers from the organizational jungle. *Overprotecting* female managers by putting them in "safe" jobs does more harm than good. First, it does not provide a chance for female managers to prove themselves. Second, by not giving women higher-risk projects, their visibility is kept low.

Overprotectiveness also occurs in situations where male superiors are fearful of being associated with a female subordinate should she fail in a difficult assignment. This often develops where chauvinistic attitudes prevail in the overall organization. Even if the male superior has had overwhelmingly positive work experiences with his female subordinate, he may feel that assigning her more challenging projects involves a personal risk. He knows that other managers are not as accepting of women as he is; if she does not succeed, his reputation and his future judgment will be on the line.

An even stronger blow to a female manager's power potential is dealt in situations where her superior shows obvious signs of lack of support and confidence in her. Lack of support is manifest in behaviors such as allowing the female manager to be bypassed easily when those reporting to her disagree with her decisions, or when her superior is always eager to listen to criticism about her and is overly concerned with any negative comment about her. This type of behavior signals to others that superiors are not confident in the female manager's capabilities. Consequently, this undercuts her authority and no one takes her seriously. It practically invites others to look for signs of failure and to lose respect for her as a manager.

Even when a female manager is respected for her competence and expertise, others may still assume they should bypass her when making important decisions because she is not connected with those on the inside and does not really know the ropes. An unusual dilemma has been created here. Even though women may be respected for their competence or expertise, they are not necessarily seen as being informed beyond the technical requirements of the job. This perception is partly in response to the staff and other "non-line" jobs women usually hold before becoming part of management. Also, business clubs and even company business lunches have typically excluded women. Consequently, women usually seek out each other for support or informal socializing. Any woman seen as politically naive and lacking organizational support will not be taken seriously and will find her avenues of communication limited.

Even when women have been able to achieve a position with power, they have not always been able to translate this personal credibility into a strong organizational power base. To create a network of supporters, a manager needs to pass on and share power. She should assure that her subordinates and peers are empowered by virtue of their connection with her. Effective interpersonal power often comes from emphasizing the dignity of others and keeping one's own sense of importance from becoming inflated.

To build a *political support base*, female managers need to share the credit and act as collegial facilitators. People will be much more apt to support you in a change if they feel that they will be seen as part of the team that brought it about.[6] Traditionally, neither men nor women have seen women as capable of sponsoring others; rather, women have been viewed as the recipients of sponsorship. Thus, a female manager's female subordinates may actually see her as a hindrance to their own careers rather than as a team facilitator.

For example, take the dilemma presented by Laura, a woman who at age 31 is head of corporate communications for a growing computer company:

> *I have a huge budget, full authority over my staff, a good salary, plus excellent fringe benefits and the confidence of management. I have little trouble being taken seriously by male superiors or subordinates. But, for some reason, women are my worst enemies. I play by the rules, try to be fair, helpful, and supportive. Yet, it seems as if every decision I make is challenged behind my back. What am I doing wrong? Or am I simply a victim of jealousy?*

Laura feels she plays by the rules and does not know why her female subordinates are undermining her authority. Chances are she is doing nothing unusual as a department manager, especially since male subordinates respond well to her leadership. Laura's problem reflects some women's inexperience in dealing with each other in a nonsocial, business environment.

Laura's age may be a factor in her dilemma; but it is probably not her youth as much as her attitude that makes her a target. Not all women born in the 1950s escaped the traditional female sex-role conditioning. Laura's age group often feels they are *entitled* to hold responsible jobs and deserve career advancements. These new age women can be a threat to the others who are victims of more traditional sex-role conditioning.

Real generational changes are apparent in organizations today. Younger women, having been raised in a different post-fifties era, are finding it easier to learn the rules of the game than older, pre-fifties women. One survey reported that women with more traditional socialization experienced more self-doubt and anxiety when they assumed a managerial role. These feelings were not shared by most younger women managers.[7] Some younger managers do report, however, an ongoing struggle to figure out how to be a good mother, wife, and corporate player all at the same time.

Many political difficulties of female managers are a result of the inexperience that surrounds them. Some women may not grasp the significance of the hierarchical system. If, for example, a female manager finds that the secretaries do not ever "get to" her work and/or her authority is undermined by public criticism, it could be that contempt is being expressed for her and/or her rank. It may also be a personality conflict, sexism, ageism, jealousy, or a variety of other human emotions are in operation. New female managers need awareness of these factors because they can get in the way of their political clout and career advancement.

Of course, there is competition among women in organizations, but the major power struggle is still with men. Unfortunately, many men in powerful positions still have traditional perspectives. Consequently, new women managers need all the power bases they can get working in their favor.

SOURCES OF POWER FOR WOMEN MANAGERS

Power is the means to get things done. Power depends on both perceived and real influence both inside and outside the work group.[8] **Influence** is the actual psychological force causing a change in another person. A manager's influence is initiated by some form of communication, whether verbal, written, or behavioral. **Interpersonal power** is the ability to influence another person to do something that he or she would not have necessarily done on their own.[9]

Samuel Johnson once said that "nature has given women so much power that the law has very wisely given them little." Historically, this appears true. Women have exerted their power mainly through informal relationships, while men have dominated formal power positions in armies, governments, and business organizations.[10] These differences in formal power are usually explained as the result of childhood socialization where boys were rewarded for competitive aggressive behavior and girls were expected to be passive and accommodating. If female managers want to achieve greater power in organizations, they are going to have to take an active stance in changing the existing organizational climate. One of the variables that can be utilized in this pursuit is the active manipulation of the basic power sources themselves.

The greater the number of power sources available to a female manager, the greater her potential influence. Seven commonly accepted bases of social power are: (1) legitimate power, (2) reward power, (3) coercive power, (4) referent power, (5) expert power, (6) information power, and (7) association power.[11]

Legitimate Power

Based on authority vested in a position or role in an organization, **legitimate power** belongs to the person who holds that position. This is a legally or socially acceptable form of power which is a part of the unwritten contract agreed upon when individuals join an organization. It is also backed by a system of rewards and punishments, which the manager may apply according to legitimate role expectations.

Since men, historically and currently, tend to hold the highest positions in organizations, they also have a greater degree of legitimate power than women. As more women rise to formal positions of authority in organizations, their share of legitimate power will increase and legitimate power could lose its predominantly masculine connotation.

Managers at the same organizational level have the same degree of legitimate power through their positions. Although their associated degrees of authority are equivalent, the managers' actual ability to influence, motivate, and direct the work of subordinates may differ widely according to their personal sources of power.

Illus. 7.1   As women rise to formal positions of authority in organizations, their share of legitimate power increases.

Reward Power

Reward power is the ability to compensate and give rewards to individuals who satisfactorily complete assigned tasks. It is based on the expectation that, if a subordinate conforms to a directive, he or she will receive a reward. The reward may be formal, such as money, public praise, or a promotion, or informal, like acceptance, self-confirmation, or attention.

Formal rewards are usually perceived as masculine modes of influence and are thought more effective when employed by male rather than female managers.[12] In order for women to use formal rewards as an effective power base, they must first have access to high positions of authority in the organization. In the meantime, however, informal rewards can be very effective in building a reciprocal social network.

Coercive Power

The ability to punish is called **coercive power**. The influence of coercive power is based on fear and the perception that subordinates will be punished if they do not conform to the manager's directives. Coercive power may take the form of physical or verbal abuse, withdrawal of desired treatment or sentiments, or withdrawal of valued resources.

Coercive power, the opposite of reward power, is also usually perceived as a masculine mode of influence.[13] Generally, the lower status of women in the organizational hierarchy is their main impediment to effective use of formal punishment as a power base. Other types of punishment can be effectively utilized by women in many informal ways, such as withdrawing emotional support, avoidance, or lack of personal interest.

These latter tactics may be perceived as petty and childish, which highlights the fact that using coercive power can have a large number of negative side effects. Punishment typically only works satisfactorily as part of a strictly defined discipline and grievance system, and even then is very tricky to apply without retaliation of some kind. Perhaps Al Capone's adage that "You can get a lot further with a kind word and a gun than with just a kind word alone," is still good advice, as long as you don't have to actually use the gun. Try all other forms of power first, and only later threaten punishment, and only as a last resort use it.

Referent Power

Referent power is based upon the attractiveness and appeal of individuals that causes them to be liked personally. Others imitate the personal style or behavior of someone with referent power because they respect or like that person. Referent power results in friendship, positive sentiments, reciprocal affection, and positive expectations. A leader who is admired and followed because of referent power is said to have charisma. Examples of individuals with referent power who have been called charismatic are Golda Meir, Mother Teresa, and Elizabeth Dole. Certain segments of the population would even include Jane Fonda and Madonna, although in a different arena.

Referent power is particularly effective for women in nontraditional occupations because this type of power has not been sex-role stereotyped as either a masculine or feminine base.[14] People with referent power are respected for their competence and personal characteristics regardless of their formal authority in the organization.

Expert Power

The influence accorded to a manager with superior knowledge, ability, or skill is known as **expert power**. Expertise may be obtained through special training, experience, access to rare information, exceptional abilities, or just a general aura of competence.

Expert power stems from the individual's abilities and is not always related to formal organizational position. Because expertise emphasizes competence and can be easily generalized, this power base can be especially valuable to women managers who want to enhance their organizational power base.

Information Power

The influence people possess through information not available to others is referred to as **information power.** Like expertise, information power is not always based on formal organizational position in an organization. Information power comes from formal or informal information held by individuals at any level within the organization.

Information power can become coercive power when necessary facts are withheld. It can become reward power when vital information is shared freely. Managers who share their information in positive ways are usually well-liked and are thought to be highly competent by subordinates.[15]

Association Power

Individuals with **association power** may have no positional or personal power of their own, but they do have influence with a person who does possess such power. Consequently, they are indirectly able to influence others who depend on the actual power holder. Family members, confidantes, and close aides of public officials have association power. In some organizations, staff members with close advisory relationships with the boss also have association power.

A new manager automatically inherits legitimate power by the authority associated with her position. Although the right to command others is a legitimate possession, exercising authority can be a very complex process. The best interests of both the organization and the individuals involved must be considered if authority is to be an effective base of power. Authority in a managerial position is often limited to the job description, the management-union contract, or the degree of acceptance by subordinates. Power, on the other hand, refers to the totality of influence derived through one's competence, valued contributions, and individual character, as well as the previously described power bases. It is much more persuasive than legitimate authority alone. In the long run, women managers, like their male counterparts, need power gained through acceptance and support in order to accomplish desired results.

Since legitimate power is limited to the authority inherent in a position, the effective woman manager must take maximum advantage of reward, coercive, referent, expert, and information power potentials. Personal influence is more important and broader than formal authority, for it is based on one's capability to personally persuade people to promote the accomplishment of the organization's goals. The key to being effective in influencing others is found not so much in the formal authority of the manager's position but instead in the personal authority she earns through referent, expert, and information power. The applications of the skills described in this book are keys to enhancing earned authority with subordinates, peers, and superiors.

POWER AND THE WOMAN MANAGER'S CAREER

Despite nearly two decades of affirmative action, steady pressure by women's groups, and increasing acceptance by corporate men, recent studies have shown that less than 2 percent of corporate officers in the country are women. It appears that the barrier against women at the senior level is holding firm, especially in senior line jobs, where the power in corporate America really lies. While professional and corporate women have made some progress over the past 20 years, they haven't yet achieved power or financial parity with their male counterparts.[16]

Many women managers find themselves in "velvet ghettos"—stuck in areas where women have typically been regarded as best suited. For example, women are clustered in staff functions like personnel, corporate social responsibility, or public relations, which are peripheral to the more directly powerful line functions like sales, production, or finance. Many women come to rest full circle in the same type of positions which inhibited their building of an adequate power base in the first place. Although these positions provide career opportunities not previously available to women, they nevertheless preserve the existing balance of power that favors the males in the organization.

Although an abundance of opportunities exists in the stereotypically female management areas like consumer relations or public relations, specializing in these areas because they represent the easiest path for advancement is not always the best career-development strategy for women. Three alternative career strategies, their advantages, disadvantages, and respective power bases are presented in Figure 7-1.

Using Feminine Characteristics to Advantage

Emphasizing traditional feminine characteristics like social sensitivity, helpfulness, humanitarian values, and awareness of feelings can facilitate a manager's advancement to positions and career paths that place high value on such qualities. These qualities are often viewed as relative strengths by both male and female superiors who are influential in her career advancement. If a manager decides to concentrate on cultivating the "feminine qualities" expected in human resource related roles and developing the associated specialized knowledge, this strategy may provide her with considerable influence in important corporate decisions

FIGURE 7-1

POWER BASES AND CAREER-DEVELOPMENT STRATEGIES AVAILABLE TO WOMEN MANAGERS

Strategy	Power Bases Emphasized	Advantages	Disadvantages
Use feminine characteristics to advantage	Expert, informational	Easily assimilated into prevailing masculine culture	Supports stereotype of women as unfit for management
		Opportunities in socially oriented functions	Leads to staff and peripheral positions
			Career stagnation
Adopt masculine standard of behavior	Referent	Easily assimilated into masculine culture	Many men reject women who possess too much masculinity
		Readily available role models	Leads to conflict between sexual identity and career identity
		Precedent established for using this model	
Seek entry into old boys' network	Referent, coercive, reward	More active strategy	Strong resistance by males
		May be used in combination with other strategies	If unsuccessful, may hinder career more than if entry was not attempted
		Both informal and formal power bases	Results not immediate
			Requires time and energy to maintain

Source: Adapted from "Career Development and the Woman Manager," by Gary N. Powell, *Personnel* (May-June, 1980): 26.

in that area. It can, on the other hand, limit the options for tougher roles in line career paths like manufacturing or general management, which frequently feed into top managerial slots.

Adopting a Masculine Style of Behavior

By conforming to the tough and aggressive masculine stereotype, women fit the dominant profile of the traditional successful manager. This strategy seems to be easiest for young females just starting their managerial careers. A study of female MBAs, all of whom were under 30 years of age and held jobs in business, found that these female managers described themselves in more masculine than feminine terms, as did their male counterparts. If this appears to be the preferred managerial style in your organization, however, a masculine self-image may not be as easy to adopt for older women who have seen themselves all of their lives in much more feminine ways.[17] Perhaps the most advantageous style is androgynous, when women preserve their femininity while at the same time incorporating certain masculine behaviors essential for being successful managers in their organizations.

Seeking Entry into Old Boys' Network

Seeking entry into the old boys' network is an action-oriented strategy to enhance the woman manager's power base by *breaking into areas of influence dominated by men*. Studies have shown that typical new women managers often naively focus on self-improvement as the critical strategy in their career advancement. Unfortunately this is a *passive*, "hope to be recognized," "wait to be chosen" approach, which ignores the political realities of social networking with the in group of power holders and decision makers.[18]

An associated strategy for building support is to set up an informal women's group or large-scale female network. Although these groupings provide a feeling of belongingness and opportunities for exchanging ideas, they provide a false sense of organizational support and still keep women out of the old boys' network where the real sources of power are reserved. In some situations, a woman who gets involved in a women's group may get written off by the men in power and effectively sever her chances of getting into the real power network.

Entering existing male networks is a more active strategy, requiring assertiveness and an ability to handle resistance. If the woman manager is successful, though, the rewards are tremendous. She will make connections with the most influential people. She will understand and be joined to key political systems. She can subsequently use her connections and knowledge to wield association power with anyone in the organization.

Each strategy has its merits and problems. Today's female manager must maintain a careful balance that is right for her between femininity and masculinity in order to succeed in any specific situation.[19] Each strategy assumes women operate from an initial power base of competence and are seeking to build on it. The feasibility and ultimate success of any strategy depends upon the prevailing culture of the organization and the additional power bases a woman manager can bring into play. Other considerations include career stage, organizational position, and characteristics of other influential individuals.

STRATEGIES FOR ENHANCING INTERPERSONAL POWER

The majority of women managers do not yet occupy positions of formal authority allowing them an adequate legitimate power base within organizations. Consequently, most of the more influential women tend to build their power bases from the more personal sources of expertise, information, and charisma. Your efficacy in wielding personal power can be enhanced through some of the more subtle strategies for building interpersonal power. Some key guidelines for success in personal politics are summarized below.[20]

Be Assertive

Be quick to seize power when opportunities arise. Someone must be in charge before anything can even get started. Therefore, although the manager may find office politics and the responsibility of power distasteful, she may wind up being manipulated by others who are more aggressive if she does not seize the opportunity.

Submissive speech patterns give power away.[21] Take the nonassertive woman asking for a raise. "I hate to ask, but would it be all right if I asked for a raise," she inquires of her boss in a weak voice with her eyes on the floor. Her boss, of course, has a perfect right to say no. Nevertheless, she should ask for that raise as though she deserves it and has every right to it. If she asks for something assertively, her boss—and others—will take her more seriously, and she has improved her chances of getting what she wants.

Be Courteous

Be courteous and cordial to people, even those one does not like. This political necessity can be as important as being good at the job one does. Managers usually expect at least nominal deference from those in lower positions. This does not mean that you have to sell out your values or throw away your pride to satisfy a superior or colleague, but energy should be expended to maintain everyone's integrity and pride. This can be accomplished via constructively working through differences as opposed to forcing others into submissive positions via inappropriate use of formal power.

Courtesy is an effective tool for getting things done. Courtesy in this context makes others feel significant in the relationship. Since a majority of a manager's subordinates may fall toward the passive end of the power scale, a woman manager should reinforce her subordinates' self-esteem frequently to help keep them at their most productive level.

Courtesy is also important for the manager's own career development since discourteous people seldom progress up the organizational ladder. It is vital for the manager's own success to have a satisfied, self-assured superior who is confident of her competence and support. By acting in a courteous, cordial manner, she will be respected and have a better chance of having her opinions count.

Direct Your Thinking

Plan, organize, and direct your thinking and actions. Directed thinking means clearly specifying what it is you hope to accomplish in an interpersonal situation and systematically considering all factors and actions that may help in achieving it. Spontaneity is often good for building strong, interpersonal relationships; but it can also hurt people if used inappropriately. For example, after insulting someone without thinking, it can often be next to impossible to undo the damage. In such situations, it is too late for hindsight unless the lessons learned are transferred to future situations. It is far better to use directed thinking to gain the foresight to prevent any undue damage in the first place.

The following questions can help the manager select and organize meaningful information so that she can behave in a directed way:

1. How has this person or group reacted to similar situations?

2. Which approaches have worked in the past? Which ones did not?

3. How does this person or group feel about me? How can I influence this impression?

4. How does this person or group feel about the change being proposed? What is the person's or group's point of view? Why?

5. What is the most effective way of communicating?

6. What unique considerations are relevant to this person or group in this situation?

Neutralize Resistance

Use disclaimers to neutralize resistance to your ideas. The context in which the manager is interacting has a great deal of influence on others' reactions. If other people involved feel that a woman manager will personally benefit from her request for a specific course of action, they may feel ripped off for the manager's personal gain. To counter this feeling, the manager needs to *disclaim* that her request is solely for her personal benefit. If she will benefit from the action, she needs to own up to this but convince others that the request is also a good thing for them. By owning up to her potential benefits—which they are aware of anyway—others may be disarmed by her sincerity and realize that she is leveling with them and striving for a joint gain. Then they may listen to her request without constantly trying to detect a hidden agenda. It sometimes helps to present both the pros and cons of a proposal being suggested to demonstrate that she has done a thorough investigation and is not just promoting something of personal concern.

Inoculate the Key Decision Makers

Refute counter arguments before they are even voiced. If you are fairly certain that others will later attempt to refute the validity of your requests, you can inoculate key decision makers against these forthcoming arguments to build their resistance to them. This strategy can be implemented by sharing and respecting possible counter arguments and then refuting these potential objections before they are voiced by the opposition. It is usually more effective to point out errors in the opposition's logic and to reiterate the advantages of your own proposal, than emotionally to try to discredit the other side.[22]

Use the Media

Disseminate ideas and proposals to others in the organization through memos or bulletin announcements. This is a relatively risk-free and effective strategy which may gain the support of influential organization members. It is a good approach to use to raise awareness about a problem and how your ideas can be of benefit. The same thing can be done on a smaller scale through word of mouth in the organization's informal grapevine.

Build Support Groups

Organize individuals who share your common concern for changing some aspect of the organization into **support groups.** They are important for testing ideas, expressing empathy, and supporting one another under heavy opposition. Group meetings can produce increased awareness about the nature and consequences of a proposed change and provide the manager with a better perspective of how to gain more control within her organization.

Gatekeep

Control the communication process so everyone has an equal chance to participate. Through such simple comments as, "What do the rest of you think?" or "We haven't heard from Jim yet," a manager can decrease the influence of her more assertive opponents and she can solicit important information from less assertive people who support her proposal.

Hold Out

Withhold support and refuse to implement plans that you are sure are inappropriate. **Holding out** is a blocking strategy that prevents a decision or calls attention to a negative aspect of a program that needs your participation to be successful. Failing to cooperate and go along with a plan of action can be dangerous and unpleasant, but in situations where you are sure that course of action is detrimental, the risk is necessary for a manager to get her point across. Be prepared to offer more appropriate alternatives and their benefits so that you will be perceived as a concerned team player and not just a sour grapes loser.

Illus. 7.2   Support groups are important for testing ideas, expressing empathy, and increasing awareness of the consequences of proposed changes.

Go Around

Contact top management when your immediate supervisor is about to do something disastrous for the organization. The manager may find herself in a situation where her superior in the organization simply will not consider a change she feels is vital, or is implementing a severely negative change. Under such conditions, the manager may feel that her only alternative is to go over her superior's head to a higher executive to gain support. This is a dangerous maneuver. It violates the trust of her superior and makes her vulnerable to any sanctions her boss may apply. **Consequently, it should be used very rarely and only in desperate situations.**

Threaten to Resign

Threaten resignation if crucial or ethical issues are being poorly dealt with. The threat of resignation is the manager's last resort. If she is a valuable manager, her opposition will listen when she lays her job on the line. Obviously this is an extremely dangerous strategy, and the warnings, as compared to the previously mentioned going around superiors, should be doubled or tripled in this case. Never cry wolf with this strategy. Do not use it unless you mean it. If your opposition senses a bluff and calls it, you will forever lose face or your job.

SEX AS A POWER TACTIC

Using sex to get power is as old as Cleopatra, but it also is a tactic still used, and an awareness and understanding of the full range of potential implications and possible consequences are vital.

Power dynamics in romantic relationships involves a social exchange of personal versus job-related resources. Typical resources exchanged include affection, companionship, sex, and services. The more powerful person in such a relationship is the one less dependent on the other person for them.[23]

Once the personal/sexual dimension is added to a work relationship, the balance of power may be altered considerably. Take the example of subordinates who desire promotion and may work hard to impress their boss in hopes of exchange for the coveted reward. If another worker is romantically involved with the boss, personal/sexual resources can be exchanged, giving this individual more influence with the boss than others not so involved.[24] For similar reasons, a romantic relationship can provide the participant with association power over others in the organization who depend on her lover.

The same special influence enjoyed by a romancer with her lover can threaten the task and career domains of others. The resulting fear, bias, and resentment can decrease the romancer's referent power considerably. It can also lead to hostile actions like work sabotage, withdrawal of assistance, and negative rumors, as peer group members attempt to balance the perceived inequity by bringing the romancer down.[25]

Using sex as a stepping-stone to power can be as brief as flirting at the drinking fountain or as long-lasting as marrying the boss's son (or daughter). Four common sexual strategies are flirtation, dating, flings, and affairs.[26]

Flirtation

Flirting is usually directed toward some powerful person, maybe even the boss himself. If the boss responds in an approving way, the flirt feels singled out and special. If that is all there is, nobody may care much or get hurt directly, but the flirt's professional image may be in jeopardy.

If the original mild overtones are encouraged and become more outrageous, there can be some unfortunate results. For one, the boss may become embarrassed or tired of the game, and he slaps the flirt down hard. On the other hand, the boss may take the come-ons too seriously and begin to expect sexual favors. Either way the flirter's ego and job prospects are bound to be hurt.

Yet, one flirt whom we surveyed denied that what she does hurts herself or anyone else. Her rules are simple: flatter men, help everyone, learn a lot, and move on, but her flirting involves more than sexual titillation (e.g., the button strategically left open, the cute smile, the joking innuendo). Her flirting includes an offer to always be available to help other powerful people when needed. She even invests time in learning about superiors' hobbies so that she can share their interests. She feels that if she limited herself to her duties, she would be just another young trainee. She believes that to be noticed as someone with potential requires more than friendliness and hard work. Thus, she believes that a bit of flirting helps.

Others surveyed indicated that office parties or picnics are prime chances for judicious flirting. These flirts know that executives use social occasions to size up the staff informally and believe that some discretionary flirting may help them get talked to, not talked about, later on. Others surveyed, however, indicated that flirting is not considered proper behavior by the majority of managerial women.

Dating

Flirting often leads to dating, a nonexclusive arrangement that may include sexual intimacy. Power-inspired dating is done with the boss or someone else higher up in the organization. It can open doors to the inner circle and provide the dater with useful information and connections for getting ahead in the job or moving on to a better one.

An attractive assistant to the personnel manager of a large Midwestern conglomerate used dating to help her get the career advancement she wanted. She had learned of a proposed purchase in California that would expand the Midwestern office. In searching for ways to be promoted to the California office, she began dating one of the financial vice-presidents. She deliberately became more involved with the vice-president, who started bringing her to company parties. There she met a variety of top-management people that she hoped would remember her favorably when the time came. She never mentioned her interest in the West Coast until the company formally announced the expansion. Then she wrote to the corporate officials she had met, expressing her interest in being relocated. Her strategy paid off, and within a year she was named personnel manager of the new West Coast division.

This dater does not feel that she did anything wrong to advance her career. She reasoned that she simply used the best route open to her to get the chance to prove herself. If she had been a man, she said, she might have played golf or kept her ears open in the men's room, but, being an attractive woman, she used that asset instead.

Regardless of the ethics involved, dating the boss or a superior can backfire, especially if higher-ups disapprove of such activities, officially or otherwise. The woman manager will never know when the date may thank her for her attention and favors but think less of her as a competent administrator. Even if the organization's culture tolerates these activities, *not* dating superiors she is less likely to go astray. People admire others who live up to their convictions and, generally speaking, societal convictions still hold out for keeping one's love life out of the office. If the woman manager is criticized for not granting a superior's request for a date, she should remember that the Equal Employment Opportunities Commission has established stringent guidelines on sexual harassment.

Flings

Short-term, hotly paced sexual interludes are another ploy in the quest for power. One survey respondent reported that a single fling is adequate if it's with the right person, at the right time, and accomplished in a sophisticated atmosphere. Her rationale was that the memory of a pleasant fling will help the boss see her in a favorable light when it's time for a promotion or a raise. On the other hand, the boss may feel that a bed partner already received her bonus for the year!

Affairs

Affairs are the next step up the power scale after dating and flings. They are exclusive, longer-term sexual relationships. They are the ultimate sex-to-gain-power ploy because they are more intense and continuous than other strategies, and because they provide more opportunities for getting and using power.

At the beginning, both partners usually are getting something that they need. Usually the female manager wants to be noticed and to enter part of the world that she feels is otherwise closed to her. Her male superior usually wants to be admired and looked up to by a pretty woman. Using an affair to get what they want works for some of the people some of the time. Since people who deliberately use sex for power are not usually looking for true love, any outcome that increases their power stands to be successful.

As with any sexual strategy, affairs are fraught with danger. They are fairly easy to begin but more difficult to continue, and usually very difficult to break off without someone getting hurt either on the job, off the job, or both. Furthermore, it is most often the woman who pays, although in one recent case a vice-president was fired because he was the senior executive and should have been more responsible.

In another situation, everyone paid. An account executive and his assistant manager were having an affair, during which he promised her a promotion. As time passed, passions cooled and the promised promotion was forgotten. The assistant manager quit, but not before she copied documents from her boss's files revealing questionable actions against a competitor. For her revenge, she passed on the copies to the competition, which resulted in a lose-lose outcome for not only her former boss, but the entire company.

The readers of this book have probably heard stories of women who have slept their way to the top, using sex as a stepping-stone up the corporate ladder. In actuality, these stories are usually just that—stories based on a desire to denigrate the accomplishments of someone else—or wishful thinking. Consider Mary Cunningham and Bill Agee, chairman of the board at Bendix Corporation. Her rapid rise from an MBA recruit to a top administrative position in less than a year, and her frequent appearances with the boss, started rumors about how Cunningham accomplished so much so fast. Eventually the relationship cost both of them their jobs considerable prestige, and a lot of emotional trauma.[27]

When a power-motivated affair works as planned, the reward can be a promotion, a raise, or easier working conditions. Rewards also include the power associated with being on the inside and backed up by the boss. Unfortunately, very often one or both partners, and sometimes innocent bystanders, end up getting hurt. Although affairs do take place, the aggrandizement of this exciting play for power should be carefully weighed against the possible long-term consequences.

Finally, a warning about being victimized sexually by powerful men. Sexual harassment is pervasive; usually a power tactic used against women who are typically victims. Today, with stringent governmental guidelines, increasing awareness, convictions and penalties, and access to all of the power bases described above, savvy women managers have a better chance of avoiding it. Using sex as a power tactic can backfire, however, and destroy many of your defenses. Severe caution is imperative.

ACTION GUIDELINES

Both acquiring and properly applying power are important issues for women managers who, for the most part, come from backgrounds that ignore or downplay power for women, or that promote more passive postures. Power and politics are realities of organizational life, and successfully coping with them is vital to managerial and career success. The following guidelines are helpful for the manager in acquiring and using power effectively.

1. Avoid peripheral job assignments and seek out those allowing maximum exposure and realistic challenge.

2. Avoid overprotective superiors and those who are cynical toward women's capabilities in general. If avoidance is not possible, the manager should try to clarify her expectations as soon as possible.

3. Use feminine characteristics to advantage, adopt masculine behaviors where appropriate, and make inroads into male-dominated networks.

4. For maximum gain, build power from legitimate, reward, coercive, referent, expert, and informational sources simultaneously.

5. Be aware of how sex is used in power politics, but be wary of using it personally.

KEY TERMS

association power — the development of power simply by being associated with a powerful person

coercive power — the ability to punish subordinates if they do not conform to the manager's directives

earned authority — the totality of one's power, which is derived through competence, valued contributions, and individual character

expert power — the influence accorded to a manager who has superior knowledge, ability, or skill

holding out — a blocking strategy in communication that prevents a decision or calls attention to a negative program that needs one's approval or participation to be successful

gatekeeping — the function of controlling the communication process so that everyone concerned has an equal chance to participate and be heard

influence — any psychological force that can cause a change in another person

information power — the influence a person has when he or she possesses information valuable to others who don't have it

interpersonal power — the ability to get another person to do something spontaneously that he or she would not have done necessarily

legitimate power — power that is based on authority vested in an organizational position and accrues to the person who holds that position

office politics — the game of getting all the different human elements in an organization working for, rather than against, a person

power — the means to get things done

referent power — the ability to cause others to imitate one's personal style or behavior because of their respect or liking for that person

reward power — the ability to compensate and give rewards to individuals who satisfactorily complete assigned tasks

DISCUSSION QUESTIONS

1. What are the forms of organizational power and how can the woman manager employ them to acquire an *earned* authority through the effective use of these forms of power?

2. What are the areas of traditional power failure for women? What strategies can be employed to strengthen these power weaknesses?

3. How can a woman adopt and refine the characteristics leading to power refinement?

4. What are some of the recommended strategies for enhancing interpersonal power? What are the merits to each approach?

5. What are the sexual strategies that can be used to access power within an organization? What are the merits/consequences of these approaches?

CHAPTER CASE

PATRICIA HILL: KING OF THE MOUNTAIN?

Patricia Hill was recently hired as an account services manager of a leading bank in the Santa Barbara county. After finishing her MBA at U. C. Berkeley, Patricia had worked for four years in a management training program at another local bank. Her new position involved supervising eight male and five female employees, as well as coordinating operations with the proof department. The latter was managed by an ambitious young man named Chuck Evans. Chuck did not have an MBA, but had received a BA in Business Economics from U. C. Santa Barbara, and had one and one-half years of banking experience. Chuck was a nephew of one of the vice-presidents of the bank.

After three months at her new job, Patricia recognized the need for a major overhaul of the structure of account services department. Account services had been run with its existing organization for nearly 15 years, and any changes that took place would have a direct impact on the functioning of the proof department. Nevertheless, through her management training, Patricia had learned of a new system that she felt would result in increased efficiency, productivity, and employee morale over the long run. The new system would require the support of her thirteen employees, and also required some minor changes in the proof department procedures.

Patricia had not yet discussed her proposal with Chuck or any of the employees involved. She knew that she would meet more resistance from her male employees than her female workers. So far, the men in her department had given her the most difficulty. Even so, she felt with a carefully planned meeting involving ideas and feedback from her employees she could win them over.

Her major problem to confront was Chuck Evans. Since she had come to the bank, Chuck had openly insulted her in front of several employees; he had purposely slowed down work in his department to make her operations suffer, and had even tried to get his uncle (a vice-president) to fire Patricia. On many occasions, Chuck had made sexist comments about managerial ability to Patricia.

Patricia knew that if she could convince Chuck to give the change a try, it could potentially save the bank thousands of dollars per month and result in the cross-training (and increased skill levels) of both of their staffs. As she sat down to write up the final draft of her presentation, she pondered over the best approach to take toward both Chuck and her employees.

QUESTIONS

1. What sources of power do Patricia and Chuck possess? How might this affect their working relationship?

2. How can Patricia use directed thinking to plan and organize her proposal? Use the six guidelines for directed thinking in structuring your response.

3. Why do you think Chuck has behaved as he has toward Patricia? What can Patricia do to help remedy this?

ENDNOTES

[1] P. D. Horn and J. C. Horn, *Sex in the Office* (Reading, MA: Addison-Wesley, 1982).

[2] Ibid.

[3] R. M. Kanter, Power Failure in Management Circuits, *Harvard Business Review* (July-August, 1979): 65-75.

[4] M. Kanabayash, The Checkoff, *Wall Street Journal* 14 March 1989

[5] D. J. Brass, Men's and Women's Networks: A Study of Interaction Patterns and Influence in an Organization, *Academy of Management Journal* (June, 1985): 327-343.

[6] J. Calano and J. Salzman, Persuasiveness: Make It Your Power Booster, *Working Woman* (October, 1988): 124-125, 160.

[7] J. Ciabattan, Managerial Courage, *Working Women* (September, 1988): 105-108, 220-221.

[8] K. Deaux, Authority, Gender, Power, and Tokenism, *The Journal of Applied Behavioral Sciences*, 14 (January-March, 1978): 22-25.

[9] P. Johnson, Women and Power: Toward A Theory of Effectiveness, *The Journal of Social Issues*, Vol. 32, 3 (1976): 99-110.

[10] N. Colwill, *The New Partnership: Women and Men in Organizations* (Palo Alto, CA: Mayfield Publishing Co., 1982).

[11] P. L. Hunsaker and C. W. Cook, *Managing Organizational Behavior* (Reading, MA: Addison-Wesley, 1986).

[12] B. Rosen and T. H. Jerdee, "The Influence of Sex-Role Stereotypes on Evaluations of Male and Female Supervisory Behavior," *Journal of Applied Psychology*, Vol. 57 (1973): 44-48.

[13] L. A. Dunn, "Consideration of Variables in Reward and Coercive Influence Attempts" (Unpublished manuscript, Tufts University, Medford, MA, 1972).

[14] P. Johnson, "Social Power and Sex Role Stereotyping" (Doctoral dissertation, University of California, Los Angeles, 1974).

[15] T. Litman-Adizes, G. Fontaine, and B. H. Raven, "Consequences of Social Power and Causal Attribution for Compliance As Seen by Powerholder and Target," *Personality and Social Psychology Bulletin*, Vol. 4, No. 2 (1978): 260-264.

[16] L. R. Gallese, "Corporate Women on the Move," *Business Month* (April, 1989): 21-36.

[17] G. N. Powell, "Career Development and the Woman Manager—A Social Power Perspective," *Personnel* (May-June, 1980): 22-32.

[18] Ibid.

[19] A. M. Morrison, R. P. White, E. Van Velsor, "Executive Women: Substance Plus Style," *Psychology Today* (August, 1987): 18-26.

[20] P. L. Hunsaker, "Strategies for Organizational Change: The Role of the Internal Change Agent," *Personnel* (September-October, 1982): 18-28.

[21] Liz Houston, "Businesswomanly Wile: A Few Rules on Disarming the Skeptic," *MBA* (September, 1977).

[22] Calano and Salzman, op. cit.

[23] S. Sprecher, "Sex Differences in Bases of Power in Dating Relationships," *Sex Roles* (December, 1985): 449-461.

[24] L. A. Mainiero, "A Review and Analysis of Power Dynamics in Organizational Resources," *Academy of Management Review*, Vol. II, No. 4 (1986): 750-762.

[25] C. Anderson and P. L. Hunsaker, "Why There's Romancing at the Office and Why It's Everyone's Problem," *Personnel* (February, 1985): 57-63.

[26] Horn and Horn, op. cit.

[27] M. Cunningham, *Powerplay: What Really Happened at Bendix* (New York: Simon and Schuster, 1984).

ADDITIONAL RESOURCES

Allen, R. W. and Porter, L. W. *Organizational Influence Processes*. Glenview, IL: Scott, Foresman and Company, 1983.

Brady, M., Dyer, L, and Parriott, S. *Woman Power!* Los Angeles: J. P. Taicher, Inc., 1981.

Connie, J. K. *The Woman's Guide to Management Success: How to Win Power in the Real Organizational World*. Englewood Cliffs, NJ: Prentice-Hall, 1978.

Hart, Lois. *Moving Up! Women and Leadership*. New York: AMACOM, 1980.

Kennedy, Marilyn Moats. *Office Politics*. Chicago, IL: Follett Publishing Co., 1980.

Kotter, John P. *Power In Management*. New York: AMACOM, 1979.

Mintzberg, H. *Power In and Around Organizations*. Englewood Cliffs, NJ: Prentice-Hall, 1983.

Pfeffer, J. *Power In Organizations*. Marshfield, MA: Pitman Publishing Inc., 1981.

CHAPTER 8

DELEGATING AND WORKING EFFECTIVELY WITH GROUPS

Delegating
  Reasons for Ineffective Delegating
  Useful Principles of Delegating
Delegating to Groups
  Formal Groups
  Informal Groups
Problems of Women in Groups
  Sex Ratios of Groups
  Overcoming of Female Stereotypes in Male-Dominated
  Groups
          The "Mass and Model" Approach
          Effective Management of Groups
Key Group Processes
  Communication Patterns
  Decision-Making Procedures
  Group Role Behaviors
          Task Role Behaviors
          Maintenance Role Behaviors
          Self-Oriented Role Behaviors

Emotional Issues
　　Identity
　　Control and Power
　　Goals
　　Acceptance and Intimacy
Emotional Expression
　Types of Emotional Behavior
　　A Show of Tough Emotions
　　A Show of Tender Emotions
　　A Denial of All Emotion
　Types of Emotional Styles
　　The Friendly Helper Style
　　The Tough Battler Style
　　The Logical Thinker Style
Team Building
　Needs Assessment
　Planning and Design
　Team Building Meeting
　Diagnosis and Evaluation
　Problem Solving
　Planning Implementation and Follow-Up
Conducting Effective Meetings
Action Guidelines
Key Terms
Discussion Questions
Chapter Case: The New Superintendent
Endnotes
Additional Resources

The previous chapter discussed the importance of managerial power for job and career success. In this chapter delegation and group facilitation are concentrated on as additional means to the same ends. We begin with the importance of **delegating** as a means of building power by giving away some power to subordinates as individuals or in groups. Then strategies for managing these newly empowered groups are described.

DELEGATING

Building a network of political supporters is one way a manager passes on and shares her power with qualified others. This builds trust and support with subordinates which can be translated into increased referent power. Paradoxically, a manager can sometimes enhance her total control and influence by giving up direct, personal control and influence in the form of delegation. This has been the hallmark of companies who have successfully renewed themselves, including IBM, which has recently changed its decades-old centralization policy by delegating authority down the organization.[1] Unfortunately, most female managers resist delegation, and this hampers their effectiveness in business. In fact, the inability to delegate ranks as a top contributor to the mortality of managerial careers.[2]

Most successful male executives break large projects down into manageable parts and parcel out pieces to others. They carefully hand out details and other tasks, especially those considered to be potentially dangerous to their own careers. Savvy managers also quickly delegate work that is tedious, time-consuming, or unlikely to be noticed by top management.

Women have a tendency to hang on to every bit of an assignment, even though it may be overwhelming. They check and recheck every detail, making sure that everything is done perfectly. The net result is they are too busy or overwhelmed to take on bigger and better challenges.

Reasons for Ineffective Delegating

Have you ever been guilty of making one or more of the following statements?[2] Many women managers are, which can make them ineffective delegators.

- It's easier to do it myself, and I know it will be done right if I do it.
- I don't have enough confidence in my subordinates.
- I'm afraid of what my boss will think.
- I like to get personal credit for these tasks.
- I thought I had plenty of time to do it myself.
- I'm afraid the worker will think I'm imposing on him or her.

Ineffective delegating can occur for a variety of reasons. Sometimes the manager is eager to prove her ability and demonstrate her assertiveness in doing things her way. At other times, she may be impatient with subordinates for taking too long to accomplish results for which she feels responsible.

Although it is understandable that managers want to show early results, not allowing subordinates sufficient time to do a thorough job may be damaging to a climate of trust and teamwork. For delegation to be effective, a manager should explain what has to be done and why. Then she should allow the subordinates to determine how the job will get done and how long it will take.

Unwillingness is usually the root cause of inadequate delegation. Unwillingness is most often based on the desire to hold on to every facet of the job and to avoid potential risks inherent when someone else does the tasks originally assigned to you. Yet even greater risks exist if you do not delegate appropriately. By delegating to others, you can multiply yourself and be more productive. Delegating effectively involves determining priorities, setting realistic deadlines, and managing time effectively.

For subordinates, delegating has both personal and job-related values. Delegating helps increase their confidence, assess their capabilities, and enhance their understanding of the business as a whole. Delegating appropriate decisions to subordinates can also lead to better decisions since they are often closest to the firing line. Accepting responsibility and having opportunities to exercise judgment make subordinates' jobs more satisfying and increase their commitment to accomplishing organizational goals.[3]

Useful Principles of Delegating

By developing an effective work team, the manager can dismiss insecurity that tasks will not be done adequately. Conversely, if subordinates do a good job, she will not have to fear the loss of power. Mutual confidence is an important foundation for effective delegation to take place. Within an atmosphere of mutual support, the series of planned steps in Figure 8-1 can enhance the delegation process.

FIGURE 8-1

PRINCIPLES OF DELEGATING

Establish goals.   Clarify objectives and the importance of the tasks being delegated including effort involved, expected completion date, and desired end product.

Define responsibility and authority.   Build the necessary legitimate and information power into the delegated assignment and clearly inform subordinates about what they will be held accountable.

Establish adequate controls.   Explain standards and expectations and provide yardsticks for assessing completed work.

Provide training.   Make sure the assigned subordinates are willing and able to do the work by selecting people with the necessary experience, education, and judgment, and then providing additional training as required.

Motivate subordinates.   Be sensitive to the specific needs and goals of subordinates and provide appropriate individual and group incentives for doing the delegated task well.

Require completed work.   Delegate the responsibility to complete the task appropriately after you provide guidance, help, and necessary information.

DELEGATING TO GROUPS

The same types of guidelines and advantages apply to delegating responsibility and authority to groups within the organization. Recognizing this, IBM recently delegated the authority for a huge number of decisions to six divisional subcommittees.[4] On a smaller scale, a manager can magnify her productive capacity immensely by delegating much of the problem solving and decision making responsibilities to work groups that are closest to the problems.

Not all decisions are appropriate for delegation, however. Appropriateness depends upon the nature of the problem being solved and the importance of the decision being made. When deciding to delegate a decision to a group, a manager should consider three questions:

1. How important is the quality of the decision with respect to its contribution to organizational goals?

2. How important is acceptance and commitment on the part of subordinates to execute the decision?

3. How much time is required to make the decision and how much time is available?

The answers to these three questions will vary from one problem to another. For decisions that only concern a manager and will be implemented by her, acceptance is not critical, so there is no need to delegate anything. If the decision is on how to program a computer for inventory control, on the other hand, it is important to involve those with the required expertise and those who will be involved in running the system to insure the essential high quality and commitment to operate it effectively. In emergencies there just is not time to delegate. If time is available and there is little quality concern by the organization about the outcome (e.g., where shall we hold the company picnic?), the problem solving process should be delegated to a concerned group for team building and member development.[5]

In general, delegating appropriate decisions to groups results in higher quality decisions plus higher degrees of understanding and acceptance of the decision, which leads to a feeling of ownership and more commitment to implement the decision effectively. On the other hand, group problem solving does take more time than just doing it alone, pulls

Illus. 8.1
Delegating decisions to groups, such as accounting or personnel, often results in higher quality decisions plus higher degrees of understanding and acceptance of the decisions.

participants away from other tasks they could be doing, and runs the risk of decisions based on values not congruent with those of the organization.[6] By considering the three criteria of quality, acceptance, and time, a manager can decide the appropriate degree of delegation to groups for each specific problem that arises.

Sometimes it is appropriate to delegate tasks to **formal groups** like cost accounting or personnel departments. Other times it is necessary to create a temporary committee to complete special projects or solve a specific problem.

Informal groups based on common interests also can be delegated tasks of common concern if there are appropriate issues they should address. An increasingly common informal group comprises women wanting to meet with other women working in male-dominated organizations. If such a group is assigned the task of overcoming common female problems in the organization, it may become more formal as a networking group responsible for aiding women in gaining and succeeding in managerial jobs.[7]

Whether formal or informal, women who find themselves in male-dominated groups can run into a variety of problems that impede their effectiveness. Some of the problems and ways to overcome them are discussed next.

PROBLEMS OF WOMEN IN GROUPS

"When a man is the rarity in a group, he is likely to be central, to be deferred to and respected. When a woman is the rarity, she is likely to be isolated, to be treated as trivial."[8] Effective intervention in such situations depends upon understanding these dynamics as a function of the group and not necessarily of the individuals involved.

Sex Ratios of Groups

All-male, all-female, and cross-gender groups differ in their content, process, and relational styles.[9] All-male groups tend to exhibit more competition, practical joking, avoidance of intimacy, and impersonality than all-female groups. All-female groups demonstrate more affiliation, concern about relationships, personal references, and concern about family than all-male groups.

In cross-gender groups, men become more tense, serious, self-conscious, less competitive, and reduce practical joking. Both men and women become more personal and share more feelings, but women speak less often than men. Sexual tensions frequently develop, and individuals may be concerned about being attractive to the opposite sex.

In cross-gender groups, both sexes will experience emotional issues regarding identity, power, goals, and acceptance with increased intensity. When a woman is the only female in a male-dominated group, however, her performance may be hindered through additional typecastings.

Overcoming of Female Problems in Male-Dominated Groups

The stereotyped female roles (mother, seductress, pet, and iron maiden) discussed in Chapter 1 are, of course, caricatures. Their more subtle, real-life applications all serve to isolate the solitary woman from the mainstream of group interaction and prevent her from demonstrating

her competencies. A solitary woman often finds it difficult to break out of
these roles. The absence of other women may lead her to believe that her
future lies in being successful according to male expectations.

The "Mass and Model" Approach. The "mass and model" approach, proposed by Rosabeth Kanter, gives women several possible
alternatives for overcoming female stereotypes and exercising their
full competence freely.[10] First, the female manager can *talk openly* in
the group about these sex-role and majority-minority problems. Second, she could seek out *female role models* in powerful positions in
her own or other organizations. These female role models may provide
her with specific feedback and advice. Using them as examples can
change her own image through association. Finally, whenever possible, she should include a **critical mass** of females in every work
group. If more than two or three women can be included in large work
groups, they can help reduce stereotyping without threatening one
another. There is strength in numbers. As enough people expose
outdated stereotypes and unproductive group expectations, positive
change in the culture of the group will occur for all participants.

Effective Management of Groups. In addition to specific female
issues, most people participate in work groups that have a variety of
problems. These problems lead many managers to the conclusion that
groups are inefficient, time-consuming, and ineffective. Yet many of
the same people have probably also participated in highly effective
and creative work groups. In order to manage groups effectively and
utilize their advantages, at least two things are necessary. First, the
manager needs to understand the fundamentals of group dynamics.
Second, she needs to know how and when to apply this understanding
to avoid problems and capitalize on strengths in order to make group
situations more effective.

KEY GROUP PROCESSES

Assume that the manager has decided to get a group involved in
helping her solve a problem. This section describes the key group processes[11] to concentrate on in order to make the group most effective. It is

important to detect these processes in action, understand their consequences, and be able to intervene to alter them when necessary.

Communication Patterns

By observing the pattern of communication in a group, a manager can determine important process variables, such as who leads whom, who influences whom, who likes or dislikes whom, and how positive and optimistic the group members feel about the task and about one another. Specific communication variables to be aware of are listed in Figure 8-2. They include: who talks, for how long, how often, who talks after whom, who interrupts whom, what style of communication is used, and body language like facial expressions, gestures, and seating arrangements.

FIGURE 8-2

COMMUNICATION PATTERNS

1. Who Talks   For How Long?   How Often?

2. Who do people look at when they talk?

   A. Individuals, possibly potential supporters

   B. Scanning the group

   C. Nobody

3. Who talks after whom?   Who interrupts whom?

4. What style of communication is used (assertions, questions, tone of voice, gestures, etc.) ?

These communication patterns will vary according to the gender composition of a group. A lone male in the group, for example, will probably tend to talk more and receive most of the attention. A lone female, on the other hand, may often be ignored or treated as trivial. The style of communication in mixed-sex groups tends to be less aggressive and more accepting than in all-male groups, but female members generally speak much less than males.[12]

Decision-Making Procedures

Some group decisions are made without much awareness of how they were made, even when they affect vital group procedures or standards of operation. Observing how decisions are made in a group can be helpful in assessing the appropriateness of the decision. A range of methods groups use in decision making are listed in Figure 8-3, and their consequences are described below.

FIGURE 8-3

DECISION-MAKING PROCEDURES

1. The Plop

2. The Self-authorized Agenda

3. The Handclasp

4. The Minority Decision

5. Majority-minority Voting

6. Polling

7. Consensus Testing

The **plop** is an assertive statement followed by silence. In essence, this silence is an indirect decision not to do whatever was suggested. For example, "I think we should appoint Fran, the first woman on our committee, as our new chairperson." Silence ensues. The group then moves to another issue, or another person is nominated. The suggested decision has not been accepted. It has plopped, but maybe for the wrong reasons.

The **self-authorized agenda** is an assertive statement followed by self-initiated action. For example, "I think we should introduce ourselves. My name is Bill Smith . . ." or "I think we need a secretary. Julie, since you're the only woman here, you're it." If Julie acquiesced and the meeting continued along, the decision was made by a self-authorized agenda.

When two people support each other to initiate a decision, the **handclasp** occurs. For example, Person A says, "I wonder if it would be helpful if we had someone to take notes." Person B then reaffirms Person A's statement with, "I think it would and, since Fran is the only woman here, let's have her do it." If no one resists this suggestion, and Fran begins to take notes, the handclasp has been effective.

The **minority decision** is made when, by asserting their agreement, **a together few** influence an **untogether whole**. For example, someone may say, "Does anyone object?" or "We all agree, don't we?" The silence which usually follows is assumed to imply agreement. In reality, some members of the group may not have had time to decide or check for support from others.

The **majority-minority voting** is simply a form of **majority wins** voting. Since women are usually minorities in groups, this means they usually lose. In any case, the ideas, rationale, and feelings among the group are not processed in a simple show of hands.

The **polling method** seeks to find out what everyone thinks about an issue. Depending upon how the outcome is perceived, the initiator may use the results as if a decision had been reached. For example, "Let's see where everyone stands on making Julie the coordinator. What do you think Jim? (pause for Jim's response), Margaret?" and so on.

The **consensus-testing method** consists of a genuine exploration to test for any opposition and to determine whether the opposition feels strongly enough to refuse to implement a decision. It does not necessarily mean that all are optimally satisfied, but an essential agreement is achieved, under the circumstances, with which everyone can live.

Since women tend to be the minority in many managerial groups, a female manager's influence is jeopardized with all except the *consensus* form of group decision making. As is pointed out later, judicious use of gatekeeping roles can help women in minority positions make sure that their opinions are heard and counted.

Group Role Behaviors

Behavior in a group (see Figure 8-4) can be classified in terms of its purpose or function.[13] Some group behavior is primarily oriented toward task accomplishment. Other behavior is aimed at improving relationships among group members. Some behaviors occur to meet some personal need or goal of an individual without regard for the group's problems. Recurring sets of behaviors aimed at accomplishing these tasks, relationships, and personal objectives are called **roles**.

Task Role Behaviors contribute to the group's task accomplishment. They include seeking information, providing information, initiating actions and procedures, clarifying issues, summarizing progress, testing the operationality of suggestions, making sure working materials are available, energizing more quantity and quality of output, and helping the group reach a consensus.

Relationship Role Behaviors help the group remain in good working order, have a good climate for task work, and foster good relationships. Some typical relationship roles are **harmonizing** to reconcile disagreements; **gatekeeping** to keep communication channels open, which is especially important for women in mixed sex groups where men usually get two-thirds of the air time; **encouraging** others to contribute; **compromising** in the interest of group cohesion, and **observing** and **commenting** on the group's internal process.

FIGURE 8-4

TYPES OF GROUP ROLE BEHAVIORS

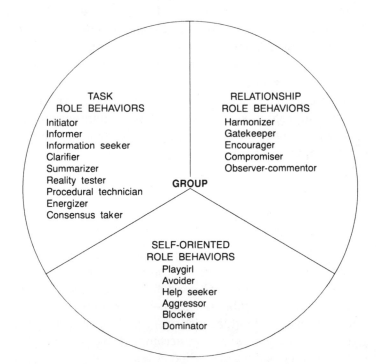

Illus. 8.2
Keeping communication
channels open and
encouraging others to
contribute help the group
remain in good working
order.

Women are more stereotyped with the roles in the maintenance behavior category than they are in the task category. Since females are traditionally thought expressive, nurturing, supportive, and cooperative, while men are thought assertive, task oriented, impersonal, and abstract, group members may automatically fall into these sex-typed specialties regardless of their own personal skills and expertise. In fact, research has shown that women are not reliably more sensitive to social cues, more affiliative, more nurturant, more altruistic, or more emphatic than males.[14] People should be aware these stereotypes trap and encourage both men and women into comfortably stereotyped roles.

If managers are really concerned about subordinates, they need to develop their subordinates' potential. This can require direct and critical feedback, with the potential for hurt feelings. Sometimes this is in the best interests of both the organization and the individual. Lulu Wong, senior vice-president of the Equitable Capital Management Group in New York, says, "Raising children is like managing subordinates. You have to be caring, but also make the hard decisions that earn their respect and trust."[15]

Concern for maintenance behaviors has a very necessary positive side. Maintenance behaviors help build a climate of openness which enhances communication and builds feelings of security with authority figures. Such "feminine" behaviors as expressing feelings, showing vulnerability, and asking for support are invaluable for building strong collaborative work teams. Men could benefit by increasing their relationship behaviors just as women could benefit by being more assertive and effective in the use of power.

Self-Oriented Role Behaviors only serve personal objectives at the expense of group task accomplishment and relationships. Examples are **aggressors** who deflate others' status, **blockers** who disagree beyond reason, **dominators** who try to constantly control others, **playgirls** who display in a flamboyant fashion their lack of involvement, **avoiders** who prevent the group from facing up to controversies, and **help seekers** who use the group to solve personal problems unrelated to the group's goals.

Effective groups need an adequate balance of task and relationship roles. As a group grows and members' needs integrate with group goals, less self-oriented behavior and more task and relationship behavior emerges. Effective group members need skills in observing what necessary roles are missing and they need the flexibility to provide these behaviors when appropriate.

Emotional Issues

Many forces are active in groups that disturb task and relationship behaviors. Underlying emotional issues also produce behaviors that interfere with effective group functioning. These issues cannot be ignored or wished away. Rather, they need to be recognized and their causes understood. As the group develops, conditions should be created to channel these emotional energies toward group goals.

There are four primary emotional issues confronting members in every group They concern the members' identity, personal goals, control, and acceptance.

Identity.   Group members ask themselves: Why am I here? How am I to present myself to others? What role should I play in the group? Many female managers awkwardly attempt to become more like their male colleagues or mentors. Attempting to act aggressively by taking charge and frequently expressing anger may cause them to feel anxious and out of character.[16] Other female managers are able to maintain their feminine nature by being assertive without being oppressive or noncaring.[17]

Control and Power. Most group members are also concerned with who has the power, how much power, control, and influence they have, and how much they need. This is a special dilemma for women who often ignore power issues in a group. These optimistic women prefer to believe a team of equals exists, when this may not be the case at all. More savvy women seek to acquire power as a transforming force for producing positive changes in the organization.[18]

Goals. All group members are concerned about personal goals. Frequent questions concern: Can any of my needs be met here? Which of my goals can this group fulfill? To which of the group's goals can I attach myself?

The personal goals that realistically can be achieved depend a lot upon the composition of the group and the nature of its task assignment. The same is true regarding individual objectives concerning increased assertiveness, independence, power, and intimacy. Goal-achievement creates positive feelings about the group, whereas, lack of opportunities to accomplish goals leads to frustration and bitterness.

Acceptance and Intimacy. Group members face the dual problem of acceptance and intimacy. Questions asked are: Am I accepted by the others? Do I accept them? Do they like me? Do I like them? How close to others do I want to become?

This is usually not a problem in all-male groups where intimacy is automatically avoided. In all-female groups, however, intimacy and openness in relationships are often of equal importance to task accomplishment. In mixed-sex groups, additional feelings arise because of concerns about being attracted to the opposite sex. When group members are successful in obtaining the degrees of acceptance and intimacy they prefer, positive sentiments develop. When their desires are blocked, negative feelings result.

EMOTIONAL EXPRESSION

Each of the four emotional issues just described create tension and anxiety for new group members. Three predominant types of emotional expression result from the tension that is created. An integral part of the manager's job is recognizing these emotions, their sources, and seeking positive resolution of the underlying issues. When people deal with these emotional issues, the way they cope with them is to show tough emotions, show tender emotions, or deny emotions altogether.[19]

Examples of *tough emotions* are anger, hostility, and self-assertiveness. These emotions are associated with fighting, punishing, controlling, or counterdependency. Tough emotions are characteristic of the stereotyped male manager who seems cool, competitive, tough, resilient, and motivated toward task achievement.

Examples of *tender emotions* are love, sympathy, desire to help, and need for affiliation with others. Behaviors associated with these emotions include supporting and helping others, depending upon others, and pairing up or affiliating with others. These are emotions and behaviors traditionally identified with women.

The behaviors associated with a *denial of all emotion* include withdrawing from others and falling back on logic or reason. This is also considered a stereotyped male response to emotional situations which is manifest in a logical, problem-solving approach.

Emotional Styles

Everyone experiences both tough and tender emotions at one time or another. How a manager deals with her own feelings depends on what has worked for her in the past and on which emotional style she is most comfortable with. This carries over to her reaction to emotional expressions from others who, of course, have different ways for reducing tension and expressing feelings. Three "pure types" of *emotional styles* (see Figure 8-5) are identified below.

The **friendly helper style** is characterized by an acceptance of tender emotions and a denial of tough emotions. The friendly helper's motto could be: "Let's not fight, let's help each other." Friendly helpers like to give and receive affection but cannot tolerate hostility and fighting. This emotional style is characteristic of women who have learned to express vulnerability, to be excessively pleasant, to smooth over conflict, to be overly concerned with having people get along well together (often at the expense of task accomplishment), to smile too much, to express their feelings, and to allow themselves to be interrupted.[20] Because of this friendly helper orientation, many female managers abandon positions of strength in order to remain charming and conciliatory.[21]

If a manager is not willing to make this tradeoff and is operating in an environment where managing in the friendly helper style will be taken advantage of, it may be in her best interests to shift styles. According to Linda Kline, president of Kline-McKay, Inc., an executive-search consulting firm, "When you're part of a male macho situation there isn't a damn thing you can do but respond in kind if you want to go anywhere at all. If most others in the organization are men who have been molded to cut all tenderness from their own psyches, they're not going to countenance too many of these traits in women."[22] It may be appropriate in this situation to shift to the tough battler style in order to survive.

The **tough battler style** thrives on the tough emotions but avoids the denial of tender emotions. The tough battler's motto is: "Might makes right!" or "Let's fight it out." Tough battlers enjoy dealing with hostility but not with love, support, and affiliation, which they see as signs of weakness. This emotional style is often manifested by men who operate from a need for power and control in the male macho style described above. One

FIGURE 8-5

TYPES OF EMOTIONAL STYLES

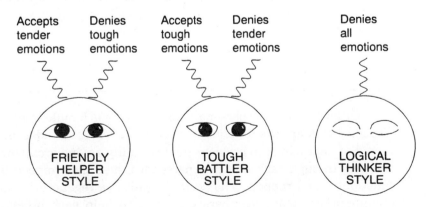

problem with women responding in kind, as advised by Linda Kline above, is that several very unflattering names exist for women who express their emotions in the tough battler style. Consequently, some women take an adult compromise position and react in the logical thinker mode.

The **logical thinker style** denies all emotion. A logical thinker's motto is: "Let's reason this thing out." Logical thinkers avoid dealing with both tender and tough emotions; and so they shut their eyes and ears to much of what is going on around them. This is probably the most acceptable mode of dealing with emotions in the rational, male-dominated business world. However, by being rational, men logical thinkers exclude needs for closeness and spontaneity even when they are very relevant to the situation.

Perhaps the best way to deal with emotions is through androgynous behavior.[23] Many women need to make their points openly, claim ownership for jobs well done, and acknowledge errors in judgment. They could benefit from more analytical thinking and healthy assertiveness. Men, on the other hand, need to be less competitive, more open, and less cool in showing their feelings. Their effectiveness would be enhanced by decreasing exhibitionism and increasing time spent on building support systems.

Whether or not a manager's specific emotional style is appropriate depends on the group situation she is in. All groups need components of all three styles at one time or another to function effectively. As a good group member, the manager needs to develop emotional flexibility so that she can exhibit the most appropriate emotional behavior when needed. "If you want to be a good manager," says Lois Wyse, president of Wyse Advertising, "first be a good mother. All the things that a mother provides for her children—comfort, praise, scoldings, motivation, entertainment, teaching, punishment, and rewards—are what shape the basic behavioral system for corporate interaction."[24]

TEAM BUILDING

Often certain interpersonal and male versus female issues appear to impede a task group's functioning. **Team building** includes all activities aimed at improving the problem-solving ability among group members by working through task and interpersonal issues that impede the team's functioning and rapport. The desired result is a regenerative interaction climate where team members cooperate to help each other grow and develop, as opposed to a degenerative climate where individuals compete at each other's expense.[25]

The objective of team building is to develop a more cohesive, mutually supportive, and trusting group that has high expectations for task accomplishment and also respects individual differences in values, styles, and skills. Successful team building should nurture individual potential and uniqueness, rather than foster conformity to smooth over differences. More specific **team building goals** are presented in Figure 8-6.[26]

FIGURE 8-6

TEAM BUILDING GOALS

1. A better understanding of each team member's role

2. A better understanding of the team's charter or purpose in the total functioning of the organization

3. Increased communication among team members about issues that affect the efficiency of the group

4. Greater support of group members

5. A better understanding of group processes

6. More effective ways of working through group problems

7. The ability to use conflict in positive versus negative ways

8. Greater collaboration versus competition among team members

9. Increased ability of the group to work productively with other groups in the organization

10. A sense of interdependence among group members

To accomplish these goals several chronological **team building steps** are required.[27] First, a needs assessment determines specific problems, what interventions are most appropriate, and what action plan for implementation should be developed. Next, team commitment is established. Individuals must feel comfortable enough with the program and facilitator to openly share and receive feedback from other members. The information gained from the assessments and exercises is utilized to pin point team problems. These are then analyzed, prioritized, and assigned to task groups to solve. Finally, ongoing follow-up is required to insure that problems are solved, solutions are implemented, and that the team continues to monitor itself on an ongoing basis. The team-building process is illustrated in Figure 8-7.

Needs Assessment

A team building program usually is initiated because someone (the leader, a higher level manager, a team member, or consultant) recognizes that the group is having problems working productively as a team. Common symptoms include overt hostilities between team members, chronic lateness or absenteeism at meetings, low quantity and quality of production, negative gossip and rumors about each other, decisions not carried out because of misunderstandings or no one takes responsibility, and apathy and lack of interest.

These factors are clearly symptoms of underlying problems that must be determined through data gathering and analysis. Two common causes, however, are (1) difficulty between team members and the team leader, and (2) difficulty among team members.

FIGURE 8-7

THE TEAM BUILDING PROCESS

PROBLEM AWARENESS ⟶ DATA GATHERING ⟶ DATA ANALYSIS ⟶

PROBLEM IDENTIFICATION ⟶ ACTION PLANNING ⟶

IMPLEMENTATION ⟶ EVALUATION ⟶ FOLLOW-UP

(Ongoing process observation, feedback, and consultation)

Successful team-development programs require accurate identification of the group's specific needs and problems. Depending upon initial needs assessment, different approaches and interventions will be more or less appropriate.

The first step gathers data about the team situation which ideally allows a correct diagnosis to be made. The group may already be experiencing "pain" as indicated through symptoms such as decreased output, hostile sentiments, and interpersonal conflicts. The next task is to determine why these negative factors exist and what can be done about them. Two common forms of data gathering are interviews and questionnaires.

Interviews. The best sensing method for getting to the core of the problem is quite often for a facilitator to privately interview each team member, assuring confidentiality of who said what. In other words, common and significant problems will later be shared with the team, but who mentioned them will not be disclosed.

Questionnaires. An alternative to face-to-face interviews is to distribute written questionnaires to team members and ask them to complete them anonymously, or signed, depending upon the climate and content of the questionnaire.

Data Analysis. Next, the facilitator analyzes the responses, determines the degree certain factors exist, and assesses how much weight team members place on those factors. These results are summarized in a presentation to team members, either written or through open sharing of data. If team building activities are required to make the team more effective, the facilitator can then plan a meeting of the team to analyze the data and generate action plans to deal with the primary concerns. If it is determined, for example, that women in the group feel discriminated against and undervalued, the manager can meet with the human resource staff to plan an awareness raising and training session for members of the group.

Planning and Design

Team members should understand clearly what sort of experience they are in for. The facilitator can describe the process to the leader and members during data gathering interviews, or at a general orientation meeting. Participant expectations need to be acceptable and congruent with the probable experience in order for them to make a commitment to fully involve themselves in the process.

At least two or three uninterrupted days away from the usual day-to-day distractions are essential to generate the climate and energy to truly investigate and improve team interactions. The physical setting should be informal, and participants should dress casually to enhance the feelings of informality and openness.

The Team Building Meeting

The session should open with a sharing of facilitator and participant expectations. Team members should have an opportunity to share their concerns, ask questions, and clarify their roles. Mutual goal setting about realistic accomplishments can be discussed and agreed upon. The result is a psychological contract among team members about contributions and likely outcomes.

Next, the facilitator explains each problem and encourages participants to ask for clarification. Everyone should understand the essence and ramifications of the problems.

After examining all available data, the consultant and group determine what is workable and which issues are most important. To make sure no hidden agendas exist, the facilitator can call for open sharing of any additional data. At this time anything that will help clarify the issues already identified can be shared, and new issues can be added.

Diagnosis and Evaluation

The next task is to set priorities and determine the group's agenda for the time they still have available. It is vital that only those issues that the team can realistically do something about be included on the agenda so that the group can accomplish something positive and feel good about itself and its problem solving abilities. Issues might be first broken down into A) those issues that can be worked on in this meeting; B) those issues that are not possible for the group to influence—things that must be lived with; C) issues that should be delegated to someone else to act on. Then items to be addressed during this session should be ranked in order of importance. If discrimination against females is the problem, for example, the group may want to prioritize the issues of pay differentials, promotion, sexual harassment, hiring practices, so that the most important issues are covered in the time available.

Problem Solving

The prioritized agenda can be worked item by item to develop action plans. The action plans should be posted on newsprint, and include a statement of the problem, solution recommended, people responsible for implementing action, and deadlines for results.

Planning Implementation and Follow-Up

If action plans are to make any difference they must be carried out and evaluated. Fairly soon—within a month—a follow-up meeting should be scheduled to determine how successful the action plans have been and what else needs to be done. The team leader also should check on progress every week before the follow-up meeting. Otherwise, enthusiasm following the team-building retreat is likely to die on the vine, as participants get back into their daily routines.

The major goal of team building is to make problem solving an ongoing process in the work group. Unfortunately, most problem-solving sessions occur in meetings that have negative images for many organizational members.

CONDUCTING EFFECTIVE MEETINGS

Ask any group member and most will agree that nearly half their time spent in meetings is wasted. If this problem could be even partially corrected, much time could be recaptured to be used on more productive tasks. To avoid unnecessary meetings, the following questions should be asked: (1) Is the meeting necessary? (2) Can the subjects to be discussed in the meeting be handled in another manner such as a memo or conference call? (3) Can the meeting be postponed to a more convenient time for all concerned?

If the answer is no to the first question and yes to either of the remaining questions, then the meeting is probably going to be a waste of time. Assuming that a meeting is necessary, the guidelines in Figure 8-8 can help make the meeting more productive.

FIGURE 8-8

MEETING GUIDELINES

1. Define the exact **purpose** of the meeting. Make sure that all who will attend are informed in advance and in writing concerning the meeting **agenda**. This will allow team members to come properly prepared.

2. **Limit the time for the meeting.** Have a specific starting time and ending time. Schedule another meeting if necessary. Remember that work expands to fill the amount of time allotted to it.

3. **Choose a good place for the meeting.** Proper ventilation, comfort, accessibility, and availability of equipment are very important. Avoid easy access to telephones.

4. **Stick to the items on the agenda.** Avoid interruptions and tangential discussions.

5. After the meeting, expedite the **distribution of the minutes** so they are to attendees no later than two days after the meeting. If any actions are to be taken, make sure that everyone knows who is accountable and what the time frame is.

ACTION GUIDELINES

1. A lone woman in a group tends to withdraw and withhold contributions because she feels isolated and unsupported. This suggests the benefits of placing several women on a team, even if other teams have no women members at all. Providing a critical mass also serves to reduce role stereotyping.

2. Analysis of communication patterns in groups can yield important information regarding feelings and influence. Appropriate gatekeeping role behavior can help maintain the minority females' influence.

3. Using the consensus decision-making procedure is an excellent way to assure acceptance of a group decision and to assure that female members have equal input and influence in decisions affecting them.

4. Encourage appropriate task and relationship role behaviors in groups and discourage self-oriented ones. Encourage role flexibility for both males and females.

5. The emotional issues surrounding identity, power, goals, and intimacy should be aired and talked through rather than suppressed.

6. Both tough and tender emotions are natural and should be expressed at appropriate times in appropriate ways through the tough battler, friendly helper, or logical thinker emotional style.

7. Group leaders should capitalize on group decision-making strengths and avoid group weaknesses by acting as facilitators, avoiding premature evaluation of alternatives, concentrating on group process as well as content, and acting in a gatekeeping role.

8. Wasted time in meetings should be avoided by defining the exact purpose of the meeting, distributing an agenda in advance, setting a time limit for the meeting, choosing an appropriate time and place, sticking to the agenda, and promptly distributing written minutes.

KEY TERMS

aggressor — a type of self-oriented role behavior by a group member who deflates others' status, attacks them or their values, and jokes in a barbed or semiconcealed way

avoider — a type of self-oriented role behavior by a group member who pursues special interests not related to the group's task, stays off the subject to avoid commitment, and prevents the group from facing up to any controversy

blocker — a type of self-oriented role behavior by a group member who disagrees and opposes beyond reason, resists stubbornly the group's wish, and uses a hidden agenda to thwart the group's movement

clarifier — a type of task role behavior where a group member interprets ideas or suggestions, defines terms, and clarifies issues before the group

compromiser — a type of maintenance role behavior where a group member offers a compromise that yields status to members involved in a conflict, admits error, and modifies a suggestion in the interest of group cohesion

consensus taker — a type of task role behavior where a group member asks to see if a group is nearing a decision and sends up a trial balloon to test a possible conclusion

consensus testing method — a method of decision making which consists of a genuine exploration to test for any opposition to an issue and to determine whether the opponents feel strongly enough to refuse to implement a decision

critical mass — more than two or three women included in large work groups in an effort to reduce stereotyping

dominator — a type of self-oriented role behavior by a group member who asserts authority or superiority to manipulate the group, interrupts contributions of others, and controls the group by means of flattery or other forms of patronizing behavior

encourager — a type of maintenance role behavior where a group member is friendly, warm, and responsive to others and indicates by facial expression or remark the acceptance of others' contributions

energizer — a type of task role behavior where a group member attempts to increase the quality and quantity of task behavior

follower — a type of maintenance role behavior where a group member serves as audience and passively goes along with the ideas of others

friendly helper style — an emotional style which consists of an acceptance of tender emotions and a denial of tough emotions

gatekeeper — a type of maintenance role behavior where a group member helps to keep communication channels open, facilitates the participation of others, and suggests procedures that permit the sharing of remarks

handclasp — a method of decision making by which two people support each other to initiate a decision

harmonizer — a type of maintenance role behavior where a group member attempts to reconcile disagreements, reduces tension, and gets people to explore differences

help-seeker — a type of self-oriented role behavior by a group member who uses the group to solve personal problems which are unrelated to the group's goals

information-seeker — a type of task role behavior where a group member asks for opinions or facts

informer — a type of task role behavior where a group member offers facts, gives expression of feelings, and gives opinions

initiator — a type of task role behavior where a group member proposes tasks, goals, or actions; defines group problems; and suggests procedures

logical thinker style — a type of emotional style which consists of a denial of all emotions **majority-minority voting**—a method of decision making by which the majority's suggestion rules over that of the minority

minority decision — a method of decision making by which a "together few" influence an "untogether whole"

observer-commentor — a type of maintenance role behavior where a group member comments on and interprets the group's internal process

playgirl — a type of self-oriented role behavior by a group member who makes a display—in a flamboyant fashion—of her lack of involvement, abandons the group while remaining physically with it, and seeks recognition in ways not relevant to the group's task

plop — a method of decision making by which an assertive statement is followed by silence which, in effect, is a decision not to do what was previously suggested

polling method — a method of decision making by which everyone's thoughts about an issue are sought so that the initiator may use the results as if a decision had been reached

procedural technician — a type of task role behavior where a group member records suggestions and distributes materials

reality tester — a type of task role behavior where a group member makes critical analysis of an idea and tests it against some data to see if it would work

role — behavior set that is aimed at accomplishing some objective

self-authorized agenda — a method of decision making by which an assertive statement is followed by self-initiated action

summarizer — a type of task role behavior where a group member pulls together related ideas, restates suggestions, and offers a decision or conclusion for the group to consider

team building — all activities aimed at improving the problem-solving ability among group members by working through task and interpersonal issues that impede the team's functioning

tough battler style — a type of emotional style which consists of an acceptance of tough emotions and a denial of tender emotions

DISCUSSION QUESTIONS

1. List and describe at least three communication patterns that may be observed in a group.

2. Describe the three main group role behaviors. Which role is traditionally attributed to women and why?

3. Describe the "pure types" of emotional style. Give an example of a situation in which you would use each style.

4. What are the steps to realizing effective managerial delegation?

5. Describe the steps necessary for effective team building.

CHAPTER CASE

THE NEW SUPERINTENDENT

The new superintendent of the school district was a direct contrast to her predecessor. Ellen Rosansky was very democratic and participative in her management and decision-making style. This new style was quite a shock for the other administrators and teachers who had become accustomed to the former superintendent's tight control and guidance. Now they were expected to make their own decisions and control their own work environments, participate in additional brainstorming meetings, and even entertain the suggestions and advice of interested parents.

Some resisted these changes as an additional burden, but others welcomed them as a chance for more independence and autonomy. It did not take long for two warring camps to develop mutual hostility and mistrust with negative impacts on rapport and productivity.

Certain male teachers commented about the lack of leadership and decisiveness that Ellen exhibited. They attributed these personality problems to Ellen being a woman who was used to working under a man, not being in charge of them. Some female teachers wished Ellen would be more forceful so that they could avoid the abuse of these males. Some male and female teachers saw Ellen's style as a chance to slack off and coast while others anticipated they would finally have a chance to make an impact on the system.

QUESTIONS

1. Although Ellen does not seem afraid to delegate, how can she be more effective in gaining cooperation and commitment?

2. What are the advantages and disadvantages of Ellen's decision-making style? What emotional issues may be generated by it?

3. How can Ellen build an effective team from the fragmented groups that now exist?

ENDNOTES

[1] J. A. F. Stoner and R. E. Freeman, *Management*, 4th ed. (Englewood Cliffs, NJ: Prentice-Hall, 1989), 315.

[2] Margaret Hennig and Anne Jardim, *The Managerial Woman* (New York: Pocket Books, 1978), 196-197.

[3] Norma Carr-Ruffino, *The Promotable Woman*, Revised ed. (Belmont, CA: Wadsworth Publishing Co., 1985), 438-440.

[4] Stoner and Freeman, op. cit.

[5] D. A. Kolb, I. M. Rubin, and J. M. McIntyre, *Organizational Psychology: An Experiential Approach*, 3rd ed. (Englewood Cliffs, N.J.: Prentice Hall, 1979), 267-268.

[6] Phillip L. Hunsaker and Curtis W. Cook, *Managing Organizational Behavior* (Reading, MA: Addison-Wesley, 1986), 439.

[7] "Women at Work," *Business Week* (January 28, 1985): 80-85.

[8] R. M. Kanter, "On Ending Female Tokenism in T-Groups: Group Norms, Processes, and Sex Role Issues," *Social Change*, Vol. 5, No. 2 (1975): 1-3.

[9] A. G. Sargent, "Training Men and Women for Androgynous Behaviors in Organizations," *Group and Organizational Studies* (September, 1981): 302-311.

[10] Kanter, op. cit., 3.

[11] D. A. Kolb, I. M. Rubin, and J. M. McIntyre, "Group Dynamics," in Chapter 5, *Organizational Psychology: An Experiential Approach*, 4th ed. (Englewood Cliffs, NJ: Prentice-Hall, 1984), 126-146.

[12] Sargent, op. cit.

[13] Kolb, Rubin, and McIntyre, 1984, op. cit.

[14] Carol Watson, "When a Woman Is the Boss," *Group and Organization Studies*, Vol. 13, No. 2 (1988), 178-179.

[15] S. Nelton and K. Berney, "Women: The Second Wave," *Nation's Business* (May, 1987): 18-22.

[16] Sargent, op. cit., 62-63.

[17] Hennig and Jardim, op. cit., 52-54.

[18] Nancy Hartsock, *Money, Sex, and Power* (Longman, Inc., 1983).

[19] Kolb, Rubin, and McIntyre, 1984, op. cit.

[20] J. B. Millen, *Toward a New Psychology of Women*, 2nd ed. (Itasca, Ill.: Beacon Press, 1987).

[21] Sherry Suib Cohen, *Tender Power* (Reading, MA: Addison-Wesley, 1989)

[22] Sherry Suib Cohen, "Beyond Macho: The Power of Womanly Management," *Working Woman* (February, 1989): 77-83.

[23] Sargent, op. cit.

[24] Cohen, op. cit., p. 78.

[25] Robert Golembiewski, *Renewing Organizations* (Itasca, IL: F. E. Peacock Publishers, 1972), 30-32.

[26] A. J. Reilly and J. E. Jones, "Team-building," *The 1974 Handbook for Group Facilitators* (La Jolla, CA: University Associates, 1974), 227-237.

[27] William G. Dyer, *Team Building*, 2nd ed. (Reading, MA: Addison-Wesley, 1987).

ADDITIONAL RESOURCES

Dyer, William G. *Team Building*. 2nd ed. Reading, MA: Addison-Wesley, 1987.

Feuer, Dale. "How Women Manage." *Training* (August, 1988): 23-31.

Goodman, Paul S. *Designing Effective Work Groups*. San Francisco: Jossey/Bass, Inc., 1986.

Janis, Irving L. *Victims of Groupthink*. Boston: Houghton Mifflin Company, 1972.

Melia, Jinx. "Wagon Train or Cavalry?" *Training & Development Journal*. (April, 1989): 50-53.

Napier, Rodney W. and Gershenfeld, Matti K. *Groups: Theory and Experience*. 3rd ed. Boston: Houghton Mifflin, 1985.

Shaw, Marvin E. *Group Dynamics: The Psychology of Small Group Behavior*. 3rd ed. New York: McGraw-Hill, 1981.

CHAPTER 9

DEALING WITH DIFFICULT EMPLOYEES

Mismatch of Manager and Employee Behavioral Styles
    The Expressive Style
    The Driving Style
    The Analytical Style
    The Amiable Style
Personality Problems of Employees
    Oversensitive Employees
    Hostile or Angry Employees
    Negative Employees
Signs of Counterproductive Behavior
    Disrespect
    Lack of Cooperation
    Passiveness and Aggressiveness
Approaches to Interpersonal Conflict Situations
    Competing
    Accommodating
    Avoiding
    Collaborating
    Compromising
Prevention of Unnecessary Conflict
    Get Initial Agreement
    Offer a Limited Choice of Alternatives
    Obtain a Commitment in Advance
    Communicate Positive Expectations
    Use Compliments as Positive Motivators
Action Guidelines
Key Terms
Discussion Questions
Chapter Case: How Would You Handle Phil Darby?
Endnotes
Additional Resources

Most managers have some exceptionally good employees but, unfortunately, they may also have their fair share of difficult ones. The difficult employees are those a manager wants to forget. As hard as she has worked with them, nothing seems to come together. She just cannot get on the same wavelength with them.

When you talk to a manager about her difficult employees, her comments generally reflect an element of despair. Typical scenarios sound like this:

Talking to Phil is like talking to a rock! I know he's bright, some people claim he's a genius, but I swear he was brought up in a test tube. It's impossible to talk to him, he never smiles, and his steely gaze just intimidates me.

Katherine does nothing but complain and gripe incessantly about the trainees, yet she never does anything about them. She whines about her powerlessness. If she'd spend half the amount of time helping them as she does complaining, the problem would be solved.

MISMATCH OF MANAGER AND EMPLOYEE BEHAVIORAL STYLES

Many times one manager's difficult employees may not be difficult with another manager. They are difficult only because their behavioral style does not match the manager's behavioral style.

A person's behavioral style is a habitual way of interacting with another person. Some people, for example, are more assertive, while others are more compliant. *Extroverts* versus *introverts* are terms commonly used to describe people who are more outgoing versus those who are more reserved when interacting with others. People with compatible behavioral styles tend to like each other and naturally get along better than people with incompatible styles. A key managerial skill is knowing how to adapt one's behavioral style for the difficult employee.

248

When people act and react, they exhibit behaviors that help define their personality. We can categorize four distinct behavioral patterns in people: (1) expressive style, (2) driving style, (3) analytical style, and (4) amiable style.[1] Each pattern is described below, along with some specific guidelines a manager can use to change his or her behavioral style to comply with the expectations of each of the four behavioral types among subordinates.

Behavioral style characteristics are especially important when an employee and a manager with incompatible styles come in contact with each other. When that occurs, tension often results. This increased tension usually pushes the employee further away from the manager and makes that person a "difficult" employee. In order to avoid this increased tension, a manager should practice behavioral flexibility: Treat employees the way they want to be treated. Not YOUR way . . . THEIR way!

The Expressive Style

The **Expressives** are animated, intuitive, and lively, but they can also be manipulative, impetuous, and excitable. They are fast paced, make spontaneous decisions, and are not very concerned about facts and details. They thrive on involvement with others.

The Expressives like to interact with other people, so the manager should try not to hurry a discussion with them. She should move at a rapid but entertaining pace. When she finally reaches agreement with an Expressive, she should make sure that both of them fully understand all the details.

The Driving Style

The **Drivers** are firm with others. They are oriented toward productivity and concerned with bottom-line results, but Drivers can be stubborn, impatient, and tough-minded. They like to take control of other people and situations.

The Drivers are easy to deal with as long as the manager is precise, efficient, and well-organized in dealing with them. She should make sure she keeps her relationship businesslike. To influence the Drivers' decisions, the manager should provide options and allow them to draw their own conclusions.

The Analytical Style

The **Analyticals** are persistent, systematic problem solvers. They can also be aloof, picky, and critical. They need to be right—which can lead them to be overreliant on data. Their actions and decisions tend to be extremely cautious and slow.

With the Analytical, the manager should try to be systematic, organized, and prepared. Analyticals require solid, tangible, and factual evidence. The manager should take time to list the advantages and disadvantages of any plan she proposes. She should have viable alternatives for dealing with any disadvantages and she should suggest ways in which the analyticals can take action. However, she should not use any gimmicks to get a fast decision.

The Amiable Style

The **Amiables** are highly responsive, relatively unassertive, supportive, and reliable. However, Amiables are sometimes complaining, softhearted, and acquiescent. They are slow to take action. Before they make a decision, they have to know just how other people feel about the decision. Amiables dislike interpersonal conflict so much that they often tell others what they think others want to hear rather than what is really on their minds.

The manager should try to support the Amiable's feelings. She should show interest in the Amiable as a person. The manager should move along in an informal manner and show the Amiable that she is actively listening. Both her approach and presentation should be low-key. She should be confident. She should make suggestions and provide personal assurances that any new actions will involve a minimum of risk.

In summary, accepting and understanding that employees are different and need to be managed differently is basic to successful management. If the manager is able to go one step further and identify critical personality traits in her employees, she can manage them the way they would like to be managed. The bottom-line pay-off will be greater productivity and more personal satisfaction in all of her relationships with her employees . . . especially the difficult employees.

PERSONALITY PROBLEMS OF EMPLOYEES

Of course, there are employees who are difficult to manage for reasons more complicated than differences in behavioral style. Certain cases are outside the manager's control, such as alcoholism or drug abuse, where outside help or referral to an employee assistance program is called for, or clear-cut cases of dishonesty or total incompetence where termination is the only answer.[2] Employees with deep-seated personality problems may exhibit work habits, attitudes, and emotional behaviors that reduce their morale and performance, as well as the work of their coworkers. Although the manager should leave the solution of such personality problems to psychiatrists or counselors, she should not ignore their existence and the disruption they cause in the workplace. People with personality problems are not easily changed, and disciplinary action is seldom effective. However, there are some positive actions the manager can take to help them.[3] As Veiga points out, name calling is the easy part![4]

Oversensitive Employees

Some employees are very sensitive to criticism and are easily hurt. They burst into tears when asked mere information-seeking questions because they assume the manager is dissatisfied with their work. They may also appear unsure of themselves and be reluctant to make suggestions for fear of criticism. With these employees, it is critical to avoid saying anything that will undermine their self-confidence. The manager should praise their work whenever possible and continually reassure them that they are doing a good job. When criticism or productivity problems do arise, she should try to eliminate the personal factor as much as possible by using words like *we* and *our department* when explaining how the work should be improved. Also, she should be careful that these employees do not misinterpret departmental decisions or job assignments as reflections on their capabilities.

Illus. 9.1   When dealing with an emotional employee, the manager should
show an interest in following up and discussing the problem further
at a later time.

Hostile or Angry Employees

Some employees are difficult because they become angry at the
slightest provocation. This type of behavior presents a problem not only to
the manager, but also to other employees who must work with them. People
who continually fly off the handle are usually emotionally immature and
often have inferiority complexes. Many of these hostile people are similar
to what Levinson labeled the "abrasive personality" and Zemke termed
"the genetic jerk."[5] Levinson believes that consistently abrasive, sharp-
tongued, self-centered, blunt people have a desperate need to be perfect,
will push themselves (and others) toward that goal with great passion, and
are prone to attack. The abrasive personality rubs people the wrong way.
Consequently, ordinary disciplinary actions may not work in stemming
displays of temper.

Talking constructively with an angry person is usually fruitless. If
someone is emotional, the best strategy is to listen, not talk or argue. Angry
people are expressing a mixture of feelings that may include resentment,
frustration, fear, prejudice, or disappointment, although none of these

might be stated directly. The manager should listen to discern what the underlying sources of hostility really are.

The manager should not try to persuade angry employees to change, nor should she talk to the company counselor on the spot, because in the employee's emotional condition that would only serve as further fuel for the fire. The best she can do, usually, is to assure a hostile employee that she understands that employee's feelings and to show an interest in following up and discussing the problem at a later time when she can check some things out (and the angry employee has had a chance to cool down).

At the later meeting, the hostile employee should be told that the company cannot tolerate such disruptive behavior. The manager should not attempt to diagnose the reasons for such behavior herself or even try to correct it. Instead, she should refer the employee to the company counselor or to an outside psychiatrist for evaluation and counseling. If the employee refuses, she must be prepared to inform the employee that such action is mandatory and that refusal will cause him or her to be dismissed from the job.

Negative Employees

Occasionally a manager will run across employees who are by nature pessimistic. They are always thinking of reasons why goals cannot be reached, why ideas will not work, and why anything different will not stand a chance. They are recognized by comments like, "Nope," "Won't ever work," or "We tried that three years ago and it didn't work. Why try it again?" It is difficult to get these employees to be enthusiastic about their work. They give up whenever confronted with a problem of any magnitude whatsoever. Even worse, this gloomy attitude may affect other workers' attitudes.

One thing the manager might try with such employees is a praise-and-compliment strategy. She might accentuate the positive aspects about everything, including the employees, by praising them for their attendance, promptness, or a job well done. This may start a self-fulfilling prophecy of optimism on their part.

If the negative employees give the manager a pessimistic response to a new plan of action, she should demand that they come up with a positive alternative. If they say that something will not work, do not rush them, but just ask them to come up with something that will. The idea is to jolt the pessimistic employees out of their negative rut. If the manager does this in a positive manner, her own optimistic attitude is apt to make a favorable impression itself.

SIGNS OF COUNTERPRODUCTIVE BEHAVIOR

Difficulties in employee relations do not always arise because of deep-seated personality problems or differences in basic behavioral styles. Sometimes difficulties arise due to employee immaturity or unprofessional attitudes. People in the work environment can be counterproductive for a variety of reasons ranging from lack of understanding to overwhelming personal problems.

There are several psychological techniques that can be used with people who are counterproductive. Some of the techniques can be used in any situation; others assume that one has formal power over the persons involved. Sometimes it is necessary to confront people because of their counterproductive behavior. This technique is not relished by many. It requires tact and confrontation skills. People are not usually amenable to change, rather they resist and fear it. When people are asked to change their behavior, they may become more defensive, angry, and hostile.

From the vantage point of a manager, signs of counterproductive behavior include (1) disrespect, (2) lack of cooperation, and (3) passive and aggressive behaviors. These behaviors are discussed below, along with the techniques that can be used to change them.

Disrespect

A newly appointed female manager should not ignore signs of disrespect from either male or female subordinates, because this could possibly erode her referent power. Although it is common to encounter resistance from male subordinates, she also can meet resistance from other women who feel resentment and inadequacy, especially when they perceive another woman has bypassed them in positions of power historically denied to them. Other women's disrespect and negative actions must be dealt with as firmly and directly as male encroachment. When the manager encounters female subordinates acting in negative ways, it may help to remember that their actions are probably based on naivete or hurt feelings rather than on maliciousness. In any case, a woman manager should calm herself and practice the techniques of coaching and confronting.

When a female subordinate acts in an unprofessional manner, the manager should call her in and explain the implications for the employee's ambitions. The manager should make sure the tone of the discussion is friendly, helpful, and calm rather than threatening or antagonistic. Male supervisors and subordinates expect this kind of coaching, and it is just as crucial to the careers of female supervisors and subordinates.

Lack of Cooperation

Signs of lack of cooperation include substandard performance or defensive and hostile actions. Look at the following scenario. Anna comes back from lunch on Friday a little giggly and light-headed from her noontime overindulgence, and does not work effectively for the remainder of the day. This leaves her boss, Stacie, with a backlog of work and many errors to be corrected. It is her responsibility to confront Anna with the effect Anna's behavior is having on her.

Although the manager may not enjoy having to deal with the above situation, some guidelines for effective confrontation can help Stacie in her chances of producing a productive and satisfactory relationship. First of all, she should try to *relax* during the confrontation. If she appears too tense, she may leave the impression that she is not confident. Sometimes a role-playing session or rehearsal will help ease the tension. She should plan carefully her words and state her feelings using "I" statements. "Anna, you are a giving person, but when you come back late, I feel. . . ."

A manager will want to vary this technique with the individual and the situation, but she should try to *get to the point* as soon as possible. She should not waste time talking about unimportant issues to ease the tension because the tension is already there!

The manager should *not apologize* or be defensive about the confrontation. This will only weaken her authority. While she wants to be considerate, she must also be firm and uncompromising. She should confront the employee in a nonhostile manner. She can share feelings of anger and frustration productively; but if she is openly hostile, her subordinate's reaction will probably be hostile also. This will lead to a counterproductive outcome.

The manager should *talk about behavior that she notices*, not about inferences that she is gathering from the behavior. For example, she should not tell Anna that something must be bothering her if Anna is drinking too heavily. Rather, she should talk about the behavior she notices. In this case, work on Friday afternoons is not being finished on time. This is a legitimate organization concern.

Many women managers prefer to avoid confrontation in order to prevent any conflict at all. Other women prefer to spend their time in noninfluential roles rather than become involved in power struggles and conflicts. In contrast, men have been taught to overemphasize power and they have been rewarded for doing so. Many even enjoy one-up, one-down interactions even when these are unnecessary or counterproductive.

Many women managers tend to resist taking charge in conflict situations, even when assertive behavior is entirely appropriate. Others actually give away their power or turn to others for help rather than confront the situation themselves.[6] Female socialization may be the cause where women are conditioned to seek help from others rather than be self-reliant. Many women managers have been socialized to accept limited resources rather than assertively hustle for the extra people or capital they need for their own projects. These habits result in failures to demand adequate resources they need. To be effective managers, women need to confront conflict situations in the most appropriate manner.

Passiveness and Aggressiveness

Some subordinates want to be led while others desire increased independence and responsibility. The manager should take the reins and provide clear directions for those who seek them. However, she should be careful not to turn over too much of her decision-making power to aggressive subordinates, since this could lead to losing part of her legitimate right to have the final say.

The manager *should not expect subordinates to do something because they "ought" to do it*. Genuine differences of opinion always occur about what should be done. The manager should observe her employees closely to learn what incentives motivate her employees to help her achieve her objectives. One important measure of managerial skill is the art of persuasion despite differing opinions.

It is not always a good strategy to be "fair" to subordinates. Being "fair" to a passive person often leads to excessive hand-holding. Being "fair" to an aggressive, manipulative person might enable that person to take over the manager's power and her job. The manager must clearly be in command. If she is not, she may be perceived as weak. Such weakness may produce rivalries and resentments among subordinates who may come to think they are more qualified to handle her position than she is. The manager should be firm, yet courteous, and she will generate respect and genuine loyalty while keeping hurt feelings to a minimum.

It is necessary to criticize subordinates for their mistakes. Without feedback, a manager's subordinates will not develop an appreciation of the manager's standards nor will they learn from their mistakes. The way she hands out criticism is what counts. Criticism without courtesy can make a passive person feel put down and defensive, or even create the desire for revenge.

A manager should level with subordinates through authentic feedback. **Authentic feedback** consists of nonevaluative interpretations of how a person's or a group's behavior affects one's objectives. It can often lead to increased understanding and decreased resistance to directions when the personal need for feedback is demonstrated and accepted. Sometimes leveling off is done in emotional and evaluative manners. While this type of confrontation may be risky, it helps to get feelings out and it opens the door to suppressed organizational problems. It is certainly better than suppressing hostile feelings and later transferring them to inappropriate people or circumstances.

Another way to suggest improvements without bringing out defensive behavior requires giving *corrective information in terms of another person or another group in a similar situation.* For this tactic to be effective, the receivers should recognize that their behavior is similar to the other reference person or group. If the awareness is present, indirect comparisons allow the employees to evaluate the manager's suggestions without losing face and becoming defensive.

APPROACHES TO INTERPERSONAL CONFLICT SITUATIONS

In each of the counterproductive situations described above, a conflict between the needs of the manager and the employee was brewing. **Con-**

flict is a disagreement between two or more organization members where the concerns of the people involved appear to be incompatible. The main sources of conflict in organizations are disputes over shared resources, differences in goals, interdependence of work activities, and differences in values or perceptions.

Although some women may have developed a tendency to avoid conflicts earlier in their careers, when they become managers they acquire the responsibility to confront and manage them productively. The specifics of how the manager deals with the person she is in conflict with will depend upon her unique situation and skills. According to Ruble and Thomas, conflict situations tend to make people primarily concerned with either satisfying their own concerns or cooperating with others to maintain a satisfactory relationship.[7] These two basic dimensions of own need versus the needs of others can be combined to define five specific methods of dealing with conflicts (see Figure 9-1). These methods are: (1) **competing**, (2) **accommodating**, (3) **avoiding**, (4) **collaborating**, and (5) **compromising**.

After reading the descriptions of common problem-solving approaches given below, the manager may feel that one is most characteristic of her. Since none of these approaches is better or worse than any other per se, she should judge the appropriateness of her preferred mode based on how effective it is for the particular situation in which she most frequently finds herself. Some guidelines for when each mode is most appropriate follow the descriptions.

Competing

Competing is assertive and uncooperative behavior where individuals pursue their own concerns at another person's expense. This is often a power-oriented mode of behavior where one uses every technique available to win one's point or defend one's position. Competing is the stereotypical male response.

Competing is most helpful in situations where quick, decisive action is vital, e.g., in emergencies. It is also useful where unpopular courses of action, such as discipline or cost cutting, must be implemented. Finally, competing is a necessary mode of behavior in conflict situations where one must protect oneself against people who take advantage of noncompetitive behavior. The manager should be careful not to be too competitive, however. If she is, she may find herself surrounded by yes men who have learned that it is unwise to disagree with her and, consequently, will close her off from sources of important information.

FIGURE 9-1

APPROACHES TO INTERPERSONAL CONFLICT

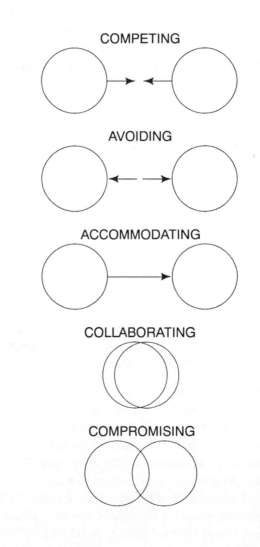

COMPETING

AVOIDING

ACCOMMODATING

COLLABORATING

COMPROMISING

Accommodating

Accommodating is the opposite of competing. It consists of unassertive and cooperative behavior. Oftentimes accommodating individuals neglect their own concerns in order to satisfy the needs of others. Consequently, this appears as a selfless generosity, or a submissive behavior in compliance with another person's wishes. Often this has been considered as the typical feminine response.

Accommodating is a useful strategy for the manager when the issue at stake is much more important to the other person than to her. Satisfying another's needs as a goodwill gesture will help maintain a cooperative relationship. It builds up social credits for later issues and is used appropriately when the manager is concerned about developing subordinates by allowing them to experiment and learn from their mistakes. She must be careful, however, not to deprive organizational members of her personal contributions or to create a climate where discipline becomes lax.

Avoiding

Avoiding is unassertive and uncooperative behavior where individuals do not pursue either their own concerns or those of others. In avoiding the conflict altogether, a person might diplomatically sidestep an issue, postpone it, or withdraw from the threatening situation. All too often this response is manifested by new female managers who are still uncertain about acting in more assertive manners.

Avoiding is useful when the issue of disagreement has passing importance or is relatively trivial to the manager. Also, if she is in a low-power position or encounters a situation that is very difficult to change, avoiding may be the best use of her time. Potential damage of confronting a conflict may outweigh its benefits. She may need to let people cool off a little in order to bring tensions back down to a productive level and regain perspective and composure. On the other hand, she should not let important decisions be made by default or spend a abnormal amount of energy in avoiding issues that eventually must be confronted.

Collaborating

Collaborating is the opposite of avoiding; it consists of assertive and cooperative behavior. It involves an attempt to work with the other person to find a solution that fully satisfies the concerns of both parties. This is a joint problem-solving mode involving a lot of communication and creativity on the part of each party to find a mutually beneficial solution.

Collaborating is a necessity when an integrative solution is required in cases where the concerns of both parties are too important to be compromised. Collaborating merges the insights of people with different perspectives. It allows the manager to test her assumptions and understanding of others, to gain commitment by incorporating others' concerns, and to win an opportunity to get rid of hard feelings. Not all conflict situations, however, deserve this amount of time and energy. Trivial problems often do not require optimal solutions, and not all personal differences need to be worked through. It also does her little good to behave in a collaborative manner if others do not do the same and take advantage of what she is trying to accomplish.

Compromising

Compromising falls somewhere between assertive and cooperative behaviors. The objective is to find a mutually acceptable middle ground which is expedient and partially satisfies both parties. It is manifested by splitting the difference, engaging in concessions, or seeking middle ground positions.

A compromise is useful when goals are moderately important and not worth the effort of collaboration or the possible disruption of competition. If the manager is dealing with an opponent of equal power who is strongly committed to a mutually exclusive goal, compromise may be the best hope for leaving both of them in relatively satisfactory positions. The same would be true if there were a high degree of time pressure and she needed to achieve a temporary settlement very quickly. Compromise is a useful safety valve for gracefully getting out of mutually destructive situations. On the other hand, concentrating on compromise so heavily might mean the manager loses sight of more important principles, values, and long-term objectives. Too much compromise can also create a cynical climate of gamesmanship.

PREVENTION OF UNNECESSARY CONFLICT

Some level of conflict may be beneficial when it opens up new alternatives and improved ways of doing things, but conflict is destructive, especially conflict generated from personality problems or counterproductive attitudes. There are some things that the manager can do, however, to prevent negative conflict from ever getting started.

Get Initial Agreement

The manager should get an initial agreement with persons or groups who object to her attempts at wielding influence. This important step insures her willingness to work with them. She has something in common with them and this then serves to favorably influence them while building her referent power. If she contradicts herself later or proposes contrary approaches, they are more apt to be open to her and her ideas if they believe that she is similar to them.

Offer a Limited Choice of Alternatives

People like to feel some power over what happens to them, but when faced with an unlimited number of alternatives to choose from, they have difficulty deciding. The strategy of providing a limited choice maximizes the manager's chances that others will accept her request. She lets them make a choice, but only from alternatives acceptable to her. One key strategy would be to phrase her questions as if a given event *will* take place, and that others would have to choose how or when this event will take place. When people are confronted with a limited choice of alternatives and asked to choose from them, most often they will do so. Only rarely will they question initial assumptions or raise additional alternatives.

Compare the following approach, "Can we get together sometime to discuss ways of improving this situation?" with one that says, "I've arranged to have the conference room available on either Monday or Friday afternoon to discuss how we can change this situation. Which day do you prefer?"

Illus. 9.2
Communicating positive
expectations makes
employees feel they are
important and are doing
something valuable for the
manager.

Obtain a Commitment in Advance

Obtaining a commitment in advance creates an obligation to implement something later. The advantages and disadvantages of a commitment become more prominent at different times. The advantages are clearer when the event is to take place in the distant future. As the event becomes more immediate, however, the disadvantages become more eminent. Since most people feel compelled to meet their obligations, it is to the manager's advantage to gain a commitment to participate in an activity well in advance of its planned occurrence. If participants feel that they have made a prior commitment, they will find it more difficult to back out when the anxieties associated with the approach of the event occur.

Communicate Positive Expectations

Communicating positive expectations fosters success. Indicating to a person that he or she is expected to be a valuable participant can often act as a self-fulfilling prophecy. That is, the employee will behave in such a way to prove worthy of the manager's high regard that the manager's expectations will be fulfilled. Successful use of this approach also decreases begrudging participation because employees feel that they are important and are doing something valuable for the manager—which they are.

Use Compliments as Positive Motivators

Compliments are positive motivators. Trying to get someone to act through criticism has negative consequences even if the strategy produces results. People usually take criticism as a slap in the face and react defensively and with hostility toward its source. The manager should phrase her criticism in positive terms and frost it with preceding compliments. For example, a line manager could say to a staff group leader, "We like your work very much. If your people would personally relate your ideas with ours, we could probably make even better use of all of our ideas." Compare this statement with, "Your people think they are such experts that they won't even come down off their high horse to relate as human beings so that we can understand what they're talking about."

ACTION GUIDELINES

Dealing with difficult employees is inevitable. A manager's effectiveness in turning around a potentially counterproductive situation depends upon her abilities to correctly diagnose what is going on, to discern the appropriate corrective behavior, and to implement that behavior effectively. The following guidelines summarize the appropriate actions to take after she has confronted a difficult situation:

1. When the manager encounters a behavioral style mismatch, she should first determine her subordinate's style and then behave so as to decrease tension and build trust. With Expressives, she shouldn't hurry; she should be entertaining and check the details of any agreements. With Drivers, she should be precise, efficient, well organized, and businesslike. With Analyticals, she should be systematic, organized, prepared, and factual. With Amiables, she should show personal interest and be more informal.

2. When dealing with employees who have personality problems, the manager should leave the solution of their personal difficulties to a qualified psychiatrist or psychologist. She should avoid disruptions and keep the subordinates productive and at work. With oversensitive employees, she should avoid undermining their self-confidence and try to praise and reassure them as much as possible. With hostile employees, she should listen for the underlying source of frustration and set up a later meeting, when feelings have cooled down, to explain the guidelines for acceptable behavior and to refer the employee for counseling. With negative employees, she should attempt to reverse their attitudes with a praise-and-compliment strategy, and always emphasize the positive.

3. When the manager encounters unprofessional attitudes or behavior in subordinates, she cannot afford to ignore them, because these could erode her managerial power base. If a subordinate treats her with disrespect, she should explain the implications of these actions in a calm, professional way. When confronting a subordinate about counterproductive behavior, she should not apologize; she should get to the point as quickly as possible, making sure that she discusses actual behavior rather than inferences regarding its source. She should not expect employees to do something because they *ought* to do it. She should be firm, yet courteous, when giving them directions. When it is necessary to criticize subordinates for mistakes, she should use authentic feedback and indirect comparisons to allow them to evaluate her suggestions without losing face and becoming defensive.

4. In conflict situations, the manager should react in the manner most appropriate for the situation. She should: *compete* in emergency situations where quick decisive action is necessary; *accommodate* when the issue at stake is much more important to the other person than to her and when she wants to build goodwill; *avoid* when the issue of disagreement is trivial to her or when the potential damage of the conflict outweighs the benefits; *collaborate* when an integrative solution is required to meet two equally important opposing needs; and *compromise* when goals are moderately important and not worth the effort of collaboration to escape a mutually destructive situation or to meet time deadlines.

5. The manager should prevent unnecessary conflicts by using the strategies of getting initial agreement, offering a limited choice of

alternatives, obtaining a commitment in advance, communicating positive expectations, and using compliments as positive motivators.

KEY TERMS

abrasive personality — a person whose primary characteristics are self-centeredness, isolation, perfectionism, contempt for others, and a tendency to attack others

accommodating — an approach to interpersonal conflict situations that consists of unassertive and cooperative behavior to satisfy the needs of the other person

Amiables — behavioral style of employees who are highly responsive, relatively unassertive, supportive, and reliable, but are slow to take action

Analyticals —tbehavioral style of employees who are persistent, systematic problem solvers and whose actions and decisions tend to be extremely cautious and slow

authentic feedback — feedback that consists of nonevaluative interpretations of how a person's or a group's behavior affects the feedback giver

avoiding — an approach to interpersonal conflict situations that consists of unassertive and uncooperative behavior in order to diplomatically sidestep an issue, postpone it, or withdraw from a threatening situation

collaborating — an approach to interpersonal conflict situations that consists of assertive and cooperative behavior in order to find a solution which fully satisfies the concerns of both parties

competing — an approach to interpersonal conflict situations that consists of assertive and uncooperative behavior in order to pursue one's concerns at another person's expense

compromising — an approach to interpersonal conflict situations that consists of splitting the difference, engaging in concessions, or seeking middle-ground positions in order to find a mutually acceptable middle ground that is expedient and partially satisfies both parties

conflict — a disagreement between two or more people where their concerns appear to be incompatible

Drivers — behavioral style of employees who are firm with others and oriented toward productivity and concerned with bottom-line results

Expressives — behavioral style of employees who are animated, intuitive, and lively but can be manipulative, impetuous, excitable, and spontaneous in making decisions

DISCUSSION QUESTIONS

1. Explain why a *Driver* and an *Amiable* might perceive each other as difficult individuals to get along with. What can either of them do to avoid this negative perception by the other?

2. What are some of the personality problems of employees that make them difficult to get along with? How can these symptoms be spotted? What should a manager do when confronted with a difficult employee who has a personality problem?

3. What are the symptoms of counterproductive behavior? What should you do when you become aware of them in a subordinate, a colleague, or a superior?

4. Name five (5) approaches in dealing with interpersonal conflict situations. Which would you select for dealing with someone who never compromises or never considers anybody else's needs? Why would you use this approach rather than one of the other four?

5. Describe five (5) methods of preventing unnecessary conflict. Which would you use when trying to reach a decision with a group of three very diverse individuals? Why?

CHAPTER CASE

HOW WOULD YOU HANDLE PHIL DARBY?

Pamela Adams graduated from the University of Texas with a B.S. degree in accounting in 1987. She passed the C.P.A. exam and took a job with Arthur Young. Recently she took a new job to become managing supervisor of the cost-accounting department at Xerox in San Diego, California.

Pamela has thirteen people reporting to her. They all have accounting degrees. They average four years of cost-accounting experience at Xerox, with a range of two to ten years. Although she has been on the job for only six months, Pamela already has some problems with employees that really concern her. Phil Darby, one of her cost-accountants, is her main problem. Phil is a bully who attempts to cow and overwhelm her. Cutting remarks, tantrums, and verbal aggression are his specialty. Also, Phil is always late for work and wants to leave early to get to the gym. Phil lives in Carlsbad (a community about 30 miles from the Xerox office) and explains that the traffic between Carlsbad and the office in the morning hours is extremely heavy. Pamela has told Phil that other people at Xerox live in Carlsbad and make it to work on time. She has also told him that his hours are setting a bad example for others in the office.

As if that weren't enough, Phil is constantly challenging Pamela's decisions as well as those of his colleagues. Phil is like a Sherman tank that always has to be right. He indiscriminately will roll over people to prove that he is right. The other accountants consider Phil to be a pain in the neck. As one colleague put it, "Our staff meetings would take half the time if Phil didn't attend. He wants to criticize and evaluate every issue. He is demeaning and rude to everyone else. Our time is valuable and most of us want to get these meetings over with quickly. I'm almost glad when he leaves early to go to the gym, even if it isn't fair."

QUESTIONS

1. If you were Pamela, how would you treat Phil's tardiness and early departures? Why?
2. What behavioral style do you think Phil exhibits? Why? How should you treat him? Explain.

3. If you were Pamela, how would you treat Phil's behavior in meetings and toward yourself and the rest of the staff?

ENDNOTES

[1] P. Hunsaker and A. J. Alessandra, *The Art of Managing People* (Englewood Cliffs, NJ: Prentice-Hall, 1980).

[2] J. Veiga, "Face Your Problem Subordinates Now!" *The Academy of Management Executive*, 2, 2 (May, 1988): 145-152.

[3] W. H. Weiss, "Supervising Employees with Personality Problems," *Supervisory Management*, 28, 2 (February, 1983): 8-13.

[4] Veiga, op. cit.

[5] Harry Levinson, "The Abrasive Personality," *Harvard Business Review* (May-June, 1978): 86-94; Ron Zemke, "Working with Jerks," *Training* (May, 1987): 27-35.

[6] A. G. Sargent, "The Androgynous Blend: Best of Both Worlds," *Management Review* (October, 1978): 60-65.

[7] T. L. Ruble and K. W. Thomas, "Support for a Two-Dimensional Model of Conflict Behavior," *Organizational Behavior and Human Performance*, 16 (1976): 143-155.

ADDITIONAL RESOURCES

Benfield, Clifford J. "Problem Performers: The Third-Party Solution." *Personnel Journal* (August, 1985): 96-101.

Peterson, Karen. "Holding Grudges Can Hold You Back." *USA Weekend* (October 18- 20, 1985): 28.

Powell, Jon. "Stress Listening: Coping With Angry Confrontation." *Personnel Journal* (May, 1986): 27-30.

Veiga, John F. "Face Your Problem Subordinates Now!" *The Academy of Management Executive* (May, 1988): 145-152.

Zemke, Ron. "Working with Jerks." *Training* (May, 1987): 27-38.

CHAPTER 10

HIRING
AND FIRING
EMPLOYEES

Recruiting Employees
   Job Analysis
   Recruitment Sources
   Laws Relevant To Equal Employment Opportunities and
     Affirmative Action
Screening the Applications
The Selection Interview
   Interviewing Candidates
   Good Questions
   Ambiguous Questions
   Poor Questions
The Hiring Decision
   Importance of the Background Check
   Methods of Checking References
Firing Employees
Action Guidelines
Key Terms
Discussion Questions
Chapter Case: Should Nancy Iverson Be Fired?
Endnotes
Additional Resources

Two important managerial responsibilities are selecting and discharging employees—responsibilities associated with the management function of staffing. More than anything else, employee selection should be seen as a *matching process*. How well an employee is matched to a job affects the quantity and quality of the employee's work (as well as the manager's subsequent work!). Workers who are unable to produce the expected quantity and quality of work can cost an organization money, time, and trouble. This chapter will be concerned with the hiring and firing of employees.

RECRUITING EMPLOYEES

In recruiting future employees, most organizations divide their recruiting function into at least two types. First, the organization uses a process called *general recruiting* for low-level positions. This continual process is directed at filling positions that frequently open up in most organizations. Examples of low-level positions include various clerical work, janitorial work, and other unskilled or semiskilled work. To fill higher level positions, an organization may opt for *specific recruiting*. This process is most appropriate for recruiting professional employees who are needed to do a specific or unique job.

For both general recruiting and specific recruiting, the two issues of job analysis and the sources of recruitment are very important for the woman manager.

Job Analysis

Before managers can recruit personnel, they must know what position is open. This is the purpose of job analysis.[1] **Job analysis** consists of a written statement that depicts the following: (1) a description that identifies the title, duties, and responsibilities for that position, and (2) hiring specifications or a definition of the desired background, experience, and personal characteristics an individual must have in order to perform effectively in the position. For example, an open position for an auditing manager in an accounting firm may state: "Position requires a BA or MS in accounting, CPA, minimum five years experience, some experience as a supervisor, and good interpersonal skills."

Recruitment Sources

Two main sources of recruitment can be used by managers: internal and external. The **internal recruitment sources** are those tapped within the organization. These may be existing employees or employee referrals (employees' friends). The recruiting is initiated by means of job posting within the organization's premises. Many organizations find it useful to recruit or promote existing employees to open positions because (1) individuals recruited from within will already be familiar with the organization, (2) it significantly reduces recruiting and placement costs, and (3) it fosters improved morale and loyalty among employees because they believe that consistently good performance will be rewarded with a promotion.[2]

External recruitment sources are also frequently used by organizations. They include walk-in applicants, placement/search firms, newspaper ads, college placement offices, unions, military services, and professional associations. The vast variety of external sources available will almost ensure that the organization will be able to find an adequate number of candidates. On the negative side, utilizing external sources can take a lot of time. Most organizations must interview between 20 and 30 candidates before one is hired. Newspaper ads also can be expensive, as is using a placement firm for more specialized or high-level managerial positions.

The growing body of research that has investigated the relationship between recruiting source and rates of turnover has yielded surprisingly consistent results.[3] These studies indicate that internal sources, particularly employee referrals, were consistently good sources of personnel who remained in the organization for a significant length of time. Employment agencies, on the other hand, were poor sources of long-term employees.

Laws Relevant To Equal Employment Opportunities and Affirmative Action

Certain laws affect organizations in their hiring practices. Since the early 1960s, the growing civil rights and women's movements called national attention to the discriminatory effects of existing human resource practices. The Equal Pay Act of 1963 and the Civil Rights Act of 1964 were important laws. These laws were expanded by the courts and most state legislatures, and through various amendments and executive orders. The implications of such legislation for managers is still evolving and being clarified by the courts.

Title VII of the Civil Rights Act of 1964 (later amended in 1972 and establishing the Equal Employment Opportunity Commission [EEOC] to enforce the provisions of Title VII), is the key legislation that prohibits employment discrimination on the basis of race, sex, age, religion, color, or national origin. These specifications for nondiscriminatory treatment are called *equal employment opportunity (EEO)* requirements. They apply to virtually all private and public organizations. Executive Order 11246 of 1965 and Executive Order 11375 of 1968 (later amended in 1977) required firms doing business with the federal government to make special efforts to recruit, hire, and promote women and members of minority groups. These requirements are called *affirmative action (AA)*.[4]

The Equal Pay Act, originally introduced in 1946, prohibits discrimination by employers on the basis of sex. Under provisions of this act, it is illegal to pay men higher wages than women for jobs equal in skill, effort, responsibility, and working conditions. The Equal Pay Act established the foundation for another concept known as **comparable worth**. Comparable worth is a doctrine that holds that jobs equal in value to the organization should be equally compensated, whether or not the work content of those jobs is similar. That is, if the jobs of secretary and draftsman (historically viewed as female and male jobs, respectively) require similar skills and make comparable demands on employees, they should be paid the same, regardless of external market factors.

Advocates of comparable worth point out that market forces and occupational segregation or the existence of an occupation dominated by one sex—such as nursing—create situations in which discrimination in pay can occur. In 1988, women made only about 68 cents for every dollar earned by men, a significant difference, which is attributed to occupational segregation. Comparable worth takes into account the actual skills and knowledge that are needed for jobs and that define a candidate's suitability for a position or category of positions; it seeks to invalidate patterns of wage and job discrimination—such as those based on sex or occupational segregation—that have often established or influenced salary guidelines.[5] The idea of comparable worth is controversial. It assumes that totally dissimilar jobs can be accurately compared and that pay rates based on supply and demand factors are inequitable and discriminatory.

Sexual harassment (unwanted sexual requests or advances or the creation of a sexually harassing environment through sexual jokes and remarks) when related to hiring or promotion decisions or the work environment violates Title VII.6 A 1978 amendment to Title VII, the Pregnancy Discrimination Act, prohibits dismissal of women because of pregnancy alone and protects their job security during maternity leaves.[7]

In the hiring process, the human resources department normally has prime responsibility for assuring compliance with equal employment opportunity and affirmative action provisions. Ultimately, all managers are affected because these provisions will determine the pool of available applicants.

Many organizations have affirmative action programs to assure that decisions and practices related to hiring do not discriminate against women and other minorities. Organizations have these programs for two reasons. First, on the ethical side, many organizations believe that they have a social responsibility to improve the status of protected group members and to redress previous inequalities in hiring, retention, and promotion decisions. Secondly, the economic cost of defending the organization against charges of discrimination can be staggering. As an example, Sears, Roebuck and Company spent over twelve years and $20 million in legal fees to defend itself successfully against accusations by the Equal Employment Opportunity Commission that its past hiring practices had discriminated against females.[8]

There have not been many new federal regulations in the 1980s on equal employment opportunity. However, the environment facing women managers remains highly dynamic. New laws and court findings concerning existing legislation will continue to influence hiring practices for years to come.

SCREENING THE APPLICATIONS

Once a position has been advertised, the manager of the unit involved may be inundated by resumes and letters of application. Many people may even call the manager directly about the position.

Certain steps are taken to process applications for jobs in most organizations. Variations on this basic progression depend upon organizational differences, including factors such as the size of the organization, nature of the jobs to be filled, number of people to be selected, and pressure of outside factors such as equal employment opportunity considerations mentioned in the previous section.

In some organizations selection activities, such as screening initial applications, may be centralized into a specialized unit within the personnel department. In others, the screening may be performed by the manager of the unit for which the position is to be filled. Regardless of who screens the initial applications, the emphasis should be on narrowing the pool of applicants generated by the recruiting activities to a select few. The emphasis should be on trying to match the best available persons with the jobs to be filled. These persons should be invited for a formal interview.

THE SELECTION INTERVIEW

Interviewing candidates is a very important step in hiring employees. First, for the organization and the candidate, it provides a great variety and volume of information about the other. Second, this face to face meeting is invaluable in determining the degree of fit or match with the organization's needs.

Three general types of interviews used most frequently are: (1) structured, (2) semistructured, and (3) unstructured. In the **structured interview**, the interviewer prepares a list of questions in advance and does not deviate from the list. This type of interview allows an interviewer to prepare questions which are job related, and then to complete a standardized evaluation. Companies under heavy pressure from the EEOC often use the structured interview because it provides documentation in the event anyone questions why one applicant was hired instead of another. The structured interview is also used when time pressures are present or when many candidates are being interviewed.

Illus. 10.1 Interviewing candidates for a job provides information for both parties and helps the employer determine the right match with the organization's needs.

The **semistructured interview** consists of a limited set of prepared questions that are asked of the candidate. This type of interview is used when there are few candidates to interview. Also, it allows for more flexibility than the structured interview.

Finally, in the **unstructured interview** little preparation other than a set of example topics is made. In this type of interview, the interviewer may ask general questions to prompt the applicant to discuss herself or himself. The interviewer then uses the applicant's responses to shape the next question. For example, if the applicant says, "I really enjoyed working with my manager at my previous job," the interviewer might then ask, "What type of manager do you most enjoy working with?"

While the interviewer/manager wants to gain as much information as possible from the candidate, limitations have been imposed resulting from antidiscrimination laws. Many questions that appear to be harmless can be construed as discriminatory in selection decisions. Unless a question relates directly to the job or to specific needs, it should not be asked. Many experts feel that the safest and fairest type of interview to use is the structured interview.[9] The structured interview is also the most *predictive* of actual job performance. This type of interview insures focused, well-organized, and more reliable outcomes.

Interviewing Candidates

Many people think interviewing is an innate talent. Just because an individual is personable and likes to talk is no guarantee that this person will be a good interviewer. The questioning techniques used by an interviewer can significantly affect the type and quality of information obtained.

Figure 10-1 (pages 281–282) provides a guide that the woman manager could use if she is interviewing applicants for a sales job. The chart identifies the relevant questions and explains the rationale behind each question. Of course, the answer given by the job applicant is assessed by the interviewer in light of what the interviewer wants in a candidate for that specific position. The purpose of the above mentioned exercise is to ask questions and find out if the job candidate will make a good employee.

Good Questions

The questioning techniques used in an interview significantly affect the type and quality of information obtained. Some types of questions provide more meaningful answers than others. Good interviewing techniques are dependent upon the use of open-ended questions directed toward a particular goal. An open-ended question is one that cannot be answered with a yes or no. *Who, what, when, why, tell me, how, which* are all good ways to begin questions that will produce longer, more meaningful, and informative answers. For example, "What was your attendance record on your last job?" is a better question than "Did you have a good attendance record on your last job?" The latter question can be answered with a simple yes or no.

The following is a list of 25 suggested questions which can elicit valuable information from an interviewee:

1. What type of job are you most interested in?

2. Why do you think you might like to work for our organization?

3. What jobs have you held in the past? How were they obtained, and why did you leave?

4. Why did you choose your particular field of work?

5. What do you know about our organization?

6. Why do you feel that you have received a good general education?

7. What qualifications do you have that make you feel that you will be successful in your field? How do they relate to the job for which you are applying?

8. What personal characteristics are necessary for success in your chosen field?

9. Why do you think you would like this particular job?

10. Do you prefer to work with others or by yourself?

11. What kind of boss do you prefer? Why?

12. What have you learned from your previous jobs that might help you in the position you are applying for?

13. What interests you in our organization?

14. What do you know about opportunities in the field in which you are trained?

15. During which hours of the day do you do your best work? Would you be willing to work at night?

16. What job in our organization would you choose if you were entirely free to do so? Why?

17. What jobs have you enjoyed the most? the least? Why?

18. What position in our organization do you wish to work toward? Why?

19. What have you done that demonstrates initiative and a willingness to work? Why do you say so?

20. How do you get along with your co-workers? Can you describe the kind of person you like to have as a colleague?

21. What is your major weakness? Why do you consider it a weakness?

22. Would you say you have an analytical mind, or are you more creative? What evidence do you have of this ability?

23. What are your unique talents or abilities?

24. What course in school did you like the best and why?

25. What course did you like least? Why?

Ambiguous Questions

Ambiguous questions often elicit important information from the person being interviewed. The questions below appear rather ambiguous on the surface. Immediately after each question is a parenthetical translation of these seemingly ambiguous questions.[10]

1. *Will you tell me a little bit about yourself?* Translates to: How much trouble have you taken to progress in your career? How well are you able to track your professional life?

2. *Why do you want to leave your current employer?* Translates to: What is the nature of your dissatisfactions and how rationally and coherently are you able to express them?

3. *Will you tell me some things about your current job?* Translates to: Give me a concisely expressed summary of your present responsibilities in a way that enables me to see how well your current work will have applications here.

4. *What do you think of your current management?* Translates to: To what extent are your present dissatisfactions likely to be duplicated here?

FIGURE 10-1

GUIDE TO IMPROVE EMPLOYMENT INTERVIEWING
FOR SALES-RELATED JOBS

Question	Purpose of Question
1. Why are you interested in a job with _____ ?	The interviewer should find out in detail what the candidate knows about the company's growth, product lines, pricing, quality, and service. How much research has the applicant done to sell himself or herself or to be familiar with the product he or she knows best? This is a good indicator of how the applicant would approach the selling of products.
2. What did you accomplish in your last job that you were most proud of?	Here the interviewer is looking for the applicant's real depth. The interviewer should listen for the applicant's figures, volumes, number of accounts opened, growth of his or her territory, increased profitability, etc., and make notes to verify the given information at a later date. The interviewer can get a good insight into the applicant from the value the applicant attaches to his or her accomplishments.
3. How did you get your previous jobs?	Here the interviewer is looking for the applicant's real depth. The interviewer should listen for the applicant's figures, volumes, number of accounts opened, growth of his or her territory, increased profitability, etc., and make notes to verify the given information at a later date. The interviewer can get a good insight into the applicant from the value the applicant attaches to his or her accomplishments.

FIGURE 10-1

GUIDE TO IMPROVE EMPLOYMENT INTERVIEWING
FOR SALES-RELATED JOBS (Cont'd)

Question

4. Which of your previous jobs did you like best and which least?

Purpose of Question

The interviewer should insist on specifics in the answer to this question! Was it the boss, the travel, the compensation plan, the product line, the territory, the opportunity, or some other element? The interviewer should keep coming back with a questioning "why?" It is normal to have preferences. Direct answers to these questions can give the interviewer specific information as to how the applicant will fit into the job for which he or she is being considered.

5. (a) What is the major asset that you can bring to _____?

Here is where the interviewer can learn about the applicant's confidence. Does the applicant really believe in himself or herself—or in the products he or she sells? If the applicant doesn't, no one else will!

5. (b) What are your major weaknesses?

The person who is aware of his or her faults can make an honest effort to correct them and, equally important, show insight and thought in evaluating his or her own situation. The applicant who candidly states that he or she has no faults is turning on the caution light—this should be followed up with straightforward, very direct questioning!

Poor Questions

The skillful interviewer will ask pertinent questions and glean much information from the applicant. However, certain kinds of questions should be avoided. Some of these poor questions are:

1. Questions that rarely produce a true answer. An example is "How did you get along with your coworkers?" This question is almost inevitably going to be answered with, "Just fine." Most job applicants are on good behavior and are not likely to reveal their weaknesses.

2. Leading questions. A leading question is one in which the answer is obvious from the way the question is asked. For example, when interviewing a person who is expected to have a good deal of public contact, the response to "You do like to talk to people, don't you?" will be "Of course."

3. Illegal questions. Questions eliciting information about race, creed, sex, age, national origin, marital status, and number of children are illegal.

4. Obvious questions. An obvious question is one for which the interviewer already has the answer (from the completed application form), and the applicant knows it. Questions already answered on the application blank should be probed, not asked again. If an interviewer asks, "What high school did you attend?", the applicant is likely to answer, "As I wrote on my application form, South High School in Milwaukee." Instead, the interviewer should ask questions that probe the information given such as, "What were your favorite subjects at South High, and why were they your favorite?"

5. Questions that are not job related. All questions asked should be directly related to the job for which the applicant has applied. Some people believe that a discussion about the weather, sports, or politics helps an applicant to relax. However, those questions consume interview time that could be more appropriately used in other ways. Also, many times the applicant does not relax; and the interviewer may not listen to the responses because he or she is using the chit-chat time to review the candidate's application

form or to otherwise make up for his or her lack of planning and preparation.

THE HIRING DECISION

Once the steps of recruiting, screening the applications, and interviewing are completed, the manager may be ready to make the job offer. At this point a background check is usually made.

Importance of the Background Check

The **background check** consists of verifying information obtained from the candidate and collecting additional references. An important group of references is the applicant's previous employers. The interviewer/manager should remember, however, that under the Fair Credit and Reporting Act, a prospective employer is required to secure the applicant's permission before checking references about the applicant's financial situation.[11]

A manager for a large petrochemical company had this to say about reference checks:

Unless you do your homework on reference checks, you may end up with good friends, relatives, and old cronies telling you that the candidate is able to do everything, including the ability to leap over tall buildings. I ask the applicant to provide me with the names of the harshest judges of his or her performance. I also like to check back over two previous employers.

Confirmation of hard data with a former employer is a worthwhile endeavor. Some studies indicate that approximately 15 percent of job applicants exaggerate or misrepresent dates of employment, job titles, past salaries, or reasons for leaving the job.[12]

Illus. 10.2   Since previous employers often hesitate to put negative information in writing, many managers prefer to have job candidate references checked by telephone.

Methods of Checking References

Several methods of obtaining information from references are available. Some managers feel that although reference checks are widely used, they are difficult to justify. Personal likes and dislikes can influence the type of reference given. Regardless, most organizations will still require reference checks. Telephoning a reference is the most widely used and preferred method because people are often hesitant to put negative information in writing. Most other methods are written ones. Some firms have preprinted reference forms that are sent to individuals who are acting as references for applicants. Specific or general letters of reference are requested by some employers and/or provided by applicants.[13] One successful woman manager commented that she telephones former bosses and asks only one question, "Would you hire this individual again if they were applying for a job with your organization?"

FIRING EMPLOYEES

When an employee is not able to perform adequately on a job, he or she may be discharged, or fired. Without a doubt, one of the most painful managerial tasks is to make the following statement to a subordinate:

"You're fired."

It is rarely said that way anymore. Today a more humanistic vocabulary exists, and a termination interview allows for more empathy. Yet, no matter what is said, the ultimate message is: You're fired, rejected, and unemployed.

Firing is the most drastic disciplinary action that a manager can take. It is done only for the most serious offenses. Altercations, theft, gambling, insubordination, and inability to perform the job are the most common reasons for firing employees.

When an employee is discharged, he or she loses all seniority standing and privileges. Since firing is such a drastic form of termination, careful documentation and consideration of the events justifying the discharge should be done by the woman manager.

It is often impossible to fire unionized workers in some organizations because of seniority rules, union-management contractual agreements, a limited supply of replacements, or the overall philosophy of the organization. In general, managers are reluctant to discharge employees. Managers often spend a great deal of energy rationalizing and procrastinating when making the decision to fire a subordinate. If a manager does not fire a problem employee, the manager is likely to become part of the problem also. According to Oberle:

Failure to administer disciplinary actions can result in implied acceptance or approval. Thereafter, problems may become more frequent or severe . . . and ultimately the supervisor will become ineffective in performing one of the primary responsibilities associated with such a position.[14]

Business Week recently advocated the following guidelines for firing employees: first, give poorly performing employees several warnings and a chance to improve before terminating them; second, make sure employees cannot claim age, gender, or race discrimination; third, be aware that oral agreements, initial-offer letters, and employee handbooks are implied contracts in some states; fourth, offer an outplacement service to senior executives, and fifth, avoid critical remarks if asked to give a reference for a terminated employee.[15]

If a woman manager, after carefully considering all factors, finds it necessary to fire an employee, she might find these guidelines useful and beneficial:

1. *Tell the employee why.* The basic requirements for firing are simple. The subordinate being fired must be told plainly that he or she has to leave the company, and must be told *why*. The woman manager should explain the dismissal in a way that allows employees to preserve their self-esteem and to explain to their friends and family why they were fired. Using tact, though, should not obscure the realities about an employee's infraction or inadequate performance.

2. *Tell the employee yourself.* A manager should undertake the firing of her direct subordinates by herself. Delegating the job to someone else is not fair to the employee being fired. Delegating the task of firing may give the employee an opportunity to muddy the issue by developing arguments about the merits of the case.

3. *Other matters.* The employee is entitled to know a number of matters. One concern involves how the employee's departure from the company will be made, and to what the departure will be attributed. A high-level employee will want to know how much time is left and whether, in the interim, he or she can use the office to arrange to have telephone messages taken. Also, the employee will want to know where the manager stands on providing future references.

ACTION GUIDELINES

The importance of staffing cannot be overemphasized. An organization needs people. Without human resources no organization survives. Each person must be attracted to that organization. It is the staffing process that matches jobs with people. The better the match, the better the performance of the organization, and the easier the manager's job!

Two of the most important aspects of the staffing process are the hiring and firing of employees. When a manager does a good job of matching the right employee with the right job, everyone benefits. The interview is of key importance and most research evidence concludes that structured and well-organized interviews are more reliable. When the manager asks good questions and makes a background check before she offers employment to an applicant, she can avoid costly mistakes and successfully complete the matching process.

KEY TERMS

affirmative action — requirement that firms doing business with the Federal government make special efforts to recruit, hire, and promote women and minorities

background check — an investigation verifying information obtained from a job candidate and collecting additional references

comparable worth — the principle that jobs requiring comparable skills and knowledge merit equal compensation even if the nature of the work activity is different

equal employment — requirements for non-discriminatory treatment in hiring

external recruitment sources — recruitment sources outside the organization

internal recruitment sources — recruitment sources within the organization

job analysis — the preparation of a statement that depicts a job description and an acknowledgment of the desired background, experience, and personal characteristics of a person to fill that position

semistructured interview — a type of interview consisting of a limited set of prepared questions to ask of the job candidate

structured interview — a type of interview consisting of a prepared list of questions to ask of a job candidate from which the interviewer does not deviate

unstructured interview — a type of interview consisting of little preparation on the part of the interviewer other than a set of example topics

DISCUSSION QUESTIONS

1. What are the merits of internal promotion, and when should a manager look to external recruitment sources?

2. What are the interviewing considerations a manager should keep in mind when determining the format and structure of the interview?

3. During an interview, what kinds of questions should a manager ask? avoid?

4. How should a manager approach the task of firing an employee?

5. What is the importance of the managerial staffing function, and what are its implications for the organization?

CHAPTER CASE

SHOULD NANCY IVERSON BE FIRED?

Sarah Darby is concerned about her employee, Nancy Iverson, and has come for advice: "I hired Nancy because we knew each other and really liked each other during our days at the University of Wisconsin. Nancy was a real leader on campus and we had always worked well together on campus affairs. Nancy was the kind of person I wanted in this organization—a lot of drive, originality, and ambition.

"Nancy has proven that she is a top-notch performer and will probably be our number one salesperson in a year or two, but she has a problem. She is the sort of person that has absolutely no respect for the organization itself. She just does not follow procedures. I am no go-by-the-book person myself, but she is unreal. For example, a really good order will come in, and Nancy will go straight to the plant and start in on the people until the order is delivered. It doesn't make any difference that other people's orders are in front of hers or how it might affect the production schedule. The order gets out because Nancy makes herself a royal pain until it does.

"But her approach has caused havoc with the production schedule. She tells the engineering people how to improve the product. She has the purchasing department people hiding when they see her coming. The other sales reps are, of course, upset with her. Her pushiness and aggressiveness cause their orders to be held up and their clients are mad. They are probably a little bit jealous too, since she is making so much more in commissions than they are. The customers think she can walk on water, though. Everyone else though hates the woman and constantly complain about her.

"I have spoken with Nancy about this on more than a few occasions. She always promises to follow the chain of command. She does for a few days, but then she reverts to her usual ways. I understand what she is doing, and in a way I admire it, but the effect it has on the other sales reps is bad and the morale of the entire organization is suffering. Should I fire Nancy and loose a star salesperson?"

QUESTIONS

1. What are the problems and issues as you see it in this case?

2. Should Nancy Iverson be fired?

3. What guidelines should Sarah Darby set up for Nancy Iverson to follow?

4. What steps should be taken if Nancy is eventually fired?

ENDNOTES

[1] James Stoner, *Management* (Englewood Cliffs, NJ: Prentice Hall, 1989), 334.

[2] Ibid., 335.

[3] P. J. Decker and E. T. Cornelius, "A Note on Recruiting Sources and Job Survival Rates," *Journal of Applied Psychology* (August, 1979): 463-464.

[4] A. Hart, "Intent vs. Effect: Title VII Case Law That Could Affect You," *Personnel Journal* 63 (1984): 31-47 and 50-58.

[5] George Ritzer and David Walczak, *Working: Conflict and Change*, 3rd ed. (Englewood Cliffs, NJ: Prentice Hall, 1986), 104-106; John B. Golper, "The Current Legal Status of 'Comparable Worth' in the Federal Sector," *Labor Law Journal*, 34 (1983): 563-580; Golper, *Pay Equity and Comparable Worth* (Washington, D.C.: Bureau of National Affairs, 1984), 13-34; and Marsha Katz, Helen Lavan, and Maura Malloy, "Comparable Worth: Analysis of Cases and Implications for Human Resource Management," *Compensation and Benefits Review* (May-June, 1986): 26-38.

[6] T. L. Leap, William H. Holley, Jr., and Hubert S. Field, "Equal Employment Opportunity and Its Implications for Personnel Practices in the 1980s," *Labor Law Journal*, 31, no. 11 (November, 1980): 669-682; and Francine S. Hall and Maryann H. Albrecht, *The Management of Affirmative Action* (Santa Monica, CA: Goodyear, 1979), 1-23. See also David P. Twomey, *A Concise Guide to Employment Law* (Cincinnati: South-Western, 1986).

[7] R. Tear and J. Ross, *Jobs, Dollars and EEO* (New York: McGraw Hill, 1983), 17-20.

[8] S. Weiner, "Sears' Costly Win in a Hiring Suit," *Wall Street Journal* 18 March 1986.

[9] R. Cochran, J. Cochran, and M. Jennings, "Legal Restrictions in Interviewing and Hiring," *Journal of Accountancy* (September, 1982): 41.

[10] S. Landau and G. Bailey, "What Every Woman Should Know," *Organizational Reality: Reports from the Firing Line*, ed. P. Frost, V. Mitchell, and W. Nord (Glenview, IL: Scott, Foresman and Company, 1982), 15.

[11] Robert Mathis and John Jackson, *Personnel: Human Resource Management*, 4th ed. (St. Paul, MN: West Publishing Co., 1985), 263.

[12] "Firms Tighten Resumé Checks of Applicants," *Wall Street Journal* 20 August 1985.

[13] D. B. Wonder and Kenneth S. Kelemen, "Increasing the Value of Reference Information," *Personnel Administrator* (March, 1984): 98-103.

[14] R. Oberle, "Administering Disciplinary Actions," *Personnel Journal* (January, 1978): 57.

15. *Business Week* (June 6, 1988): 168.

ADDITIONAL RESOURCES

Braham, James. "Hiring Mr. Wrong." *Industry Week* (March 7, 1988): 31-34.

"Fire Power." *Fortune* (May 30, 1983): 48.

Powell, Gary. "The Effects of Sex and Gender on Recruitment," *Academy of Management Review* (April, 1987): 731-743.

"Privacy." *Business Week* (March 28, 1988): 61- 68.

INDEX

A

acceptance, defined, 46
accessories:
   and image, 72
   guidelines on use of, 72
accomplishments:
   and career planning, 90
   defined, 46
   documenting, 106
active listening, 159, 162
adaptation techniques, 134-136
affairs and power, 206-207
affirmative action, 274, 275:
   laws relevant to, 274, 275
Agee, William, 207
aggressive behaviors, 10, 254,
    265-257
aggressor, 228
Alpander, G. G., 18
American Management
   Association, 46, 74
amiable behavioral style, 249, 250
analytical behavioral style, 249,
   250
Anthony, S.B., 44
appearance, and first
   impressions, 66-68
applications, screening, 276
association power, 194
attending, and listening, 162
authentic feedback, 257
authority:
   and age, 96
   and confrontation with

   uncooperative employees, 255
   and dress, 66
   and legitimate power, 191
   and use of apologies, 154
   and women managers, 186, 188,
    189, 191, 198
   delegation of, 50
   earned, defined, 208
avoider, 228

B

background check:
   defined, 284
   importance of, 284
Barnett, R. 142
barriers, 6:
   and controlling, 49
   between doing and managing,
    6-9
   external, 5
   internal, 6
   overcoming, in communication
    process, 163
   to career development, 92, 96
Barton, C., 4
Baruch, G. 142
behavioral flexibility, 249
behavioral styles:
   amiable style, 249, 250
   analytical style, 249, 250
   driving style, 249
   expressive style, 249

293

mismatch of, manager and
  employee, 248-251
behaviors:
  adopting a masculine style of,
    197
  aggressive, 10, 256-257
  and personality, 248
  assertive, 256, 261
  cooperative, 261
  corrective, 262
  counterproductive, signs of,
    254
  emotional, and styles, 230
  group role, 189, 225-228
  language, 154
  learned, 15
  maintenance role, 227
  passive, 9-10, 256
  power-oriented, 256
  relationship-oriented, 46
  self-oriented, 228
  task-related, 48, 226
biofeedback, and stress, 136
Birdsall, D., 16
blocker, 228
breadth of knowledge, 66:
  defined, 77
  increasing, 77
Brief, A. P., 16
business etiquette, 66, 75

C

career:
  advancement, strategies for,
    96-98
  and adopting a masculine
    style of behavior, 197
  and being visible, 99
  and courtesy, 199
  and delegation, 216
  and feminine characteristics,
    195-196
  and high performance, 99
  and human emotions, 190
  and image, 66
  and mentors, 102

  and seeking entry into old boys'
    network, 197-198
  and sex-role conditioning, 190
  barriers to development, 92-96
  defined, 88
  meanings of, 88
  planning, 90-92
  setting goals, 91
  steps in planning, 90-92
  strategies, 96-98
  woman manager's, and power,
    195-198
career alternatives:
  entrepreneurs, women as, 114
  home, working out of, 114
  job sharing, 115
career concepts, 89
career dilemmas:
  commuter marriage, 111
  dual career couples, 111-112
  linear career crisis, 113
  mommy track, 111, 112-113
career development strategies,
    196
career management, 128
Carr-Ruffino, Norma, 19, 67
Chusmir, L., 16
Cinderella complex, 17
Civil Rights Act, 274
clothing:
  and authority, 66
  and image, 66, 69-72
  specific guidelines on, 70-72
coercive power, 192
Colwill, Nina, 7, 9
communication:
  and distortions to match
    expectations, 158
  and distrust, 159
  and emotional involvement,
    158
  and group decision making,
    223
  and group processes, 225
  and hidden intentions, 157
  and maintenance role
    behaviors, 226-228
  and misperceptions, 158-159
  and preoccupation with tasks,
    157

as component of leadership, 44
as management skill, 151
effective, and management
    functions, 151
effective, need for, 151
patterns, in groups, 223
persuasiveness, developing,
    166-168
process, 151
roadblocks to effective two-
    way, 156-159
special problems for women,
    150-156
time spent on, 150
variables, 223
communication effectiveness, 150-
    151:
    and hypercorrect or
        excessively polite speech,
        153
    and weak speech patterns,
        152-154
communication process, 150:
    and gatekeeping, 202
    ways to overcome barriers to,
        163-166
commuter marriage, 111
comparable worth, 276
conditioning, traditional
    cultural, 108
conflict
    and accommodating, 258, 260
    and avoiding, 258, 260
    and collaborating, 258, 261
    and competing, 258
    and compromising, 258, 261
    and emotional styles, 230
    and mentor relationship, 108
    as opportunity for growth and
        creativity, 35
    between manager and
        employees, 257
    between manager and
        organization, 97
    defined, 257-258
    interpersonal, approaches to,
        257-261
    unnecessary, prevention of,
        262-264
consensus-testing method, 225

control and power, 229
controllers, women as, 49
controlling, 48-50:
    aids, 49-50
    and lower-level supervisors, 51
    as management function, 36,
        48-49
    defined, 48
    percentage of workday spent
        on, 54
coping techniques, 133-137
credibility:
    and clothing, 68
    and communication, 164-166
    and depth of knowledge, 76-77
    and self-fulfilling prophecy,
        166
    and speech characteristics,
        164-166
critical mass, 222
Cunningham, Mary, 207

D

dating, and power, 205-206
decisions:
    advantages of groups in
        making, 224-225
    hiring, 284-285
    made by others, 68
    minority, defined, 225
    procedures for making, 225
    weaknesses of groups in
        making, 224-225
Decyk, R., 22
delegating:
    and building power, 216
    ineffective, reasons for, 217
    to groups, 219
    useful principles of, 218
delegation:
    and female managers, 216
    defined, 40
    effective, steps for, 41
Department of Health, Education,
    and Welfare, 137
depth of knowledge, 66:

defined, 75
discrimination:
    and compensation, 274
    and EEOC, 274
    based on sex, 276
Dole, E., 44, 193
dominator, 228
Donnell, S., 16
Dowling, Colette, 17
Driver, M., 89
driving behavioral style, 249
dual career couples, 111-112
Durand, D., 16

E

Eisenhower, Dwight D., 40
emotional behaviors:
    and styles, 230-232
    denial of all emotion, 230
    show of tender emotions, 230
    show of tough emotions, 230
    types of, 230-232
emotional styles, types of,
        230-232:
    friendly helper style, 230-231
    logical thinker style, 232
    tough battler style, 231-232
empathy, and feedback, 173
employees:
    and manager, mismatch of
        behavioral styles, 248-251
    firing, 286-287
    hostile or angry, 251-253
    negative, 253
    oversensitive, 251
    personality problems of,
        251-254
    recruiting, 272-275
    selecting and discharging of,
        272
enthusiasm:
    and finding a mentor, 105
    and image, 66, 78-79
entrepreneurs, women as, 114
Equal Employment Opportunity
    Commission, 272

equal employment opportunity,
    laws relevant to, 274-275
Equal Pay Act, 274
Etiquette, business, 66, 75
Executive Order 11246, 274
Executive Order 11375, 274
exercise, and stress, 134
expert power, 193
expressive behavioral style, 249

F

Fair Credit and Reporting Act,
    284
feedback:
    adequate, need for, 169-173
    and controlling, 49
    and empathy, 173
    and mixed signals, 171
    and performance, 93
    authentic, defined, 257
    defined, 169
    direct and critical, 227
    effective use of, 173-176
    fact, 172
    feeling, 173
    nonverbal, 171-172
    types of, 169-173
    verbal, 170
female sex roles, pressures of,
    7-9
Fenn, M., 6
firing employees, 286-287
firing, guidelines for, 287
first impressions:
    based on appearance, 66-68
flexibility, 36:
    in leading, 46
flings, 206
flirtation, and power, 204
Fonda, Jane, 193
Foxworth, J., 4

G

game playing, 4, 11
Gandhi, Indira, 44
gatekeeping, 202
glass ceiling, 22, 23, 94
goal balancing, 32-34
goal setting, 91
goals:
    and emotional issues, 229
    and finding a mentor, 106
    clear-cut, and career
        satisfaction, 97
    planning for, 37
    specific, setting of, 91-92
group processes:
    and communication patterns,
        223
    and decision-making procedures,
        224
    and emotional issues, 228-229
    key, 223-229
group role behaviors, 224-228:
    and group processes, 225
    maintenance 227-228
    self-oriented, 228
groups:
    advantages in decision making
        by, 224-225
    and emotional behaviors and
        styles, 230
    and emotional issues, 228-229
    and identity, 228-229
    communication patterns and
        sex composition, 223
    delegating to, 219
    decision-making procedures,
        224-225
    effective management of, 232
    key processes, 222-229
    male-dominated, overcoming of
        female stereotypes in,
        221-222
    problems of women in, 221-222
    sex differences in, 221
    sex ratios of, 221
    weaknesses in decision making,
        224-225

H

Hall, J. 16
Hancock, E., 22
handclasp, defined, 224
Handlon, Joseph H. 17
Harris, D., 22
Heinen, J. S., et al., 17, 18
helpmate role, 7
help seeker, 228
Hennig, Margaret, 7, 11
hiring decision, 284-285
Hollander, E. P., 15
home, working out of, 114
Horn, J. C. 186
Horn, P. D., 186
Hull, J. B., 17
human resource planning, 42

I

image:
    and assertiveness, 73
    and career tactic, 66, 67
    and clothing, 66, 69-72
    and hypercorrect or
        excessively polite speech,
        153
    and mixed messages, 108
    and proper business etiquette,
        75
    and role models, 222
    defined, 66
    overall, 73
influence, defined, 190
information power, 190, 193-194
initiative, defined, 46
interpersonal conflict:
    and accommodating, 258-260
    and amiable style, 212
    and avoiding, 258, 260
    and collaborating, 258, 261
    and competing, 258
    and compromising, 258, 268
    approaches to, 257-261
interpersonal power:
    and being assertive, 198

and being courteous, 199
and building support groups,
    201
and directing your thinking,
    199-200
and gatekeeping, 202
and going around, 203
and inoculating key decision
    makers, 201
and neutralizing resistance,
    200-201
and threatening to resign,
    203
and using media, 201
defined, 190
strategies for enhancing,
    198-203
interviewing candidates, 276:
    ambigous questions, 280
    good questions, 278-280
    illegal questions, 283
    leading questions, 283
    obvious questions, 283
    poor questions, 283
interviews:
    and EEOC, 276
    guide to, 281-282
    importance of, 276
    selection, 276
    semistructured, 277
    structured, 276
    unstructured, 277
iron maiden, 8, 188

J, K

Jardim, Anne, 7, 11
job:
    analysis, 272-273
    previews, realistic, 98-99
job sharing, 115
judgment, good, 46
Kanter, R., 7, 222
Kline, L., 231
Koff, Lois A., 77
Korda, Michael, 186
Kosaba, S., 130

Kripke, _. 71

L

Lakein, Alan, 138, 139
lateral transfer, 43
leaders:
    effective, 48
    well-known, examples of, 44
    women as, 45
leadership:
    and acceptance, 46
    and accomplishment, 46
    and communication, 46
    and flexibility, 46
    and good judgement, 46
    and initiative, 46
    and objectivity, 47
    and performance, 46
    defined, 44
    dilemmas for female manager,
        47
    guidelines for, 46-47
leading, 44-48:
    as management function, 36, 44
    defined, 44
    percentage of workday spent
        on, 54
legitimate power, 191
Levinson, H. 252
linear career crisis, 113
listening, 159-162:
    active, 159, 162
    defined, 159-160
    poor habits, 160-162
Loden, M., 4

M

Madonna, 193
Maddi, S., 130
Marram, E., 22
McGregor, D., 45
maintenance role behaviors,
    226-228

and communication, 228
compromising, 226
encouraging, 226
folowing, 226
gatekeeping, 226
harmonizing, 226
observing-commenting, 226
majority-minority voting, 225
male-female roles, 11, 227
management:
    defined, 36
    effective, of groups, 222
    functions, and communication,
        151
    functions of, 36-50
manager:
    and dress, 69
    and employees, mismatch of
        behavioral styles, 248-251
    as conceptual thinker, 34
    as effective communicator,
        151, 163
    as mediator, 35
    as motivator, 35
    as politician, 35
    as problem solver, 34
    as representative, 35
    balances competing goals,
        32-33
    makes difficult decisions, 36
    number one high-stress job,
        137
    roles of, 32-36, 51
managerial process, variations of,
    50-55
mass and model approach, 222
meetings:
    effective, conducting of,
        237, 238
    team building, 236
meditation, and stress, 136
meetings:
    effective, conducting of, 237,
        238
    team building, 236
Meir, Golda, 193
mentors, 102-111:
    benefits of, for woman manager,
        105
    career functions, 102

defined, 102
functions of, 103
how to find, 105-106
need for, 104
psychosocial functions, 102
women as, 110-111
mentor relationship:
    and sexual attraction, 109
    difficulty letting go, 110
    problems encountered in,
        108-110
Miller, M., 93
minority decision, 225
Mintzberg, Henry, 51
mixed signals, defined, 171
Molloy, John t., 70, 71
mommy track, 111, 112-113
Morrison, A., 5, 22
mother role, 7, 155, 159
Mother Teresa, 193
multiple roles:
    and stress, 129
    benefit of, for women, 130

N

Nelson, D., 129
networking:
    groups, 107
    system, 106
networks:
    and organizational politics,
        35, 187
    female, 197-198
    male, 197
    old boys', 14, 197
Nightingale, Florence, 44
Nolan, Helen D., 104

O

Oberle, R., 286
objectivity, defined, 47
office politics:
    and sex, 186

defined, 186
old boys' network, 14:
    seeking entry into, 197-198
Oliver, R. L., 16
organizers, women as, 40
organizing, 39-41:
    aids, 41
    as management function, 32,
        36, 44
    defined, 39
    percentage of workday spent
        on, 54
OSHA, 137

P

passive behaviors, 254, 256-257
perfectionism, avoiding, 140-141
performance:
    and controlling, 49
    and feedback, 93
    and typecasting, 222
    defined, 46
    expected, cues for, 92
performance appraisal:
    and staffing, 42
    regular, 92
pet, 8, 22
physical exercise, and stress, 134
planners, women as, 37
planning, 37-39:
    aids, 37-38
    and upper-level executives, 51
    as intangible work, 6
    as management function, 36
    career, long-term, 88
    career, steps in, 90-92
    defined, 37
    effectiveness, evaluation of, 39
    human resource, 42
    percentage of workday spent
        on, 54
playgirl, 228
plop, defined, 224
politics, 35:
    and power, 186
    and women managers, 99

organizational, 186-187
polling method, defined, 225
power:
    and affairs, 206
    and career, woman manager's.
        195-198
    and control, 229
    and dating, 205-206
    and delegating, 216
    and emotional style, 231-232
    and flings, 206
    and flirtation, 204
    and office politics, 198
    and seeking entry into old boys'
        network, 197-198
    and sex, 203-207
    and women managers, 186, 195,
        228
    association, 190, 194
    bases, 196
    coercive, 190, 192
    defined, 190
    expert, 190, 193
    failures of women managers,
        187-190
    information, 190, 193-194
    interpersonal, 190, 198-203
    legitimate, 190-191, 194
    referent, 190, 193
    reward, 190, 192
    sources of, for women
        managers, 190-194
    tactic, sex as a, 203-207
Prather, Jane, 16
Pregnancy Discrimination Act,
    275
pressure, and stress, 132
pressures, of female sex roles, 7-9
primacy effect, defined, 67
priorities:
    and time management,
        138-140
    establishing, in planning, 39

Q, R

Queen Bee syndrome, 9, 110

Queen Elizabeth I, 44
Quick, J. C., 129
reality shock syndrome, 92:
    and lack of regular
        performance appraisal, 93
    and low initial challenge, 92
    and low self-actualization
        satisfaction, 93
    and the Glass Ceiling, 94
    and threat to superiors, 94
    and unrealistically high
        aspirations, 93
recreation, and stress, 131, 134
recruiting:
    and job analysis, 272-273
    general, 272
    specific, 272
recruitment:
    defined, 42
    sources, 273
reentry, for women, 95
references:
    methods of checking, 285
referent power, 190, 193, 216
relationship-oriented
    behaviors, 48
Renwick, P. A., 16
responding, and active
    listening, 162
responsibility
    as role of manager, 32
    delegation of, 40
reward power, 192
Rivers, C., 142
role constraints, 13-14:
    gender-related, 13
role models:
    female, 222
    few women, 45
    provided since birth, 10-13
roles:
    and group behaviors, 225-228
    decisional, 54
    informational, 52
    interpersonal, 51
    manager's, 32-36, 51
    of mentors, 102
Rubin, Zick, 67
Ruble, T. L., 258

S

Schoonmaker, Alan N., 97
Schwartz, Felice, 4
screening applications, 276
seductress, defined, 8
selection, and staffing, 42
self-authorized agenda, 224
self-esteem:
    and firing employees, 287
    and grade point average, 16
    low, 16, 17
self-fulfilling prophecy, 166, 175,
    253, 264
sensing, and listening, 162
separations, and staffing, 43
servant trap, 110
sex:
    and office politics, 186
    and power, 203-207
    as a power tactic, 203-207
sex-role stereotyping, 15, 193:
    self-fulfilling, 21
sex roles:
    and groups, 222
    iron maiden, 8, 222
    mother role, 7, 222
    pet, 8, 222
    pressures of female, 7-9
    seductress, 8, 222
    traditional conditioning, 189
sexual attraction:
    and group processes, 229
    and mentor relationship, 109
sexual harassment, 7, 207
Simmons College, 96
sincerity:
    and image, 66, 79-80
    and power, 172
Smith College, 96
socialization:
    and role constraints, 13
    traditional process for women,
        6, 9
society, historically sexist, 9-21
speech patterns:
    hedging or modifying phrases,
        153
    hypercorrect or excessively

polite speech, 153
questioning intonation, 153
submissive, and power, 199
use of apologies, 154
use of disclaimers, 153
use of empty adjectives, 152
use of fillers, 154
use of tag questions, 153
weak, ways to overcome,
    155-156
women's, characteristics of,
    152-155
staffing, 41-43:
and human resource planning,
    42
and orientation, 42
and performance appraisal, 42
and recruiting, 42
and selection, 42
and separation, 43
and training, 42
and transfer, 43
and women, 43
as management function, 36, 41
defined, 41
percentage of workday spent
    on, 54
process of, 41-43
Stanek, Lou W., 16
stereotypes:
and critical mass, 223
and group role behaviors, 227
and mentor, 108
cultural, 10
defined, 14
emotional, and males, 230
female, overcoming of, in
    male-dominated groups, 222
gender-related, 9
masculine, women adopting,
    197
men as inherently more
    assertive than women,
    18-19
men as intellectually superior
    to women, 15-16
men as valuing achievements
    and meaningful work more
    than women, 16-18
myths and realities, 14-19

negative, 5
solutions for overcoming,
    221-222
women don't work for money,
    19-21
women waste time, 138
strategic openness, 159
stress:
ability to handle, 130
adaptation techniques, 133,
    134-135
and lack of control, 132
and conflicting demands, 133
and overload, 132, 137
and physical exercise, 134
and pressure, 132
and recreation, 131, 134
and relaxation exercises, 135,
    136
and uncertainty, 131-132
as dysfunctional, 129-130
as functional, 129
coping techniques, 133-134
defined, 128
methods of dealing with,
    133-137
sources of, 131-133
stress management, 128-131:
and managerial life-style, 129
defined, 128
stressors:
body reaction to, 129
causes, 129
defined, 128
stress response, 128
support base, 188

T

task behaviors:
and relationship behaviors,
    47-48, 226
defined, 47
types of, 226
team building:
goals, 232
needs assessment, 234

planning and design, 235-236
meeting, 236
steps, 233-234
team efforts, collaborative, 6
team member, 4
Thomas, K. S. 258
time management, 137-143
    establish priorities for,
        138-140
    techniques, 138-143
time orientation, 6
timesaving ideas, 141-142
time wasters:
    defined, 140
    control of, 140
Title VII of Civil Rights Act, 274,
    275
training, and staffing, 42
Transcendental Meditation, 136
transfers:
    and staffing, 43
    lateral, 43
    vertical
Turla, P., 140

U, V, W, Y, Z

uncertainty, and stress, 131-132
Van Velsor, E., 5
versatility, and image, 66, 78
vertical transfer, 43
visibility:
    and mentors, 106
    and power, 187
    as career tactic, 99
Wellesley College Center for
    Research on Women, 142
White, R., 5
women, reentry:
    competition with younger
        women, 95
    problems, 95-96
    relating to younger supervisors,
        96
    strategies for, 95-96
Wong, L., 227
Wyse, L., 232
yoga, and stress, 136
Zemke, R., 252